TAKING CARE

TAKING CARE

*Supporting Older People
and Their Families*

Nancy R. Hooyman
Wendy Lustbader

THE FREE PRESS
A Division of Macmillan, Inc.
NEW YORK

Collier Macmillan Publishers
LONDON

Copyright © 1986 by The Free Press
A Division of Macmillan, Inc.

All rights reserved. No part of this book may be reproduced
or transmitted in any form or by any means, electronic or
mechanical, including photocopying, recording, or by any
information storage and retrieval system, without permission
in writing from the Publisher.

The Free Press
A Division of Macmillan, Inc.
866 Third Avenue, New York, N.Y. 10022

Collier Macmillan Canada, Inc.

Printed in the United States of America

printing number

1 2 3 4 5 6 7 8 9 10

Library of Congress Cataloging-in-Publication Data

Hooyman, Nancy.
      Taking care.

      Includes index.
         1. Aged—Home care—United States. 2. Aged—United
States—Family relationships. 3. Aged—United States—
Care and hygiene. 4. Aging—United States—Psychologi-
cal aspects. 5. Old age assistance—United States.
I. Lustbader, Wendy. II. Title.
HV1461.H66 1986   362.6'3   85-15870
ISBN 0-02-914900-2

In memory of my mother,
Doris Stratton Runkle (1904–1978).
                    N. R. H.

In memory of my friend,
Edna Whitman Chittick, (1883–1984),
who showed me how to live well.
                    W. L.

Contents

Preface

Most books about aging are targeted to either professionals or families, artificially separating these audiences. This book attempts to reflect the partnership between professionals and families that is a vital part of successful care arrangements. Theory and practice are blended, with the goal of suggesting solutions to care dilemmas that are clinically sound and applicable to everyday life. The book has been designed for use by social workers, clergy, nurses, physicians, home health aides, and occupational and physical therapists as well as family members. Included in the text are practical tools, such as a medical bill accounting sheet, a guide for delegating tasks among family members, a checklist for comparing retirement homes, and a chart for keeping track of progress with rehabilitation exercises. Each tool is introduced in the context of the clinical rationale that underlies its usefulness.

Throughout the book, the word "family" is defined more broadly than blood ties, encompassing anyone who plays a family-like role in an older person's life. Older people without biological family, those estranged from family members, and those who live at a great distance from relatives often receive family-like support from friends, neighbors, and other natural helpers. These critical forms of support are explicitly acknowledged in Chapter 4, but are also implied in the sections addressed to "family members."

The authors have purposely grappled with taboo topics and ethically complex issues. Discussions of older people's racist reactions toward service providers and abusive caregiving relationships explore ways to approach these problems, rather than give superficial answers. Other difficult areas confronted include the special needs of lesbian and gay caregivers, the older person who wants to die, concerns about inheritances, and caregiving as a traditional woman's role in need of redefinition and increased public support.

While raising difficult issues, the book does not attempt to provide comprehensive legal or medical advice. Instead, appropriate professional assistance is recommended and the reader is referred to additional readings and organizations at the end of each chapter. Because community resources are limited and constantly changing, the suggestions for services are initial guidelines rather than directives.

Specific cultural, ethnic, and religious differences are not covered in this book. Instead, an effort was made to note aspects of caregiving where these differences are most apparent in order to alert professionals who may need to do further reading in these areas. At the end of Chapter 1, readings are suggested which portray diverse cultures in a way that does justice to their complexity and the importance of professional sensitivity.

To simplify reading and avoid both awkwardness and sex stereotyping, masculine and feminine pronouns are alternated throughout the text. Case illustrations are presented in the gender most appropriate to the issues under discussion, or for ease in pronoun references. When gender differences are important, they are explicitly acknowledged.

Perfect solutions do not exist for the difficult choices faced by professionals and families. The question of how much to give and sacrifice is a highly personal issue for every caregiver, with care arrangements requiring constant readjustment as needs change. Rather than trying to address the full range of human variability, this book presents the most typical problems and then models strategies for prevention or resolution that can be generalized to a variety of caregiving situations.

Acknowledgments

This book grew out of our friendships and working relationships with many older people and their families. The questions and concerns they raised made the need for such a book clear to us. It was their voices that motivated us when other professional and caregiving demands pressured us and made the task arduous.

Special appreciation to my boys, Kevin and Christopher, who were often wakened by the click of the computer or printer late at night, who wondered when "that book" would ever be done, and who kept me laughing through the process.

To my husband, Gene, who grew in his support during our continual juggling of family and professional responsibilities, who shared the many weekends dominated by the book, and whose gentle caring kept me going through the stressful periods.

To my father, Hugh Runkle, whose pride in my accomplishments is a source of strength.

To our after-school sitter, Cynthia Lombardi, who cheerfully put in long hours.

To Laurie Pollack, Suzanne Condict, Cheryl Yates, Sharon Evans, Gail Nyman-York, and Darrell Thomas from the University of Washington School of Social Work, who assisted with many of the production details.

N. R. H.

Many thanks to Sharon Gray for making order out of chaos during the early stages of the manuscript and for encouragement throughout.

To Kathy Sullivan for demonstrating home nursing care at its best and for inspiration on clinical issues.

To Sue Tomita for vicarious experience during many months of authorial hibernation.

To Barry Grosskopf for helping to work out the ethical knots in the manuscript.

To Adrienne Robbins, John Freeman, and Tracy McAvoy for friendship through the long haul.

To the staff of Pike Market Community Clinic for reviewing the manuscript and for their practice of humane health care.

Special thanks also to my grandparents for their example of aging with vitality.

W. L.

Introduction

Family caregiving for older persons has recently received widespread attention from both policymakers and gerontology practitioners. Fiscal restraints, scarcer public resources for long-term care, and increased expectations of private responsibility for older persons have resulted in a growing awareness of the major roles played by families in caring for their older members. Despite the apparent discovery of family caregiving by gerontologists in the 1970s, it is not a new phenomenon. Family caregivers have served for years as the invisible laborers, essential to the survival of both the long-term care system and disabled older persons. Yet their invisibility has excluded family caregivers from the planning of programs and services which could ease their stress, improve their caregiving ability, and enhance their older relatives' lives.

Professionals have only recently recognized families' needs for information, social support, respite, and financial assistance in providing care to older relatives. The focus of research and practice has begun to shift from the older person alone to the family system, with some gerontologists predicting a crisis in family caregiving and an escalation of nursing home placement, unless additional professional interventions to support family caregivers are developed.[1] This chapter begins by examining the centrality of family caregivers in the long-term care system and the demographic and social trends that intensify demands on family

1

caregivers. The book's underlying assumptions, focus, and organization are then presented.

The Importance of Family Caregivers

Contrary to the myth of family abandonment of older persons, most older people are integral members of family networks, see their adult children and other close relatives at least several times a week, and interact regularly by telephone or letter with relatives living at a distance.[2] Approximately 94 percent of people age sixty-five and over have family members. Married couples are the most common family structure among older people. More than half of the population over age sixty-five is married and lives with a spouse in independent households. Significant differences exist, however, in the family arrangements of men and women age sixty-five and over, with 37 percent of the women in this category married as compared to 77 percent of the men. Accordingly, women are more likely than men to live alone, especially after age seventy-five, and to care for a disabled spouse. Women caring for their husbands have been referred to as "the hidden victims," experiencing emotional, financial, and physical burdens in addition to their own aging changes.[3]

The second most frequent family pattern involves older parents and their adult children. Seeking to maintain their privacy and independence, most older people prefer to live near, but not with, their adult children. Although only 18 percent of older persons live in their children's households by choice or out of health or economic necessity, this percentage increases for widowed, separated, and divorced older persons. One-third of all men age sixty-five and over in this situation share a home with their children, as do one-half of all women age sixty-five and over who are widowed, separated or divorced. Even when older parents and their adult children do not share a household, they see each other frequently. Approximately 80 percent of people age sixty-five and over with children live less than an hour away from at least one child.[4] Families generally experience a pattern of reciprocal support across the lifespan, with older parents providing aid to their children and grandchildren and later receiving assistance when they face chronic illnesses.

Families provide the majority of in-home services to the older generation, resorting to institutionalization only after exhausting their resources. Families have been estimated to furnish 80 percent of the in-home care of persons age seventy-five and over with chronic disabilities.[5] Nearly 10 percent of older people who live in private homes would require nursing home placement if family support were withdrawn.[6] Although chronic illness prevents approximately 18 percent of older people from carrying out

2

their daily activities, their family's support enables the majority of them to remain in the community. Family assistance initially tends to be financial, such as gifts of cash, and emotional, through visiting, companionship, advice-giving, and phone checkups. Families also advocate their older relative's receipt of services from social and health agencies. As their relative's health declines and needs increase, families provide more concrete daily services, such as cooking, cleaning, shopping, bathing, dressing, feeding, and transportation, often struggling to maintain two households. Spouses frequently find themselves virtually homebound by caregiving tasks, unable to leave to grocery shop or take a short walk.

The majority of primary caregivers of older people are women—wives for men and daughters or daughters-in-law for women.[7] Adult daughters predominate in caregiving networks, in a secondary role for those with surviving spouses, but as principal caregivers to widowed older persons.[8] Men's caregiving tends to be indirect, such as assisting with financial affairs and running errands. Men generally assume primary care responsibilities when a female relative is unavailable.[9]

Trends Affecting Family Caregiving

The number of families providing long-term care to older relatives is expected to increase substantially in the next few decades, as a result of major demographic and social trends. In the past century, changes in mortality and fertility rates and patterns of migration have contributed to dramatic increases in the absolute number and proportion of older persons in the population. In 1900, approximately three million persons aged sixty-five and older formed 4 percent of the total population. By 1980, an estimated twenty-five million persons age sixty-five and older comprised 11 percent of the population. The fastest-growing segment of the older population is age seventy-five and over. The frail elderly, composing 38 percent of the aged population, are the segment most likely to suffer chronic illnesses and disabilities, which require medical care and limit their ability to function independently.[10]

The increase in life expectancy and the growth in the number of frail elderly have resulted in a demographic shift toward the multigenerational family. Older people with children comprise four-fifths of the elderly population, a proportion unchanged over the past twenty years. What has increased is the number of four-generation families. Among older people with adult children, about 40 percent are heads of four-generation families, 94 percent have grandchildren, and 46 percent have great-grandchildren. Among adult children, over 80 percent of middle-aged couples have at least one living parent, compared to fewer than half at the turn of the century.[11] Even among those in their early sixties, 20 percent have a surviving parent.[12] As a result, some adult children, coping with their own health problems and life transitions, are also faced with caring for frail parents. Most frequently, middle-aged children care for two older generations, but in some instances, the grandparent generation assists great-grandparents. With technological and medical advances, these trends will continue.

Along with the growth of multigenerational families, the number of older people is greater than the pool of younger family members available to assist them. The low birthrate of the current cohort of frail elderly has resulted in a smaller number of adult children as potential caregivers. At the turn of the twenty-first century, the chances that an older person will have at least one living child will be greater than they are today. With declines in birthrate and family size, however, adult children may find the burdens of caring for older parents to be greater. Older people will also have fewer available siblings to provide assistance.[13]

Many middle-aged individuals, commonly referred to as the "sandwiched" generation, are faced with competing responsibilities of simultaneously caring for parents and children, as young adults remain economically dependent longer and as parents live longer. The "empty nest" is being filled by the frail elderly and by grown children who cannot afford to leave or who return home.[14] These multiple responsibilities are magnified for women. As women advance from forty years of age to their early sixties, those with surviving parents or parents-in-law are increasingly likely to be providing hands-on care to older relatives who are living with them.[15] Ninety percent of middle-aged women have dependent children, resulting in their juggling full-time work along with their nearly full-time family responsibilities. Middle-aged married women comprise the largest category of working women, with 60 percent of married women between the ages of forty-five and fifty-four and 42 percent of married women between the ages of fifty-five and sixty-four in the work force.[16] Women's paid employment generally does not reduce the hours of assistance, even though most women do not have the job flexibility or the income to incorporate these additional demands into their lives.[17] Without affordable community alternatives, the financial and psychological rewards of employment may not compensate for the tensions generated by prolonged elder care combined with work. Some women attempt to resolve such multiple demands by quitting their jobs. The majority, however, remain conflicted, oftentimes reducing their working hours in order to fulfill their filial responsibilities.

Another social trend affecting the adult child–parent relationship is the increase of "serial monogamy" among people experiencing a series of

4

divorces and remarriages throughout their lives.[18] As a result, the number of "reconstituted families" is growing. Adult children may thus be caring not only for their biological parents and parents-in-law from their current marriage, but, if previously divorced, may be emotionally tied to their former spouse's parents, especially through the children of the earlier marriage. Such ties can create multiple responsibilities for former parents-in-law, now older and requiring care. Difficult definitions of family membership and loyalties may complicate the distribution of time, attention, and money across generations. Alternatively, adult children experiencing divorce may not have the time or emotional stamina to assist older generations.[19] Further, within the past two decades, new and diverse family structures have emerged, such as communal living, cohabitation by unmarried couples and gay and lesbian partners. Whether these various family forms will result in more obligations, commitments, or resources to meet older persons' needs is as yet unknown.

The Stress of Caregiving

Despite these changing family configurations, most families attempt to maintain their older members at home as long as possible, generally at considerable personal sacrifice. Most prefer, however, not to be the sole source of help,[20] but are selective in their requests for assistance, asking primarily for homemaking and home health care to provide immediate relief from daily responsibilities.[21]

The primary reason for families' desire for assistance is that long-term caregiving is physically, financially, and emotionally burdensome. The physical strains of back-breaking lifting, washing urine-soaked sheets late at night, and doing chores for two households have emotional costs. Likewise, income forgone through reduced employment and extra medical, food and transportation expenses can intensify worry, disrupt sleep, and result in lifestyle changes, such as sacrificed leisure time and delayed vacations. Experiencing a narrowing of their life space, and confined by their care tasks, family caregivers may feel helpless to control their lives.

Emotional burdens are complicated by the lack of behavioral norms and models for caring for older family members. Our society does little to prepare families for this nearly universal role of caregiver to older relatives. Compared to the extensive child-rearing literature, guidelines on how to care for an older relative, to get support, or to cope with ambivalence about caregiving responsibilities are scarce. As another contrast to child-rearing experiences, most families have little hope that their older relative will become more independent. Not knowing the length of the caregiving situation compounds the difficulties of making a commitment to assist an older relative.

The long-term care of an older parent poses complex value questions about what adult children should do. Although it is a predictable and nearly universal experience, caring for parents is generally not planned for. Even spouses who earlier vowed "in sickness and in health" usually do not anticipate the duration of care required by chronic conditions. Both adult children and spouses are often dismayed by the lack of societal supports for their efforts. Most policies and programs, for example, have focused on the older individual alone, with scant recognition given to the special needs of the total family system.[22]

This absence of supportive resources for families heightens their feelings of isolation and stress. The tendency for burdens to intensify over time can lead to family disruption, neglect or abuse of the older person, and mental or physical impairment of the caregiver. Under such conditions, the caregiver not only becomes a hidden victim of stress, but the older person may be institutionalized. Approximately 25 percent of nursing home placements are precipitated by the caregiver's illness or death.[23] Thus, expectations that families will care for their older relatives in stressful situations can be inappropriate for both the family and the older person.[24] Unless family caregiving efforts are supported, emotional and physical problems may spread throughout the family system, ultimately increasing the costs to society.

Social Policy and Family Caregivers

Social and health policies set the parameters within which professionals and families strive to meet older persons' needs. Policies are, in turn, strongly influenced by society's values about who is responsible for the care of dependent persons, by public perceptions of the elderly, and by resource limitations. While agreement exists that both the government and the family are responsible for the care of older persons, disagreement persists about how to translate this concept of "shared responsibility" into specific policies and programs. Historically, U.S. social welfare policies have been organized on the premise that the family is responsible for caring for dependent persons. The state has intervened only after the resources of the older person and the family have been exhausted or the family has been incapable of meeting certain standards of care. The assumption of primary family responsibility is reflected in the fact that twenty-five states have laws, though rarely enforced, which require financially able children to contribute to their parents' long-term support.

Since the 1930s, government has expanded its contributions toward maintaining older people's independence, exemplified by Social Security, the Older Americans Act, and Medicare. As costs for long-term care have escalated, public dollars have shrunk and a vocal public has demanded limits on government expenditures and on intrusion into private spheres. Increasingly, the family is viewed as a cost-effective alternative to institutionalization. For example, limits on the length of stay and treatment of Medicare- and Medicaid-funded patients have shifted long-term care expenses to families. Defined as effective and inexpensive service providers, families are increasingly faced with relatives prematurely discharged from hospitals.

Most health and social service programs do not have caregivers' welfare as a central goal. The United States is one of the few industrialized nations that does not provide a stipend to family caregivers, compared to more than sixty countries with provisions for attendant allowances under social security programs.[25] Policymakers may even disregard or denigrate programs that relieve families of caregiving responsibilities. For example, a 1982 General Accounting Office report criticized home health programs for performing custodial functions suitable to families, and therefore, as costly compared to nursing home care.[26] A 1980 California ruling on Title XX funds prohibited in-home supportive services to an "able and available spouse."[27] A growing number of states have reintroduced family responsibility amendments, requiring adult children to contribute 25 percent of the cost of nursing home care prior to application for Medicaid. Yet the amendments' rationale of cost savings and deterred institutionalization is not supported by data which show that wealthy children are "dumping" their parents in nursing homes. Instead, most nursing home placements involve older people who do not have family or who lack suitable housing.

In some cases, existing policies may serve to discourage family supports. Medicaid and Medicare, the major reimbursement mechanisms, focus on institutional care, with less than 2 percent of their budgets allocated to home care services that could relieve caregiving families. Medicaid funding of home care services is determined on the basis of income eligibility requirements, not on the older person's level of functional disability, even though their incapacity creates the daily burdens for caregivers. The families of older people who are ineligible for Medicaid and lack funds to hire private services often must shoulder caregiving responsibilities alone. Husbands or wives who "spend down" in order to be eligible for publicly supported services face the risk of destitution after their spouses die. Caregivers thus bear the financial costs of home care in addition to the unestimated value of their nonpaid work.

Some policies also have an effect of penalizing family caregivers and their relatives. For example, a two-tier entitlement policy has been proposed: one tier would provide comprehensive services for older people without family supports, while the second tier would allow only modest benefits to complement family assistance.[28] When resources are limited, service providers have been found to target in-home services to those without family supports, on the rationale of cost-effectiveness.[29] As another example, Supplemental Security Income benefits can be reduced by one-third and, in some cases, Medicaid eligibility lost when families contribute housing, cash, or in-kind assistance to low-income older relatives.[30] In addition, an older SSI recipient may lose the opportunity to contribute to the family's household. In seven states, an older person can be declared ineligible for SSI if relatives provide financial support.[31]

Incentives for family caregivers have been debated in Congress since 1975. Financial incentives, such as more liberal tax credits and deductions and tax-free stipends, have been proposed to offset home care costs. While possibly benefitting families already committed to care, these incentives fail to address families' nonmonetary and nonrational motives for care decisions. In addition, financial incentives do not provide relief from the daily care tasks that intensify the emotional burdens. They also ignore caregivers' preference for supportive services rather than financial aid.[32]

Although respite and adult day care programs are being developed at the state level, they are not universally funded. Demonstration educational and training programs for caregivers are scarce. Such programs are also constrained by the assumption that one family member, usually a woman, is willing to provide care, and needs knowledge and skills to perform her numerous tasks efficiently. Yet increased efficiency is not a sufficient antidote to the stresses created by multiple demands. The recent expansion of family support groups is an important resource for caregivers, but it may require that families locate respite help and transportation in order to attend.

More importantly, none of the current or proposed programs adequately addresses the critical policy issue that our society is running out of caregivers. A "typical work cycle" or "life course" of school, work, marriage, and caregiving no longer exists for most women. In a study of three generations of women, a majority of the middle generation daughters and young adult granddaughters stated that adult children should not adjust their work schedules in favor of parent care. All three generations, however, were more likely to expect working, married daughters, rather than sons, to make adjustments. While women strongly favored sons providing the same amount of care as daughters, the middle generation daughters actually performed most of the care themselves.[33] Influenced by the women's movement and socialized in a different economic climate, future cohorts of women may be less willing to make sacrifices for caregiving. Even if women in the future are willing to provide care, they may be unable to afford to, given the higher proportion likely to be divorced or living on limited incomes. Proposed programs not only fail to address the future shortage of potential family caregivers, they also do not resolve whether and under what conditions responsibility for elder care should be private.

Why This Book?

These policy dilemmas underlie the need for books in support of older people and their families. The emotional, financial, and physical costs of maintaining older persons in the community are too great for the family, and particularly for women, to bear alone. Professional interventions supporting family caregivers are essential. These interventions can be two-pronged: (1) to enhance older people's competence and independence, thereby decreasing their care needs, as for example, through in-home chore services or adult day care programs, and (2) to minimize family care burdens and increase the resources for sustained assistance, through respite, education and mutual support, or work flex-time and released time for caregivers. Professionals and families are thus viewed as collaborators, each supporting the other's efforts to enable the older person to remain in the community.

This book begins by questioning "why care?", given the multiple demands created by dual-career marriages, divorce and single parenthood, increased geographic mobility of adult children, and limited public support for caregiving. For some spouses and adult children, past negative relationships with older relatives lead to caring out of obligation, not affection. For such families struggling to answer "why care?", clear-cut guidelines do not exist. How they answer varies with caregiving demands and dynamics created by the type of relationship. Some caregivers are supported by rich extended family networks with siblings and other relatives while others resent needing to assist in-laws or stepparents. Others are only children, biologically, or through estrangement from siblings, or from geographic isolation from other supportive family members. The need to negotiate shared caregiving responsibilities, as discussed in Chapter 3, is common to all these different types of caregivers. All caregivers, especially those without supportive blood relatives, need to build familylike networks. Strategies for identifying and building such helping networks among friends, neighbors, and acquaintances in the community are discussed in Chapter 4.

Caregivers' ability to cope with stress varies considerably. Some with round-the-clock responsibilities show few signs of stress, while others with fewer tasks feel unable to manage. The caregiver's physical and mental capacity, the nature of the relative's illness and configuration of care needs, the degree of vigilance required or the amount of disruption created by the older person's illness, the home's physical arrangements, and the extent of social support all affect the degree of stress which the caregiver experiences. Chapter 4 focuses on strategies for taking care of the caregiver to prevent exhaustion, depression, and abusive behavior.

Family caregiving is a dynamic process, constantly changing as the older person's needs and the family's life circumstances alter. Caregiving can extend over many years, as the older person gradually declines, or it can be precipitated by a sudden illness or accident and experienced intensely for a short time. As the older person's physical and mental health changes, the family's roles, tasks, and problem-solving abilities are altered along with the appropriate living situation for their relative. Chapter 6 discusses techniques families can use to cope with common changes in memory, vision, hearing, mobility, sexuality, and incontinence. With physical and mental losses, the need for preventing depression among homebound older people also increases, as discussed in Chapter 7.

Decisions about the older person's living arrangements are critical transitions for both families and their older relatives. While the mental and physical well-being of both the caregiver and the older person often determines when such transitions occur, financial constraints particularly affect where and how an older person can safely live. Chapter 8 describes the primary health and income maintenance programs for older people and addresses critical financial management issues. The family's ability to locate in-home services and to encourage their older relative to use out-of-home services are also powerful determinants of the older person's independence. Chapter 9 discusses locating and bringing services into the older person's home, including surmounting their resistance to services, and adapting their home environment for safety. Chapter 10 identifies strategies to overcome transportation difficulties and psychological barriers to using services outside the home, including adult day care, senior centers and support groups.

Although families attempt to maintain their older relatives in their own homes as long as feasible, some are faced with choosing other less independent living arrangements, as described in Chapter 11. In many cases, such decisions are made hurriedly in response to a crisis, such as the older person's imminent hospital discharge or the family's cross-country move. The family's ethnicity, urban or rural location, or the value placed on providing personal care may tip the decision toward the older person's move into a family member's home. Such decisions, with major repercussions for the lives involved, are often made without consideration of the long-range consequences created by multiple generations sharing a household. Typical problems arising in intergenerational households and

10

techniques for addressing them are presented in Chapter 12. The book concludes with the recognition that family caregiving does not necessarily cease with nursing home placement, even though family roles and tasks shift. Ways to ease this transition and maximize the older person's competencies and contributions to family life are discussed in Chapter 13.

Notes

1. Elaine M. Brody, "Women in the Middle and Family Help to Older People," *The Gerontologist* 21, 5 (1981): 471–480.
2. Ethel Shanas with Peter Townsend, D. Wedderbuin, H. Friis, P. Mihoj, and J. Stehouwet, *Old People in Three Industrial Societies* (New York and London: Atherton and Routledge Kegan Paul, 1968); Lillian E. Troll, "Life in Middle and Old Age: The Generation Gap," in F. Berbardo, "Middle and Late Life Transitions," *The Annals of the American Academy of Political and Social Science* (November 1982): 38–47; Brody, op. cit. (1981): 471–480; Judith Treas, "Family Support Systems for the Aged: Some Social and Demographic Considerations," *The Gerontologist* 17, 6 (1977): 486–491.
3. Alfred P. Fengler and Nancy Goodrich, "Wives of Elderly Disabled Men: The Hidden Patients," *The Gerontologist* 19, 2 (1979): 175–183.
4. Ethel Shanas, "The Family as a Social Support in Old Age," *The Gerontologist* 19, 2 (1979): 169–174; Ethel Shanas, "Social Myth as Hypothesis: The Case of the Family Relations of Old People," *The Gerontologist* 19, 1 (1979): 3–9; Betsy Robinson and Majda Thurnher, "Taking Care of Aged Parents: A Family Cycle Transition," *The Gerontologist* 19, 6 (1979): 587–593.
5. Comptroller General of the United States, *Report to the Congress: The Well-Being of Older People in Cleveland Ohio* (Washington D.C.: United States General Accounting Office, 1977).
6. Shanas, op. cit. (1979a): 3–9; Brody, op. cit. (1981): 471–480.
7. Lucy Steinitz, "Informal Supports in Long-Term Care: Implications and Policy Options," presented to the National Conference on Social Welfare (1981): 7; Lillian E. Troll, "Intergenerational Relations Throughout the Life Span," in B. B. Wolman, ed., *Handbook of Developmental Psychology* (Englewood Cliffs, N.J.: Prentice-Hall, 1982).
8. Brody, op. cit. (1981): 471–480; Marjorie Cantor, "Strain Among Caregivers: A Study of Experience in the United States," *The Gerontologist* 23, 6 (1983): 597–604; Colleen Johnson and Donald Catalano, "A Longitudinal Study of Family Supports to Impaired Elderly," *The Gerontologist* 23, 6 (1983): 612–619.
9. Amy Horowitz and Rose Dobrof, *The Role of Families in Providing Long-Term Care to the Frail and Chronically Ill Elderly Living in the Community*, Final Report to the Health Care Financing Administration, (1982): 132–137; Elaine M. Brody with Pauline T. Johnson and Mark C. Fulcomer, "What Should

Adult Children Do For Elderly Parents? Opinions and Preferences of Three Generations of Women," *Journal of Gerontology* 39, 6 (November 1984): 736–747; Elaine M. Brody with Morton Kleban, Pauline Johnson, and Christine Hoffman, "Women Who Help Elderly Mothers: Do Work and Parent Care Compete?," paper presented at the 37th Annual Scientific Meeting of the Gerontological Society of America, San Antonio, Texas (November 1984): 3; Elaine M. Brody, "Parent Care as a Normative Family Stress," *The Gerontologist* 25, 1 (1985): 19–30.

10. Elizabeth Kutza, *The Benefits of Old Age: Social Welfare Policy for the Elderly* (Chicago: University Press, 1981): 6–10.

11. Peter Uhlenberg, "Death and the Family," *Journal of Family History* 5 (1980): 313–320.

12. Brody, op. cit. (1981): 471–480.

13. Judith Treas, "The Great American Fertility Debate: Generational Balance and Support of the Aged," *The Gerontologist* 21, 1 (1981): 98–103.

14. Brody, op. cit. (1981): 471–480.

15. Abigail M. Lang and Elaine M. Brody, "Characteristics of Middle-Aged Daughters and Help to Their Elderly Mothers," *Journal of Marriage and the Family* 45 (1983): 193.

16. U.S. Bureau of Labor Statistics, "Employment and Earnings" (January 1984), Table 3.

17. E. P. Stroller, "Parental Caring of Adult Children," *Journal of Marriage and the Family* 45 (1983): 851–858.

18. L. Tiger, "Omigamy: The New Kinship System," *Psychology Today* (July 1978): 14–17.

19. M. Smyer and B. F. Hofland, "Divorce and Family Support in Later Life," *Journal of Family Issues* 3 (1982): 61–77.

20. V. G. Cicirelli, *Helping Elderly Parents: The Role of Adult Children* (Boston: Auburn House, 1981): 65–92; Horowitz and Dobrof, op. cit. (1982): 229–252.

21. Amy Horowitz and Lois Shindelman, "Social and Economic Incentives for Family Caregivers," Paper Presented at the 33rd Annual Scientific Meeting of the Gerontological Society of America, San Diego, California, 1980; Marvin B. Sussman, *Social and Economic Supports and Family Environment for the Elderly*. Final Report to the Administration on Aging, AOA. Grant # 90-A-316, January 1979.

22. G. M. Nelson, "Support for the Aged: Public and Private Responsibility," *Social Work* 27, 2 (1982): 137–143; Robert M. Moroney, *Families, Social Services and Social Policy: The Issue of Shared Responsibility* (Washington D.C.: United States Government Printing Office, 1980).

23. A. S. Kraus with R. A. Spasoff, E. J. Beattie, D. E. W. Holden, J. S. Lawson, M. Rodenburg, and G. M. Woodcock, "Elderly Application Process: Placement and Care Needs," *Journal of the American Geriatrics Society* 24 (1976): 165–172; Stanley J. Brody with S. W. Poulshock and C. F. Masciocchi, "The Family Caring Unit: A Major Consideration in the Long-Term Support

System," *The Gerontologist* 18, 6 (1978): 556–561; Jeanne A. Teresi with John A. Toner, Ruth. G. Bennett, and David E. Wilder, "Factors Related to Family Attitudes Toward Institutionalizing Older Relatives," paper presented at the 33rd Annual Scientific Meeting of the Gerontological Society, San Diego, Calif. (November 1980): 19–22.

24. Sheldon S. Tobin and R. Kulys, "The Family in the Institutionalization of the Elderly," *Journal of Social Issues* 37 (1981): 145–157; George L. Maddox, "Families as a Context and Resource in Chronic Illness," in S. Sherwood, ed., *Long-Term Care: A Handbook for Researchers, Planners, and Providers* (New York: Spectrum, 1975).

25. M. J. Gibson, "Women and Aging," paper presented at the International Symposium on Aging, Georgian Court College, Lakewood, N.J. (October 19, 1984).

26. Tish Sommers, "Cost of Care: What Do We Do With Grandmother?" *Gray Panther Network* (September/October 1983): 5.

27. Sandra J. Newman, "Government Policy and the Relationship between Adult Children and Their Aging Parents: Filial Support, Medicare and Medicaid," Institute for Social Research, Ann Arbor, Mich. (1980, unpublished): 10–19.

28. Dwight L. Frankfather with Michael J. Smith and Francis G. Caro, *Family Care of the Elderly: Public Initiatives and Private Obligations* (Lexington, Mass.: Lexington Books, 1981): 87–89.

29. Urban System Research and Engineering, "In-Home Services and the Contribution of Kin: Substitution Effects on Home Care Programs for the Elderly," Washington, D.C. (1982).

30. Carroll Estes, Robert Newcomer and associates, *Fiscal Austerity and Aging* (Beverly Hills, Calif. Sage Publications, 1983).

31. Newman, op. cit. (1980).

32. Horowitz and Shindelman, op. cit. (1980); Sussman, op. cit. (1979).

33. Brody, Johnson and Fulcomer, op. cit. (1984).

CHAPTER 1

Why Care for Aging Parents?

Deciding whether to sacrifice personal goals for a parent who needs care is a distinctly modern question. In preindustrial societies in which a 50-year-old was considered elderly, generations remained in their towns of origin, and with each other, throughout the life span. Expectations were as clear as what could be seen firsthand: people who survived to old age were cared for by their relatives. Although responsibility may have been abdicated or interpreted less generously in individual instances, the notion of giving care to parents was rarely questioned in most societies.

The separation of the home and the workplace is a characteristic of postindustrial society which makes giving care to parents especially difficult. Even those who do not leave their hometowns are likely to face the problem of working a distance from where they live. Adult children of the twentieth century can take an ailing parent into their homes, but their need to drive ten miles to work leaves the parent without assistance during the day. In the first half of this century, a woman would undoubtedly have been home to care for a parent. Now that women's responsibilities have expanded, they are also driving to the workplace. In the second half of this century, the home and workplace are becoming increasingly segregated, with people paying others to care for their children, and their parents, during the workday.

Caregiving now tends to be viewed in both the public mind and the professional literature as a restrictive burden that limits adult children's opportunities to pursue their own goals. Both the need to make money and the emphasis on a social identity derived from attainments in the workplace have made the care of a parent an interference, no matter how loving the relationship between a parent and an adult child. The emotional benefits derived from giving care to parents are not widely acknowledged, detached as they are from economic gain or social achievement.

This chapter first describes the opportunities for personal growth and satisfaction inherent in caregiving, and then explores two obstacles to taking advantage of these opportunities: the changes in the woman's role in modern society and the increasing geographic mobility of younger generations.

Caregiving as an Opportunity

By changing family rules, caregiving can be a primary opportunity for adult children to develop better relationships with their parents. Implicit rules and longstanding patterns within their families limit what people do and say. Many people move beyond these patterns of relating—outside their families—only to resume them in the presence of parents and siblings. For instance, a daughter who easily hugs her friends may find that a deeply established pattern of reserve within the family prevents her from hugging her mother. Similar familial constraints can keep certain topics off-limits, with family members feeling at a loss as to how to break through these verbal barriers.

The touching that is inherent in assisting with personal care almost always makes family members speak more tenderly and intimately than would otherwise be possible between them. For example, a daughter who helps her mother button her blouse each morning while recovering from a stroke may talk on a more personal level than she has ever previously ventured with her mother. It is difficult to hold on to past anger or resentment while buttoning someone's clothes or helping with other tasks requiring physical contact. The sight of a parent unable to get out of a chair or into a nightgown without assistance is emotionally moving to even the most embittered children, often provoking conciliatory gestures and remarks that have been absent for years.

Discovering strengths in siblings is another insufficiently heralded component of taking care of parents. Siblings are undeniably linked with each other through their parents, a connection that reasserts itself most intensely when parents become ill in later life. Needing to deal with adversity outside themselves, siblings who unite to battle the physical and practical encroachments on their parent's independence often come to appreciate each other in new ways. For instance, a daughter may be compelled by exhaustion to allow her historically unreliable sister to take over their mother's care on weekends. In doing so, she may find that her sister has overcome the faults of her past. For her sister, taking care of her mother may be a chance to redeem herself in the eyes of family members who live too far away to see how she has grown and changed.

In many families, comfortable ways for individual members to obtain time alone with each other are scarce, unless pretexts arise in the natural course of events. Caregiving offers tasks that can serve as pretexts for one-on-one time, without worry about hurting others by excluding them. A son may have spent most of his adult life visiting his mother in the company of his wife. While performing the most mundane chore, such as driving his mother to the pharmacy to pick up a prescription, he finds an opportunity to be alone with her. The kind of conversation which requires open-ended time and freedom from interruption can be accomplished during longer errands, such as a child accompanying a parent to the doctor. People who are unable to sit down and have emotionally significant conversations often lapse into them while driving a car or during other activities which divert their attention.

The sheer fact that adult children will take time out of their lives to help often moves parents to express greater warmth toward their children. A son who devotes two successive weekends to building his father a wheelchair ramp may receive the thanks and recognition from his father that he has yearned for all his life. This appreciation might then instigate a spiral of good experiences between them, as the son is spurred on to complete other vital projects and his father reacts with increasing warmth. Seeing each other more often under the guise of working on these projects can itself promote their closer acquaintance, perhaps also heightening their interest in each other's daily lives. Acts of helping have more power as communicators of love and respect than the most costly gifts sent in the mail or the most ardent claims of love over the phone.

Parents are commonly reluctant to grant their grown children equal footing with them as adults. This delay can persist long into later life, especially if geographic distance prevents parents from witnessing their children's success in jobs and relationships. More decisively than most life experiences, illnesses can cause a change in such a relationship by forcing parents to accept help from their children. A father who decides to rely on his son to do his banking, for example, implicitly affirms his son's capacities as an adult. Such reliance conveys a trust that may be deeply satisfying to the son. By allowing his son to be a provider of help, the father actually gives more emotionally than he receives practically.

Similarly, adult children often have difficulty seeing their parents as people. Many do not realize this perspective until they become parents themselves. Making mistakes with their own children, they begin to see how it might have been for their parents. Remarks such as, "Mom, now I know what you went through" or "Now I see why you worried about us so much" can open up discussion of what took place for the parent during the family's earlier years. Instead of harboring early resentments, adult children can liberate themselves through a willingness to look at the circumstances in a parent's life that may have contributed to poor parenting. Parents who feel forgiven and understood are much more likely to speak honestly about the past than those who detect that old resentments still deprive them of the right to be fallible human beings. Toward the end of their lives, parents often find it a relief to express their regrets—and their wisdom—when they sense this kind of openness from their children.

Confronting serious illness quickly accelerates the pace of change between adult children and their parents. Each realizes that time is running out, with no further chances to reach understandings. The sight of a parent in a hospital bed is a frequent catalyst for sons and daughters to put aside their hesitations and broach topics they have long wished to discuss. Parents' own confrontations with illness and dying often provoke a receptivity to such conversations, sometimes astonishing their children. Previously intractable conflicts may become amenable to resolution; family secrets that have gone unexplained or unspoken for years may be exposed and put to rest. From this perspective, participating actively in the last months of a parent's life can be a privilege for adult children wishing to achieve resolution of early life issues.

For some, early life issues cannot be resolved through this means. Adult children who were physically or emotionally abused as young children may have chosen to establish totally separate lives as adults. Their way of coping with negative memories may be to avoid contact with their parents or to keep communication at a controlled minimum. When phoned by a hospital discharge planner, for instance, a daughter of a formerly abusive parent may refuse to pick up the parent at the hospital and take him into her home for his recuperation period. She may reason, "I had a rotten childhood, so why should I go out of my way now?" Sensitivity to ambivalence is a critical prerequisite for professionals who encounter children of formerly abusive parents. In such situations, suggesting indirect helping tasks may enable estranged adult children to satisfy their sense of personal decency while still protecting themselves.

Women in the Middle

Value conflicts often make it difficult for women to derive satisfaction from giving care. Most women hold the traditional value that care of an older relative is a family responsibility, but they are increasingly confronted with, and often espouse, new competing values that women should be free to work outside the home and pursue their own interests as well. The value of being a good daughter or daughter-in-law may thus conflict with that of pursuing a career, returning to school, accepting a promotion, or simply having time for personal projects. At the same time that the proportion of older people in the population is rapidly growing, the numbers of middle-aged women entering the labor force have reduced the pool of people at home during the day to give care. These shifts in values and demographics have combined to pressure women from several directions, making the question of giving care to parents particularly painful for them.

The "woman in the middle" tends to be between 35 and 55 years of age. She is in the middle from a generational standpoint, with demands from younger and older relatives converging at once. The intensity of these demands may be heightened by their occurrence at a time when she is reevaluating her life and eager to pursue her own interests. Perhaps freed for the first time by her children being in college, she may experience a mixture of sadness and relief at endings, joy and fear of beginnings. Her recently gained sense of freedom and her ability to make long-range plans could be abruptly interrupted by an adult child who returns home after a divorce, by a spouse struggling with his midlife issues, and by aging parents. Other women in the middle who were born to older parents may face their parents' aging while pressured by the early stages of their careers. Those who bore children late have to cope with the demands of small children as well as with their aging parents.

Although many men provide care for their parents and children, the reality is that women are the primary caregivers to older and younger generations. Even when men and women rotate care responsibilities, women are more likely to find such demands burdensome to the extent that they internalize a sense of themselves as caregivers. Socialized from childhood on to attend to others' needs, women often have difficulty refusing requests for attention and nurturance from employers, workmates, and subordinates, as well as from relatives. If a family member is ill or in need, the emotional pull to be helpful generally takes precedence over intellectual demands to complete pressing work. Most women will drop a project at work or leave a half-finished manuscript to attend to family needs, while men more easily insist that they are too busy. At work and at home, men tend to be the symbolic fathers, too preoccupied with the large tasks of life and too busy to be disturbed; women remain the symbolic mothers, always available and nurturant, even when at work.

A woman's employer, spouse, and children tend to reinforce these sex-based distinctions by their expectations for her to be "superwife" and "supermom" who can work, drive the carpool, respond to another's illness, and still have time to exercise and entertain. As a result of these competing demands, employed women who are also primary caregivers often end up feeling they are not doing any job well. They may try to resolve such conflicts by quitting work or reducing their hours. Such modifications, however, generally do not remove the source of their conflicts, leaving a residue of resentment and frustration to accumulate. The reality is that the combination of work and the care of dependents does not involve a redistribution of existing tasks, but rather creates a larger total package of responsibilities for women to complete or delegate. The hours in the day are simply insufficient to perform their conflicting roles and still have time for themselves. Although some women may cope efficiently in meeting their multiple demands, they may do so at expense to their sense of self. Continuously confronted by others' demands during the workday, evenings, and weekends, such women may long for the time to sit alone for even five minutes or take a bath without being interrupted. They may come to resent the phone ringing or a knock at the door, which represent yet another request and therefore another intrusion.

Although increasing numbers of women are working because of career commitments or a desire for self-fulfillment, the majority do so because of economic necessity. Financial pressures are intensified by inflation, as well as by familial expectations of two salaries to assure a certain standard of living. For many women, no spouse is available to provide economic and social support. Given the high rates of divorce and widowhood, women are more likely to face caregiving and financial responsibilities on their own as they get older. Since on the average women earn considerably less than men, their employment status does not ensure that they will have extra money to purchase services to cover the surplus of responsibilities they face. Single parents with dependent children are especially unlikely to have the resources needed for child care, respite, in-home assistance, or even labor-saving appliances. In addition, divorced or widowed women may remain emotionally tied to their in-laws, assisting them as well as their own parents while trying to attain economic security on their own.

Not only do women earn less than men, but they also are concentrated in jobs such as teaching, nursing, social work, or service occupations that emphasize tending to the needs of others. As a result, women are likely to give more support than they receive, and create an imbalance in both their work and home relationships. Moreover, women's interactions with people dependent upon them may be more aversive than pleasant. Interacting with a feverish toddler, a rebellious teenager, or a cognitively impaired older person can be singularly unrewarding. Skilled at nurturing and serving others, many women in the middle receive little nurturance themselves. This "support gap" can be a major source of stress for many women.

Another problem with the lower-status jobs generally filled by women is that they often do not permit the flexibility of taking time off during the day to attend to a sick child or parent. Hourly-pay jobs usually require a deduction in pay for missed time. Lower-status jobs may include the further pressure of close supervisory scrutiny of the ways that sick time is used, whereas a higher-status employee does not need to feign illness as a cover for helping a family member. For women in such lower-status jobs, their vacations, sick leaves, and holidays may be filled with attending to others' needs, rather than providing time for activities which renew their stamina.

Women who are employed in higher-status positions may possess greater worktime flexibility, which allows adjustments for caregiving demands. Ironically, however, utilizing this flexiblity may place women at a disadvantage for promotions, juxtaposed to male colleagues who do not take time off for caregiving. For instance, an attorney's contract negotiations may be interrupted by her daughter or her mother calling to ask her for help. Trying to complete her negotiations, she may find herself distracted by the problems at home.

Caregiving remains central to women's identity, even among those efficient and successful in the business world. What has happened with women's movement into careers is an expansion of their spheres, without a compensatory reduction in their other responsibilities. Simply urging such women to manage their time more efficiently does not address the unequal distribution of responsibilities inherent in traditional sex-role socialization and societal expectations.

These responsibilities may be further complicated by geographic distance. For instance, a daughter may take a month's emergency leave from work in order to help her mother with the difficult weeks following a stroke. By midmonth, the daughter may realize that her mother is not improving rapidly enough to be left on her own. Hiring someone to provide round-the-clock home care would exceed the cost of nursing-home care. Yet if the daughter lived in her mother's community, she could hire outside help during the work hours, requiring that she fill in only on weekends and evenings. Without this option, she is faced with the dilemma of staying longer than a month and possibly losing her job or resorting to a nursing home.

Women who leave the work force in response to such dilemmas often confront others' assumptions that they have gained free time and relief from pressures. The reality is that caring for children or parents requires the management of multiple details—which child to drive to basketball practice and pick up from piano lessons, the date of a parent's doctor appointment, the sequence of a parent's daily medications, and whether the meat has been removed from the freezer. The psychological burden of remembering what to do can be greater than performing the acts themselves. Although these matters may not be inherently stressful, their accumulation day after day can become taxing to the point of mental and physical exhaustion. A husband returning home from work may complain about his wife not spending enough time with him, without perceiving that household, child-care, and kin-keeping responsibilities add up to more than a full-time job.

Having internalized social expectations, many women resist setting limits on their helping efforts and refuse offers of help from others. To say "no" to unreasonable requests goes against their moral grain, despite the most emphatic professional encouragement to take care of themselves. In some instances, professionals may need to focus on persuading overloaded women to give up caregiving, at least for a respite period when they can give credence to their own needs: "Look, you're not sleeping at night, you've lost weight, and you look terrible. You've done everything you can for her, and it's time to admit that it's not working out." Helping such women recognize the line between doing their utmost and threatening their own health and well-being, in addition to teaching them to use supplementary community resources, is a critical professional responsibility.

Another professional imperative is to try to involve resistant husbands and brothers in caregiving, rather than following the path of least resistance with their wives and sisters. When assisting families in negotiating their division of care tasks, professionals should take steps to ensure that physical care and housekeeping responsibilities are distributed fairly, rather than according to traditional sex roles. Discharge planners in hospitals should attempt to contact sons as well as daughters. Professionals need to be sensitive to how they inadvertently reinforce women's inclinations to try to "do it all" through subtle remarks or through failure to expect more from male members of caregiving families.

These emotionally charged issues, woven in the fabric of our society, are not easily confronted by either professionals or family members. Such fundamental assumptions about men's and women's roles and responsibilities must be questioned in order to assure the long-range well-being of both the women in the middle and persons dependent upon them for care. Accessible day care for both children and older adults, additional flex-time and job-sharing arrangements, and financial subsidies for caregiving are only a few of the societal responses which could ease pressures on women.

Long-Distance Caregiving

Geographic mobility often separates children from parents in early adulthood and, to a large extent, slows down the development of bonds between them. Although most older people who have adult children live near one of them, growing numbers of adult children live at a distance from parents. Problems frequently arise between siblings who live near parents and those who do not, due to differences in perspective and attitudes toward the parents. Giving care to parents from out of town poses tactical and emotional challenges which are even more difficult when no family member lives in their local area. A further pressure entailed by long-distance caregiving is deciding whether or not parents in this position should move to be closer to their adult children.

Differences in perspective cause conflict between even the most harmonious out-of-town and local family members. Care tasks glimpsed for a week or two can seem less burdensome than when experienced on a daily and protracted basis. Visiting family members may offer innocuous suggestions such as, "Why don't you take Mom out to dinner more often?," without realizing that the local helpers already feel weary from accumulated errands and dinners. This perceptual gap widens even more when the older person improves in response to the visit of a rarely seen family member, failing to display the difficult behaviors and symptoms that will resume after the visitor departs.

Daily contact with the older person often prevents local relatives from noticing health changes that are obvious to infrequent visitors. When out-of-town family members arrive after a long absence, their shock at their parent's deterioration may be matched only by their local relative's unawareness of these changes. Functional losses from arthritic diseases, for instance, can occur so gradually that helpers close to the situation do not realize that they have gradually taken over many household tasks. Instances of memory loss are especially prone to this phenomenon, with visiting family members berating local relatives for being poor informants, for example, "Why didn't you tell us Mom's memory has gotten so bad?"

When they are hit abruptly with the sight of a parent's deterioration, adult children tend to direct their reactions of helplessness and outrage toward their siblings. On a rational level, they know that their relatives are not responsible, but there is no other way to vent these accusations: "Why didn't you get her to the doctor sooner? How could you let her live like this?" Local relatives become understandably defensive in response to such remarks: "It's easy for you to come into town for one week and tell us what to do, then disappear for months while we're stuck with all the work." A commonly used silencing technique in these instances is to play on out-of-town family members' guilt. To help prevent hurt feelings from escalating, professionals can point out to local people that their relative's anger is most likely at the older person's illness rather than at them.

Another disparity in perspectives arises from the fact that most care arrangements are the result of a gradual, ongoing process rather than clear choice. As the older person's health status deteriorates, local helpers accept imperfect solutions to the problems that emerge gradually. A son may struggle for months to persuade his father to accept a chore worker's services, and finally settle for the insufficient but tolerable compromise of having the worker come once a week. Arriving in town for her annual visit, his sister may assail him for "letting Dad live like a pig" when she sees the cluttered condition of their father's household. Visiting family members often do not realize that they are witnessing the outcome of a carefully considered series of compromises, rather than neglectful or irresponsible care.

During the initial days of the visit, both local and out-of-town family members may need professional reminders to give each other time to adjust. Simply being made aware of these differences of perspective prior to encountering them often helps family members avoid conflict. It is particularly important for out-of-town family members to refrain from criticizing the care until they have gathered information; likewise, local people need to realize their advantage in being able to adjust incrementally to what visitors encounter all at once. The recognition that care dilemmas cannot always be resolved to satisfy all family members may also reduce pressure on families to achieve solutions during the concentrated time they are reunited.

Another discovery out-of-town family members often make during their visits is that the older person's situation is worse than communicated by letter and phone. Making the most of geographic privacy, some older people exclude their problems from phone conversations with family members. In this way, they can screen evidence of their decline for long periods of time, until an acute crisis reveals their level of need, for example, "My daughter's got her own worries. What could she have done about my swollen foot from 2,000 miles away?" The older person may not intend to deceive family members, but rather to make the best of the situation on her own. Coming upon such surprise problems during visits, family members may regard the concealment as deception rather than protectiveness.

Trying to cope with an older person's care needs when there are no involved local relatives is another matter entirely. Family members are faced with the need to solve as many problems as they can within the duration of their visit, aware that follow-up on any actions they initiate will be limited to phone calls and subsequent visits. In addition to their time constraints, they may be pressured by a lack of familiarity with the older person's community and worries about their unattended commitments at home. For those who visit without a partner, the separation from personal sources of support can also heighten the difficulty of the situation. Working people who are conscious of using up precious vacation time for the visit tend to feel an added urgency to try to resolve everything in order to avoid using up their next vacation for the same purpose.

Prior to visiting or immediately upon arrival, out-of-town family members should contact a professional in their relative's community who can provide an appraisal of the local services. Staff persons of organizations which are targeted to serve older people, such as senior centers and senior hotlines, possess more useful information about a community's specialized resources than could be obtained by randomly calling agencies out of the telephone book. Associations such as the American Cancer Society, the Arthritis Foundation, and the Lung Association can be particularly helpful in recommending services for specific health problems. Some communities have private agencies that specialize in assisting out-of-town relatives with coordinating services for older people.

The amount of lead time needed to set up care arrangements can be exasperating to visiting relatives. For example, the older person may be eligible for the state's chore-service program, but the delay before someone does the required home assessment may be up to a week. Another waiting period may occur before the service actually begins. In addition, the older person may initially resist strangers' assistance in the home and need time to become accustomed to the sense of intrusion and loss of control. Hiring someone through a newspaper advertisement may not be feasible because of the need to stay in town long enough to ensure that the person is trustworthy and can handle the care responsibilities. Private-pay services through agencies, which require only a day's notice, are the most convenient in these instances, but the hourly rates may be prohibitive for many families.

Another problem produced by time constraints is the tendency for visiting family members to try to obtain as much information as they can during their limited contact with health professionals caring for their relative. They may have the unrealistic expectation that health-care providers should go out of their way to spend time with them because of the distance they have traveled to be there. Pressured by their heavy caseloads, the health professsionals may try to conduct briefer discussions than family members feel is their right or need. The contradictory pressures of such discussions can frustrate all participants. A helpful strategy is for families to contact the health care professionals by telephone first, notifying them of the impending visit and letting them know the specific kinds of information they will be seeking, rather than expecting the professional to drop everything when they arrive.

When family members plan to visit in response to their relative's hospitalization, calling ahead to the primary nurse or discharge planner also personalizes the care provided by hospital staff. Information about the older person's life history, family relationships, and present lifestyle helps hospital staff establish realistic posthospital plans. In addition, discharge planners need to know the names and capabilities of people in the local support system who have most actively assisted the older person. By saving hospital staff the time and effort needed to identify such helpers, out-of-town family members hasten the planning process and ensure that necessary community resource referrals are made in a timely manner.

After the stress and expense of flying back and forth to repeated crises, out-of-town relatives are often attracted to the idea of moving the older person to their community: "Mom, if you lived near us, we could really help you instead of just putting out fires." From the older person's perspective, the losses in such a move may seem much greater than the gains. The thought of leaving lifelong friends, moving out of a long-term home, and learning a new area implies an immensity of effort that some find overwhelming. The older person may also wonder if she will find a physician with as much skill and warmth as her family doctor or if she can build a social network of helpful and supportive neighbors.

Despite these objections to leaving her community, an older person may tell herself, "At my age, I should be near my kids." She may be afraid of delaying the move until "something happens" which will make her regret having waited. Many people believe that it is always better to move near family in later life, no matter how rooted they have been in their long-term communities. Even though decades may have elapsed since they last had daily contact with their adult children, they assume that bonds of blood are the most crucial toward the end of life.

The major problem with an older parent's move to an adult child's community is that it can abruptly overload their relationship. Having left support systems behind, the parent becomes entirely dependent on family members for social contact and practical assistance. Renewing family relationships requires a certain amount of emotional stamina under any circumstances. Doing so under the compulsion of care needs does not allow an approach that is gradual enough. For instance, a daughter may pressure her mother to move to her community after an unsuccessful cataract operation. Her mother's extensive needs for assistance due to vision problems would change their relationship from infrequent long-distance calls to daily face-to-face contact, with no transitional time to reestablish their bonds on a happier basis.

25

The daughter is likely to discover that she cannot possibly fill in for the friend with whom her mother talked on the telephone every morning for 20 years. The daughter may realize that she is making room in her life for someone she calls "Mom" but whom she does not know very well as a person. Even when healthy, independent parents announce that they are thinking of moving near their adult children, their offspring often react with anxiety: "Will we get along if we see each other more often?" Relationships which have succeeded within the limits imposed by geographic distance require extensive readjustment when this limitation is removed. The pragmatic decisions of how often to see each other and how often to call, in addition to the deeper questions of privacy, become subject to sensitive renegotiation. These renegotiations, combined with the intensification of contact, may strain the relationship in ways that neither wants, but feels at a loss to prevent.

Her mother may find herself missing everyone from her beautician to the custodian in the senior high-rise where she lived for several years. Trying to reenact these bonds in a new community, she may find that natural helping networks that evolved over a span of years are not easily replaceable. Many older people are not cognizant of the value of remaining in their own communities until after they move away. To avoid situations of regret, families should urge their relatives to view the move in terms of a trial period. One option is for the older person to rent an apartment for a few months in the new community. It is usually not difficult to convince someone that the cost of maintaining two residences for a few months is worth preserving the possibility of moving back. Such trial periods are especially useful following a spouse's death or another event that may have hastened the decision to move.

Professionals in the field of aging often feel especially neglectful about living at a distance from their older relatives. In their daily work, they see the difference it makes when family members are actively involved in older people's lives. They tend to carry an extra degree of guilt about their own parents and grandparents: "Here I am helping everyone else's grandmothers, while mine gets hardly any help from me." Such professionals are keenly aware of the difficulty of practicing their expertise over the phone or through brief visits. They also hear themselves giving advice to others that they are unable to follow in their own lives, for example, "How can I counsel other people to do what I'm not doing?" Furthermore, experienced professionals, who are able to extrapolate from current circumstances to what the future is likely to bring, do not have the luxury of ignorance about the implications of their choices.

In trying to answer "why care?," most adult children face a continual tug of war between what they feel they *ought* to do and what they *want* to do. Although they may crave a single decision which resolves the matter, this conflict between duty and personal choice tends to erupt over and over again as their parents get older and need more from them. The chapters which follow survey the wide emotional and practical territory of giving care to parents in a modern society. The dynamics between spouses as caregivers are presented first, since they struggle with earlier versions of these same dilemmas.

Suggested Resources

Caregiving Dilemmas Faced by Adult Children

BRODY, ELAINE. " 'Women in the Middle' and Family Help to Older People," *The Gerontologist,* 21, 5, (1981): 471.
> Examines the phenomena of middle-aged women whose work competes with their caregiving demands. Compares attitudes of those generations of women toward filial responsibility, gender-appropriate roles, and preferences for types of service providers.

Change, Newsletter of National Support Center for Families of the Aging, P.O., Box 245, Swarthmore, PA 19081.
> Focused on caregivers, this newsletter includes articles by caregivers and practical tips for coping.

CICIRELLI, VICTOR. *Helping Elderly Parents: The Role of the Adult Children* (Boston: Auburn House, 1982).
> Findings of a survey of adult children's attitudes and caregiving behaviors toward their parents.

Family Seminars for Caregiving: Helping Families Help. (Seattle: Pacific Northwest Long Term Care Gerontology Center, University of Washington, 1985).
> A manual for professionals to aid them to prepare and present a series of six seminars for caregivers of chronically impaired older persons. Each set of topics includes content outline, suggested readings, handouts, and group activities.

FINCH, JANET, AND DULCIE GRAVES. *A Labor of Love: Women, Work and Caring* (London: Routledge & Kegan Paul, 1983).
> An insightful analysis of women's caregiving for dependent persons and how social policies fail to support their efforts. The analysis is based upon the tension between women's economic independence and their traditional role as caregivers.

GORDON, MARY. *Final Payments* (New York: Ballantine Books, 1978).
> A novel which powerfully portrays the isolation of caregivers. A young woman of thirty reenters the world of paid work and social relationships after caring for her father for ten years.

L'ENGLE, MADELINE. *The Summer of the Great-Grandmother* (New York: The Seabury Press, 1979).
> A beautifully written, moving account of a daughter's caring for her mother and the daughter's approach to her mother's dying.

RUBEN, DIANE. *Caring: A Daughter's Story* (New York: Holt, Rinehart & Winston, 1982).

> A personal account of a daughter's care and concern for two ailing parents and the maturation of the relationship between mother and daughter. Openly expresses her ambivalent feelings about caregiving.

WHARTON, WILLIAM. *Dad* (New York: Avon Books, 1981).

> A fictional account of a middle-aged son's coping with his parents' aging. Emphasis on intergenerational dynamics.

Ethnic and Cultural Differences

How families care for their older members varies with ethnic and cultural values. For additional reading about ethnic differences, the following resources are suggested.

JACKSON, JACQUELYN J. *Minorities and Aging* (Belmont, Calif: Wadsworth Publishing, 1980).

> Includes an excellent bibliography and annotated references on minority aging. Maintains that extended family caregiving, characteristic of minorities, has developed partially in reaction to being excluded from programs, not necessarily out of preference.

Minority Elderly: A Historical and Cultural Perspective (Corvallis: Oregon State University, Division of Continuing Education, 1979).

> Examines different needs and expectations among Black, Native American, Pacific Asian, Hispanic older people.

STANFORD, E. PERCIL (ed.). *Minority Aging: Policy Issues for the 80s* (San Diego: San Diego State University, Campanile Press, 1981).

> A collection of conference proceedings on the health status, economic conditions, and social services of minorities.

WOEHRER, CAROL E. "The Influence of Ethnic Families on Intergenerational Relationships and Late Life Transition," *Annals of the American Academy of Political and Social Science*, no. 464 (November 1982): 65–79.

> Examines how ethnic values, family patterns, and socialization influence intergenerational interaction in adulthood among a wide range of ethnic groups.

Also of interest is a series published by San Diego State University, Campanile Press, including the following:

EVA CHENG, *The Elder Chinese*, 1978.

KAREN ISHIZUKA, *The Elder Japanese*, 1978.

FRANK DUKEPOO, *The Elder American Indian*, 1980.

ROBERTA PETERSON, *The Elder Philipino*, 1978.

RAMON VALLE AND LYDIA MENDOZA, *The Elder Latino*, 1978.

E. PERCIL STANFORD, *The Elder Black*, 1978.

CHAPTER 2

Spouses as Caregivers

Spouses are the most frequent caregivers. Adult children and other relatives generally assume daily caregiving responsibilities only when a spouse is absent. Most frequently, an older wife is caregiver to a disabled husband. Caregiving demands are intensified for spouses who are coping with declining reserves of energy, physical illness, and the stresses of medical expenses. In addition, few community resources are available to support spouses in their caregiving efforts. In fact, an implicit but unspoken assumption has been that when a wife is present, she can and should care for her husband. Accordingly, such women are often hidden victims, whose isolation, loneliness, and fatigue may be overlooked by service providers.

Regardless of the partners' ages or the caregiver's gender, illness can exacerbate a marriage's weaknesses or benefit from its strengths. Chronic illness challenges the coping skills inherent in the best marriages, especially when combined with other difficult aspects of aging, such as friends' deaths and the loss of former occupations or activities. It should not be assumed that a spouse will provide daily care; rather, a variety of factors which affect a couple's ability to cope with illness in old age need to be assessed. The viability of particular care arrangements should be evaluated when spouses first assume care responsibilities, as well as periodically throughout the caregiving process. The questions below suggest critical factors to be considered when spouses give care, followed by a discussion of the effects of illness on marital relationships. The ways that caregiving issues may vary for gay and lesbian couples are then examined, with particular attention to helpful responses professionals can employ.

Factors to Consider When Spouses Become Caregivers

1. *What was the length of the marriage prior to the onset of the illness?* Is it a marriage of convenience or a deep bonding?
2. *What is the health status of the caregiving spouse?* Is he or she healthy enough to meet the care demands without physical or emotional harm to him or herself?
3. *What were the predisability marital patterns?* Did the couple previously face adversity in a unified or divided way? Has there been a high degree of emotional abuse?
4. *What is the timing of the onset of the illness relative to retirement plans?* Was the couple about to enact long-awaited plans? Does the healthier partner feel cheated as a result of the illness?
5. *What is the nature of the symptoms produced by the illness?* Is the care particularly difficult or repugnant? Is depression a component of the illness?
6. *How adaptable is the couple's residence?* Can adjustments be made to accommodate the care needs?
7. *What are the couple's cultural or spiritual attitudes toward illness and caretaking?* Does each believe in marriage until death, with care during illness as an essential part of the commitment?
8. *What is the nature of the sexual adjustment entailed by the illness?* Does the couple need to begin sleeping separately? Has the illness made sexual activity frightening or painful?
9. *What is the impact of the illness on the couple's financial resources?* Is there an added stress from uncovered medical expenses? Is the need for hiring extra help eroding their life savings?
10. *To what extent is the couple receiving support from family members, friends, and community-based services?* Are financial considerations limiting vital forms of assistance?

Marital Belief Systems

Any analysis of spouses as caregivers is at its basis an examination of varying conceptions of marriage. Whether consciously or unconsciously, individuals marry and remain married for a wide range of reasons, some of which have little to do with the notion of being in love. Among these are the desire for children, physical attraction and sexual need, parental and societal pressures, economic security, unmet dependency needs, and the desire for companionship. Based on varied reasons, the meaning of the marital commitment for particular couples can range from, "I'll stay with you so long as you enhance my life and meet my needs," to "I'll stay with you through sickness and health, till death do us part."

In some versions of marriage, the underlying belief system supports caregiving only to the extent that it does not curtail one partner's personal needs or life plans. For example, a later-life marriage may occur more for economic convenience and the need for companionship than from a deep love commitment. The healthier spouse would then be left in a bind if the other became ill, with medical bills and limited mobility disrupting the financial and social basis of the marriage. In this situation, legal separation and nursing home placement may appear to be the only way to gain desired security and freedom to seek another companion. Similarly, a spouse in an unhappy marriage of long duration might choose to reject caregiving if it impedes retirement plans to which she has looked forward for many years.

In other types of marriages, the personal sacrifice accompanying the provision of care becomes a meaningful way to express gratitude for years of mutual devotion. Cultural and religious values, personal creeds of loyalty, or beliefs that caregiving in old age is an irrevocable marital responsibility may underlie such partners' reactions to disabling illness. Within this concept of marriage, the healthier spouse tends to regard nursing home placement as a failure to live up to the marital commitment, no matter how seriously placement is warranted by the nature of the care. In such instances, the spouse may need help relinquishing care that has become detrimental to her own health.

Since marital belief systems arc rarely articulated until challenged by life crises, partners with contrasting beliefs often discover these differences for the first time during the crises themselves. A person who believes that caregiving in old age is an irrevocable part of the marital bond may discover that the spouse leans more toward a belief in individual life enhancement. Although it may be impossible to mitigate the disappointment of such a discovery made during a disabling illness, the couple may find professionals helpful in articulating their inner beliefs and moving beyond the hurtful particulars of their situation.

Difficult Kinds of Care Between Spouses

Guilt-Laden Caregiving

Some spouses feel that enjoying their own mobility while their partners suffer illness and confinement is contrary to the meaning of marriage. As a result, they curtail out-of-home activities and personal pleasures. Such individuals often bear an unrelenting sense that they should be doing more for their partners, despite their inability to conceive of what additional efforts could be helpful. This type of caregiver tends to feel guilty during outings which family members try to provide, as if they are luxuries obtained at the ill person's expense. Such a wife or husband needs the encouragement to view rest and pleasure as essential to competent caregiving, for example, "What would happen to Dad if you got worn out?" Family members may need to emphasize repeatedly that by taking care of themselves, spouses prolong their ability to give care and increase the quality of their care.

Guilt arising from past conflicts is also detrimental because it makes spouses easy to manipulate. Spouses who feel the need to perform acts of penance or to repay the emotional debts are vulnerable to demands for inordinate amounts of service. If control through manipulation of guilt has been a long-standing dynamic in the marriage, this pattern tends to become exaggerated under caregiving pressures. A husband who has been paying emotionally for an affair since the early years of his marriage may become servile as a caregiver, waiting on his wife and giving up his own needs in response to her demands. Such a spouse essentially joins his partner in using caregiving as a punishment for a wrong which could not be righted. Whatever the source of guilt, a sense of debt of this magnitude can be imprisoning to a spouse and may require marriage counseling as an intervention.

Another kind of guilt stems from forbidden feelings which a spouse tries to suppress. One of the most common of these is anger at the partner for becoming ill. Although the caregiving spouse knows rationally that the person could not help becoming ill, anger can arise in reaction to the immensity of the disappointment. For example, a couple planning to embark on a cross-country trip in their new camper may find their plans terminated by the husband becoming disabled by a stroke. Providing 24-hour care instead of touring the country, the wife is likely to feel angry, no matter how loving their relationship or how clearly she acknowledges to herself that the stroke is not her husband's fault. Guilt from suppressed anger can be most detrimental when it prevents the spouse from obtaining necessary rest or is expressed in subtle hostility.

Dislike for a spouse whose personality has changed in response to illness is another forbidden feeling conducive to guilt. Some formerly expansive personalities contract or withdraw when chronic pain or physical dependency come to dominate their existence; they may become focused on somatic complaints or disinterested in others' lives. A spouse may miss her partner as he used to be, and suppress her dislike of spending time with this previously admired person. Family members can provide valuable help by acknowledging these unappealing personality changes and admitting their own difficulties in coping with them. When the feeling of dislike is thus released from its taboo, the spouse gains relief from some of this isolation and guilt.

Excessive Caregiving

Some spouses carry caregiving to an extreme. Although the types of guilt depicted previously can be the causes, excessive caregiving can also stem from the healthier spouse having no other meaningful activity on which to focus. In such instances, the partner's illness produces something to do and talk about in an otherwise uneventful life. It yields appreciation from family members which was otherwise scarce, as well as increases the frequency of their visits and calls. When well-meaning family members attempt to assume some of the caregiving tasks, they may encounter resistance deriving primarily from the spouse's need to fill open time and to possess an important role. When family members point out improvements in the ill partner's health status, the caregiving spouse may present them with an onslaught of evidence to justify her gains in role status and contact.

A spouse's need to keep her partner in a sick role can produce roadblocks to the partner's regaining independence. By providing unnecessary help, the caregiver removes opportunities for stimulation and exercise, as well as chances to practice self-care skills. If the ill partner welcomes the excessive care, family members and professionals may find it difficult to break this mutually satisfying cycle. One strategy best attempted by a professional is to ask the caregiver to visualize what her sudden illness or death would mean for her partner should the state of dependency persist.

Learning how to withhold help is a challenging aspect of caregiving for most spouses. When assistance can be granted in a matter of seconds, forcing a partner to tolerate discomfort requires a great deal of mental fortitude. For example, a man wanting to facilitate his wife's recovery from a stroke may know that he should let his wife struggle to get her arm into her blouse. If she yells at him during the course of her frustration, his ability to withhold help may falter. A helpful technique in such situations is for the couple to agree on a set number of minutes that the disabled partner will attempt to accomplish a task on her own. The caregiver then takes on the role of the timekeeper, while the disabled partner focuses on a defined period of effort during which pain must be tolerated. Both partners may need to be reminded that future gains are more important than immediate discomfort.

Impact of Physical Changes

The degree to which the illness produces body-image changes is particularly crucial for spouses. Limb amputation, colostomy, breast removal, and one-sided paralysis are among the most visible of such changes, and among those most difficult with which to deal. More subtle shifts in body image can also occur with open sores, severe weight loss, skin problems, and arthritic deformities. People experiencing such bodily changes often try to avoid contact with the altered body part and to prevent others from seeing the changes. Spouses may be reluctant to have their partners participate in their personal care out of fear that their revulsion will be shared. To guard further against this vulnerability, they may distance themselves from all forms of physical contact, often to the caregiver's bewilderment and dislike. If educated to anticipate such defensive reactions, their partners may be able to avoid interpreting them as personal rejection or uncooperative obstinacy. Couples who are financially able to hire supplementary caregivers to handle intimate personal care tasks involving body contact may be better able to adjust to such physical changes.

In some instances, the caregiver has difficulty accepting the partner's physical changes. Using supplementary caregivers then serves to prevent the hurt that would occur if the caregiver's nonacceptance should become evident. Irrespective of any change in a body part, physical aversion may affect a caregiver when stool, urine, or soiled clothing must be handled. Additionally, if the couple has been sexually active prior to the onset of the illness, some spouses may find their sexual feelings incompatible with their functioning as caregivers. For others, simply the image of their spouse needing bathroom assistance may conflict with a need to retain the partner in a protective, dominant role.

Another aspect of illness which affects spouses is the frequency of contact required by the care. For couples whose marriages have survived largely on the basis of minimal contact, the addition of disabling illness to retirement can be markedly disruptive. The sheer amount of time spent together in the home may multiply to the point at which both partners experience feelings of encroachment. As longstanding boundaries are violated, the losses in solitude and privacy can themselves produce irritability and conflict. If both become homebound as one attempts to take care of the other, or as each experiences confining mobility problems, the loss of buffers, such as recreational and volunteer activities, may uncover marital problems previously masked by the couple's ability to avoid each other. Rather than attempting to mediate such conflicts, family members and friends can often do the greatest service by helping such couples recover some of their time separate from one another.

Illnesses with ambiguous symptoms pose special dilemmas. The more symptoms fluctuate, the more difficult it is to establish and maintain care routines. Respiratory illness, heart conditions, and arthritic diseases can produce such variability in levels of functioning that a caregiver may be unable to arrive at a stable set of expectations for her partner or herself. The caregiver may wonder why her partner is able to perform certain tasks on one day but not the next. Such circumstances contrast with more clearly demarcated situations, such as paralysis or amputation. Even if their preillness relationship did not involve manipulation, the caregiver may feel that the partner uses physical complaints for power or convenience rather than actual need. Illnesses with ambiguous symptoms allow room for conflict over who does what in the household and how strenuously a caregiver should push toward the ill person's resumption of independence.

Role Disruption

The disruption of longstanding marital roles can be the most devastating of all the effects of illness on spouses. Along with patterns of proximity, partners tend to evolve a division of labor in which each has responsibility for different areas of their mutual life. Such role differentiation in the relationship can become deeply habituated over time. In some marriages, the distribution of roles is skewed, with one partner assuming the protective, managerial role and establishing a parentlike relationship to the other. If the more dependent person in such a marriage becomes disabled, the couple can often absorb the change into its ongoing pattern of interaction. If the parentlike person becomes disabled, however, the reversal of the dependency can cause chaos in the marriage.

The spouse with longstanding dependency needs tends to seek gratification from the nearest outpost of strength. Upon losing the partner's protection, the more dependent spouse is likely to try to place other family members in the directive or decision-making roles vacated by the ill partner. Family members may find themselves suddenly responsible for two older people, one weakened by illness and the other left newly vulnerable. The partner unaccustomed to sharing control is likely to suffer deeply from the need to compromise and negotiate. At the same time, the other partner tends to experience anxiety, sleeplessness, and other signs of stress, resulting from the double tension of the caregiving needs combined with new feelings of vulnerability. Family members stepping into the protective role can themselves become the object of the disabled partner's frustration and may need to find ways to restore portions of the lost control (see pages 151–158).

35

Family members can also attempt to help the caregiver obtain competence in areas of life not previously mastered. Frustrated from seeing someone else perform in her domain, the disabled partner may repeatedly focus on the tasks her spouse does incorrectly. Thereby, the disabled partner undermines the spouse's efforts to master new roles as cook, housecleaner, car mechanic, or financial manager. Learning new tasks can create situations ripe for verbal explosions, which can leave residual damage in the relationship. Family members observing this dynamic around role changes can help by regularly providing the missing appreciation which the disabled person is unable to give to the caregiver and offering specific instruction on the mechanics of the new roles. Once a degree of mastery is attained, the caregiver should be cautioned to expect expressions of rage which have nothing to do with the quality of the efforts involved, but rather relate to stylistic differences in the way tasks are accomplished. Divergent opinions as to how neatly clothes are to be folded, the way dishes are to be washed, the degree of exactitude necessary to balance a checkbook, how carefully a car is to be handled, and the way a garden is to be maintained—all of these can be infuriating to a person who has lost control over areas of life previously managed without interference.

When Both Partners Become Ill

Marital coping with illness can be exponentially more complex when both partners need to give and receive care. Given the increasing incidence of chronic illness with age, older couples are likely to have simultaneous care needs. The following chart depicts examples of disparities between spouses' abilities and their partners' needs which can be particularly difficult to resolve. This chart can also be used to assess the caregiver's capability over time.

The prospect of either living apart or leaving a long-term home is often more abhorrent to an older couple than the awareness that their mutual caregiving is detrimental. A man with cardiac problems may persist in picking his wife up off the floor after her frequent falls, despite his physician's warnings against such lifting and his family's pleading not to endanger himself. His reluctance to call on family members for help each time his wife falls may arise from fear that the family would insist on her going to a nursing home if they knew how often the falls occurred. Realizing that they possess a different conception of how much danger is acceptable, older couples frequently choose to keep their private adaptations and compromises out of family members' view. In fact, this type of concealment may be at the basis of apparently irrational behavior, such as

Care Needs	Caregiver Characteristics Which Can Interfere with Caregiving
• Help getting dressed, preparing meals, and other activities of daily living.	Arthritis, Parkinson's disease, and other illnesses which impair fine motor ability, such as fastening clothing, opening jars, and so forth.
• Help locating things in the home. • Keeping track of bills, medications, needed grocery items.	Vision or memory impairment that cannot be solved by establishing routine locations for household items and memory aids.
• Assistance with transfers, such as getting in and out of a wheelchair, getting up off the floor after falls, getting in and out of the tub.	Back problems, respiratory diseases, or cardiac conditions which preclude lifting or strenuous exertion.
• Help with unpredictable needs and highly variable forms of assistance for which care patterns cannot be established.	High blood pressure, respiratory diseases, conditions for which stress is harmful; advanced memory loss, severe hearing loss, visual impairments, or other disability for which set routines are vital.

the postponement of needed surgery and the refusal to accept home-care services.

The systems of mutual helping evolved by couples can leave family members unaware for years of the extent of their care needs. For example, a woman with a declining ability to use her hands may employ her intact memory to compensate for her partner's progressive memory loss, giving him step-by-step directives for the completion of the physical tasks she can no longer manage. Similarly, a man needing assistance with walking may use his eyes to help his visually-impaired wife, while she uses her physical agility to help him. The inventiveness of the methods used by such couples to meet the demands of daily life tend to reflect the intensity of their motivation to remain together in their home. Their interlocking methods may produce a reasonably safe situation as long as they are able to remain together.

When mutual caregiving does endanger the welfare of one or both spouses, family members may find it difficult to allow them the choice of remaining together. For example, adult children may become angry at their mother for sacrificing her health for their father's care. If the parent with the greater care needs is resented by adult children, this emotional cargo can interfere with their ability to face the dilemma constructively.

Professional help may be needed for them to avoid venting this anger and adding to the favored parent's stress. Since a parent's refusal to relinquish caregiving can stem from aspects of the marriage which are not visible to adult children, the professional's intervention in such instances may focus on helping the children understand these hidden aspects of their parents' relationship.

Worry About Who Will Die First

The dynamic of care between spouses is often powerfully affected by their unspoken worry about what will happen when one dies before the other. Couples may go to elaborate lengths to avoid mentioning each other's death. Family members may vent such worries among themselves while omitting them in the couple's presence. A primary reason for such silence is that discussing someone's death makes the reality of losing that person painfully evident. Anticipatory sorrow can be sufficiently intense to block attempts to plan rationally, no matter how necessary it is to weigh future possibilities. With some couples, one of the partners may initiate talking about these concerns while the other denies them; with others, both may contribute to the maintenance of the silence. Months can be spent lingering over decisions, such as a move to a retirement home, which could have been resolved quickly if the essence of these private worries could have been revealed.

The diagnosis of cancer is one of the most common triggers of worry about death. A man confronting a recent diagnosis may feel an urgency about taking steps to ensure his wife's financial and emotional welfare before he dies. With this underlying motivation, he may perceive several advantages to their moving to a retirement home, such as his being able to assist with the sale of their home and helping with investing the proceeds in a way that would assure his wife sufficient income. In addition, he may want to know that his wife has the security of established social routines that will help with her loneliness after his death. Should the topic of his dying remain unmentionable between them, however, he cannot use potentially persuasive arguments to overcome his wife's resistance to leaving their long-term home.

Worry about having enough money after a partner's death can also impede decision-making and planning. For example, a wife may resist spending money to hire extra help, regarding the high hourly rates as too severe a drain on their life savings. Pleading with her to purchase assistance vital to her own health and the quality of her caregiving, frustrated and concerned family members may not realize that her reluctance stems from an area which she finds unmentionable. Their pleading may serve only to further isolate her in her fears, since she may also feel guilty about allowing future concerns for herself to interfere with her partner's needs.

A professional can allude to death without being inhibited by personal grief and therefore may be better able than family members to bring up these difficult topics. For instance, if home-care services are provided after hospitalization, family members can request that a social worker visit the older couple to hold planning sessions with them. A professional can clarify death-related concerns through guided discussion, generally yielding significant relief for older partners. Provided with this opportunity for discussion, older caregivers initially react with tearfulness or solemnity at facing their dreads; they then tend to vent their concerns in great detail and make substantial progress toward resolving their worries.

Expressions of gratitude are among the most important feelings likely to surface when a couple is released from the taboo of discussing dying. A husband may remark about his wife, "She gets short with me sometimes, but she's done a heck of a job taking care of me through all this." During bereavement, spouses frequently remember and regret moments of impatience that occurred during the caregiving period. Therefore, such statements can help prevent the guilt otherwise felt for years. Similarly, remarriage guilt can be reduced if spouses have the opportunity to express both verbal appreciation for their years together and a hope for the partner to achieve companionship with someone else.

Discussion of the event of death itself is of both practical and emotional value. A statement such as, "I want to die in my own bed, but it's okay to call an ambulance if you get scared," can release a spouse from self-berating behavior for allowing her husband to die in an intensive care unit. If various responses to medical emergencies are explored in depth, each partner's ability to make decisions on behalf of the other during a crisis can be immeasurably improved. Permission not to prolong the other's life needlessly may particularly bring relief. Finally, specific preferences for funeral arrangements can be clarified, and the location of vital documents can be determined.

Lesbian and Gay Couples

Professionals need to be alert to issues distinct to lesbian and gay older people, estimated to be up to 10 percent of the older population.[1] Professional sensitivity is especially crucial when family members are not supportive toward the older gay or lesbian couple. Community-based services, such as widow's groups, tend to be oriented toward heterosexual caregiving partnerships, or lack provisions for sexual minorities. Because policies of hospitals and nursing homes may serve to discriminate against homosexual partners, the successful use of home-care services is especially critical for gay and lesbian caregivers. This section surveys the needs of older gay and lesbian couples, particularly the problems they confront as caregivers, and suggests nonhomophobic professional interventions.

Professionals working with long-term gay and lesbian partners need to recognize their life histories of coping with discrimination. Faced with negative responses from family members, friends, and employers, most gay and lesbian couples have paid a high emotional and sometimes economic price for living out their sexual orientation. Siblings and parents may have rejected them, or families may be split concerning acceptance of their sexual preference. As a result, lesbian and gay older people tend to have keenly hewn survival skills and may cope with the aging process and illness better than heterosexual individuals. They also may have developed alternatives to the usual kinship networks, devoting themselves to lifelong friendships equivalent to family bonds in loyalty and long-term consistency of contact. Without expectations of children to care for them in their old age, they may have cultivated friendships with younger people.

On the other hand, the absence of family support when confronted with long-term illness can result in extreme bitterness for lesbian and gay couples. For instance, those who were parents and then divorced were probably deprived of custody or even visitation rights to their children. In later life, when they observe other parents receiving assistance and advocacy from adult children, a resurgence of bitterness can precipitate periods of depression.

For people who express their homosexuality after long-term heterosexual relationships, their adult children's reactions can also be a source of pain. For instance, a daughter may refuse to meet her mother's lover, resisting such a profound change in her view of her parent. Some adult children may become openly antagonistic toward the parent, eliminating all contact or making hurtful remarks when they do interact. Facing adult children's rejection may be particularly painful for people who have delayed coming out until after their own parents' deaths. The potential for healing such rifts between adult children and homosexual parents is one consolation often accompanying late-life care needs. Previously resentful adult children may rethink their prior rejection when they witness the care sacrifices of their parent's partner. Working together to care for the parent may present opportunities for adult children to bond with the parent's partner as an individual, with the provision of care a unifying experience.

One of the most painful predicaments that gay and lesbian couples encounter is nonacknowledgment by medical professionals when one of the partners is ill. Since such couples are not blood relatives or legal spouses, they are generally not accorded the recognition and support during medical crises extended to husbands, wives, and adult children. Health care providers may refuse to release medical information or allow special visiting status to a gay or lesbian partner, irrespective of any explanation of the nature of the bond with the sick person. Already vulnerable in reaction to the partner's illness, the partner may have difficulty asserting rights to have questions answered and contact assured. In contrast, a partner's brother or sister is likely to be allowed immediate access on the basis of a blood relationship, no matter how weak the emotional bond may be.

One way that a gay or lesbian person can assure partner access to medical information during health crises is to sign a release of information form at the hospital or clinic where the services are received. This form designates the person's name to whom information can be released and becomes part of the permanent medical record. Another strategy is for partners to assign durable power of attorney to each other, specifying within the agreement that the partner has the power to make medical decisions on the other's behalf in the event of physical or mental incapacity. Making these arrangements in advance of the occurrence of medical problems is advisable, despite the human reluctance to face the prospect of incapacitating illness.

Health care providers tend to assume heterosexuality when they interview older people. Questions about marriage, children, and sexual activity are asked within the context of mainstream expectations, and opposite-sex pronouns are used when asking about the person's partner. Omitting heterosexual references encourages gay and lesbian people to express their particular needs to health providers. Using the term "partner," rather than asking about a husband or wife, leaves the issue open, implicitly cueing the person that the health provider is sensitive to the concerns of sexual minorities and will act upon this sensitivity.

On the other hand, some older people in later life same-sex relationships do not identify with the term "lesbian" or "gay". An older woman may develop a sexual relationship with a close woman friend, but not perceive herself as a lesbian or feel kindred with the community of sexual minorities: "I am in love with this friend of mine." Especially in current generations of older people, lifelong scorn toward sexual minorities can be a powerful block against using certain words or categorizing a love relationship as gay or lesbian. Professional tact with the use of labels is crucial when people do not want to define themselves as lesbian or gay. Watching for cues about how an older person defines a relationship is the best strategy for finding the appropriate language during discussions.

When assisting gay or lesbian caregivers with their care arrangements, professionals should realize the potential difficulties they may have taking time off from work to help ill partners. For instance, an older woman who has not discussed her sexual orientation with her coworkers may find that she does not have the automatic claim to personal leave commanded by a woman with "a sick husband at home." Informing a boss that, "My roommate is getting out of the hospital tomorrow, so I need to take a week of medical leave to assist her," may elicit neither sympathy nor the necessary permission. Her other option, revealing the nature of her "roommate" relationship, can create consequences she does not want to face while also coping with the stress and worry about her partner's condition.

An area where professionals can be of concrete assistance is to discuss homophobia in their training of chore workers and home-health aides. The personal nature of in-home care makes these workers' acceptance of gay and lesbian choices more crucial than in other kinds of services. Providing in-home workers with an opportunity to ask questions about sexual minorities and to practice nonhomophobic responses is crucial, given the myths and taboos surrounding homosexuality in our society. A supervisor who has discussed these issues with the staff is then in the position to assign the most accepting workers when services are requested by gay or lesbian caregivers. A gay or lesbian couple will undoubtedly be relieved by a professional's sensitive advocacy to spare them the intrusion of prejudiced strangers into their private realm.

As indicated for heterosexual spouses, arranging for substitutes to provide personal care may be necessary for the continuation of a couple's sexual relationship. Many people find the roles of caregiver and lover incompatible, needing to be one or the other. An older gay man may fear losing his lover if he asks him to wash soiled clothing or change the bandage on a bedsore. Their relationship may have formed too recently for him to hope to retain companionship if care demands take precedence over sexual needs. Fiscal constraints on in-home services frequently place low-income gay older people in such impossible binds, whereas wealthier partners can afford to limit their lovers' direct caregiving.

The quest for partners in later life is challenging for anyone whose mobility is reduced by physical problems, but gay and lesbian older people face the added constraint of their numerical minority and the scarcity of convenient meeting places. A man accustomed to meeting partners in bars may be forced to forgo this option because of medical prohibitions on his alcohol use. Finding a partner in his neighborhood senior center may not be a feasible alternative. In addition, the apparent emphasis on youthful attractiveness within the gay world may cause an older man to withdraw from attempts at sexual exposure, responding to such a suggestion, for example, with "Who would approach someone like me in a gay bar?" Organizations for gay and lesbian older people's socializing and support are just beginning to form in communities with large populations of sexual minorities.

Another avenue of professional assistance is to urge older gay and lesbian couples to obtain competent legal advice regarding issues of finances, inheritance, and funeral arrangements. For example, state laws are skewed toward the ability of blood relatives to contest wills when a gay or lesbian person leaves them out of an estate in preference to a partner. Since living trusts and bank accounts with rights of survivorship are less vulnerable to legal challenge than wills, these options may be particularly attractive to gay and lesbian couples who anticipate familial interference.

An overall area of professional sensitivity relates to discarding stereotypical views of the nature of gay and lesbian relationships. Contrary to commonly held images, the varieties of bonding are the same as within the heterosexual community, ranging from monogomous life-partners and nonmonogomous primary relationships to serial monogomy and episodic liaisons. Gay and lesbian life-partners have the same issues to confront that were described earlier for long-term heterosexual spouses, such as the disruption of retirement plans by a partner's becoming ill and role changes in response to illness. One positive difference is that same-sex couples may not have instituted separate breadwinner and housekeeper roles to the degree of their traditional heterosexual contemporaries, possessing more flexibility when one of the partners becomes ill.

Similar to heterosexual marriages, long-term gay or lesbian partnerships are more likely to accommodate difficult care needs than recent partnerships. In either community, older people who practice serial monogamy or other less committed forms of relationships are likely to feel threatened by health problems in the periods between relationships or during the formative stages of new partnerships. When sacrifices to provide care are necessary, a bond based on an extensive shared history and loyalty for help rendered in the past can usually sustain the pressure more than ties lacking such emotional foundations.

Note

1. Douglas C. Kimmel, "Adult Development and Aging: A Gay Perspective," *Journal of Social Issues*, 34, 3 (1978): 113–135.

Suggested Resources

ALMVIG, CHRIS. *The Invisible Minority: Aging and Lesbianism* (Utica College of Syracuse, N.Y.: Institute of Gerontology, 1984).
Study of lesbians' concerns about aging, difficulties with the health care

system, and inability to grieve the loss of a loved one who is not always viewed by family and friends as the loss of a significant other.

BERGER, RAYMOND. *Gay and Gray: The Older Homosexual Man* (Chicago: University of Illinois Press, 1982).
Based on intensive interviews with a small sample of gay men.

BERGER, RAYMOND. "Realities of Gay and Lesbian Aging," *Social Work*, 29, 1 (1984): 57–62.
Presents the findings of interviews with eighteen homosexual men and women aged 40 to 72. Includes recommendations for the provision of social services by both peers and professionals.

CANTOR, MARJORIE. "Strain Among Caregivers: A Study of Experience in the United States," *The Gerontologist*, 26, 6 (1983): 597.
Spouses were the highest risk group among the caregivers studied. The caregivers who were children were primarily married, middle-aged women. All caregivers expressed emotional strain and negative impacts from sacrifices. Spouses expressed a need for relief and respite.

CROSSMAN, LINDA, CECILIA LONDON, and CLEMMIE BARRY. "Older Women Caring for Disabled Spouses: A Model for Supportive Services," *The Gerontologist*, 21 (1981): 464.
Describes a multiservice support program for older women caring for disabled husbands at home. Began as a peer support group and through the wives' advocacy developed into a respite project.

FENGLER, ALFRED P., and NANCY GOODRICH. "Wives of Elderly Disabled Men: The Hidden Patients," *The Gerontologist*, 19, 2 (1979): 175.
Study of how the husband's disability impacted the wife's morale. Morale scores of husbands and wives were associated. Wives in low-morale group more frequently mentioned the problems of isolation, loneliness, economic hardship, and role overload. The most important supports for high-morale wives were children, relatives, and friends who visited.

MOSES, A. ELFIN, and ROBERT HAWKINS. *Counseling Lesbian Women and Gay Men: A Life-Issue Approach* (St. Louis: Mosby, 1982).

SAGE: Senior Action in a Gay Environment, 208 West 13th Street, New York, NY 10011, 212-741-2247.
Provides services to older lesbians and gay men, but in the New York City area only. Maintains a list of other groups around the country and provides information for starting groups dealing with lesbian and gay aging. Newsletter available.

Till Death To Us Part: Caregiving Wives of Severely Disabled Husbands, 1982, Gray Paper #7, Older Womens League, 1235 G. St., N.W., LLB, Washington, D.C. 20005.
Presents the major problems, especially lack of supports, faced by spouses as caregivers. Urges mutual support group projects and advocacy efforts.

WOLF, DEBORAH COLEMAN. *Growing Older: Lesbians and Gay Men* (Berkeley, CA: University of California Press, 1982).

44

CHAPTER 3

Sharing the Care
Among Family Members

When family members come together to provide care for an older relative, their efforts to cooperate may be hindered by inheritance anxieties, factional splits, and traditional sex role expectations. Efforts to distribute tasks fairly among members can be still more difficult when in-laws or stepparents require care. Grandchildren may experience negative repercussions from the caregiving situation, although they can also make substantial contributions. This chapter explores a variety of family relationships and the use of family meetings as one strategy to address problems that arise within families. The chapter concludes with a discussion of the adult child who has a limited pool of supportive relatives and is alone with caregiving responsibilities.

Siblings

Those who work with families are often struck by how vividly unresolved issues from early life reemerge in caregiving situations. Coming together to face a parent's illness requires an altogether different degree of cooperation and communication among siblings than organizing holiday dinners and family reunions, the type of joint ventures which usually characterize siblings' adult relationships. Stresses rooted in early life can both impede efforts to plan fair and realistic distribution of caregiving tasks and produce severe emotional suffering as difficult decisions are confronted. Siblings may use their parents' illness and care needs as ammunition to express old grievances. In many instances, professional interventions remedy workload imbalances or accelerate the resolution of painful conflicts. These resolutions can improve the older person's comfort and safety, relieve stress on primary caregivers, and prevent unnecessary nursing home placement.

This section identifies typical sibling relationship patterns which interfere with collaborative caregiving efforts. Difficulties can be mitigated when professionals help siblings to learn to recognize negative patterns and to employ problem-solving strategies to address them. The questions below can be used by professionals and families to anticipate areas of conflict and to begin devising such strategies.

Factors to Consider When Siblings Need to Share the Care

1. *Are worries about a potential inheritance straining the relationship between siblings?* Are the worries coloring their attempts to work out caregiving conflicts?
2. *How spread out are the siblings geographically?* Does only one live locally, or are the majority nearby?
3. *Does a large financial disparity exist between siblings?* Does one possess much greater financial latitude than the others? Has one depended on the others for financial assistance?
4. *What has been the nature of the siblings' adult relationships with each other?* Have they developed active friendships, or have they maintained minimal, family-related contacts?
5. *How obviously do the parents sustain a preference or a grudge toward one of the siblings?* Have patterns toward a favorite or scapegoat of the family been carried on into their adult lives?
6. *Is there a natural leader among the siblings?* Has one tended to mediate conflicts within the family and consistently provided assistance to the others?
7. *Is there a health-care professional among the siblings?* Do the others view this person as the one who should provide the care or make the care decisions?
8. *Does the family contain stepsiblings?* Were the families joined during their early lives, or have they become acquainted only as adults?
9. *Does the family view female siblings as the expected caregivers in preference to the male siblings?* Do the females accept this traditional role?

10. *What is the nature of the personal obligations each sibling must meet in addition to the parents' care needs?* Do some have young children or older in-laws for whom they are already providing care?

Inheritance Anxiety

Most families find discussion of inheritance to be volatile and difficult, especially when open discussion of money violates past family norms. When the potential inheritance is sizable enough to be significant to the adult children, or when family possessions have a high degree of emotional value, inheritance issues often surpass all others in their power to disrupt relationships. The choices involved in "who gets what" have the power to symbolize who is loved, respected, or trusted most among siblings. When facing distribution decisions and their associated battles, older people can experience severe stress that hastens the decline of health. The consequences for siblings can be that caregiving arrangements, which might otherwise have succeeded to their mutual satisfaction and to their parents' benefit, dissolve for lack of cooperation and leave a legacy of injured relationships behind.

The major portion of an inheritance battle tends to be carried out while one or both of the parents is alive. The conflicts can also start long before the actual care needs arise. A common point of onset is when parents leave a private house for a smaller, easier-to-manage apartment. With an item such as an heirloom piano which will not fit in the apartment, an older couple may be forced to consider who among their children would take the best care, feel the keenest attachment, or make the greatest use of it. After finally offering the piano to one of their children, the couple may find themselves barraged by the hurt feelings of the others, who interpret the choice as a negative judgment against themselves or a positive judgment in favor of the selected sibling.

When anticipating the need to distribute possessions, an older couple can defuse the potential for hurt by asking adult children to identify which household items have the greatest emotional significance to them. This strategy places the discussion out in the open and incorporates the adult children as participants in the choice process. Adult children's lists of the items to which they are most attached function as a survey of the emotional territory. They also provide the older couple with an advance view of items which may be disputed. Preventive discussions can then be initiated by questions such as, "If you had to choose between the Oriental rug and the piano, which would you take?" The essence of this strategy is for older persons to remove themselves from the judgmental role as much as possible, thereby stripping the distribution process of its symbolic power.

Similarly, the choice of an adult child to serve as a money manager or to be assigned power of attorney can seem to the siblings to contain implications of emotional and financial favoritism. They may suspect that the sibling chosen to oversee the parents' investments has been targeted to receive a disproportionate share of the estate. The parents may find it difficult to persuade them that the money-management tasks were assigned on the basis of skill rather than favoritism. If such mistrust persists, the family member selected to help with the finances can often allay worries by opening up the bookkeeping function to the other adult children's view. Similar to companies issuing financial statements, a family financial manager who wishes to dispel anxiety can periodically report to the others, specifying the nature of the investments and itemizing the ways income has been spent or reinvested.

Another type of inheritance anxiety arises in disagreements between siblings over how extensively the parents' life savings should be drained by the care expenses. One sibling may regard hourly payments to a private-duty nurse as unnecessary, preferring that family caregivers organize to spend their time sharing care tasks rather than spending their inheritance. Conversely, others in the family may view the purpose of the life savings as funding for care in later life, indifferent to the inheritance value of the money or simply preferring to protect their time. Those who do invest their time often see themselves as deserving a larger share of the inheritance than those who do not exert themselves to provide care. Although adult children generally do not express these feelings directly, they may nevertheless hope that parents notice the disparity in effort and reward it in the will. To prevent later resentment, family members can calculate the cost equivalents of the services they are willing to provide and negotiate a method of ongoing compensation.

Finally, professionals may be drawn into such a fray concerning inheritances by becoming privy to family financial secrets. An older person who has become close to a visiting nurse may confide her inheritance plans, asking that the nurse not reveal certain aspects of them to her adult children. Although such confidences may be harmless as long as advice is not offered, the professional may be placed in an awkward position among family members excluded from secret information. The worst situations are those in which professionals inadvertently stumble upon financial secrets. While assisting with a Medicaid application, a hospital discharge planner may learn that a son secretly arranged with his mother years ago to put her savings in his own name. If exposed during the already emotionally charged medical crisis, such secrets can trigger explosive conflicts between siblings. Professionals perform an important service for families by warning them not to establish such secrets and by helping them once such inopportune discoveries occur.

Factional Splits

A particularly problematic situation arises when two siblings with different perceptions of a parent's needs both attempt to control the care decisions. Factions develop within the family as these would-be leaders enlist alliances with other family members who support their opposing points of view. Unless reconciled, such splits can force the older person into the center of an uncomfortable tug-of-war as each side attempts to undermine the others' efforts. Splits within families commonly revolve around two conflicting beliefs: that the older person should be placed in a nursing home "for the sake of health and safety," and that the older person should be maintained in the community "no matter how much the family has to do" to preserve the person's health and safety at home.

As compromises are made in the home environment, these conflicting points of view can intensify over time and erupt into open battles during a hospitalization. A medical crisis provides a focal point for the conflict in which family members who prefer nursing home placement attempt to accomplish during the hospital stay what they have deferred doing in the home setting. Using hospital staff as resources, they may seek advice about local nursing homes or request help with the mechanics of the placement process. Such family members may also try to make the most of the momentum of change generated by the older person's separation from the routines of home.

When opinions are divided to this extent, the sibling leaders from each faction are prone to try to recruit the support of the medical professionals involved in the older person's care. The "keep-at-home" faction may seek reassurance that the new care demands are manageable, requesting specific forms of training and referral to community resources to aid their home care effort. The opposing faction may request that the weight of a medical recommendation be used to support their belief in nursing home placement as the preferred option. At such junctures, medical professionals decisively influence the course of events to the extent that they provide information to one of the factions or lend an authoritative stance to another. For example, a physician's passing remark that the older person's medical condition is "too much to handle at home" could bolster the position of family members eager to be released from home care responsibilities, and could break the will of those not ready to stop trying.

Since each faction's information will be colored by their point of view, hospital professionals trying to advise such a family are likely to hear two separate versions of the home situation. Hidden agendas within the rivalry of the two family leaders can so widen the gap between the two versions that professionals may be at a loss regarding which reality should inform their recommendations. In such instances, professionals may more readily side with the keep-at-home faction, because of their professional stance toward noninstitutional alternatives. They may also be influenced by the pragmatic realities of scarce nursing home beds and pressured by shorter hospital stays for Medicare patients. Just as divisively, however, professionals' global pronouncements of support for nursing home care can alienate the other side of the family, deepen the split, and intensify the emotional strife which the older person is likely to experience if returned home.

A more productive professional strategy for the welfare of the older person and the siblings in conflict is to propose a time-limited trial period at home. Without excluding the option of nursing home placement, the trial period can be presented as a chance to assess the effects of changes in the older person's condition on the family's caregiving capacity. Before housing arrangements are relinquished and helping networks disbanded, the older person can test her new needs against the realities of her home situation. When an older person is thus permitted to reconcile herself to the necessity of placement, family members who have difficulty with the idea of a parent residing in a nursing home often become more accepting. During such a trial period, family members in favor of nursing home placement should be assured of an end point if the situation does not improve. With a shortened interval during which to cope, family members frequently experience a renewed ability to manage home care demands.

For the time between hospital discharge and the date set for reevaluating the situation, the older person's physician should request the services of home care professionals who can directly assist family members with the care needs. Based upon firsthand observations of the home setting, these professionals can formulate recommendations for care. They can also help resolve the factional differences by suggesting revisions in the division of tasks and facilitating family meetings. A critical factor in establishing such trial periods is the physician's willingness to rehospitalize the older person if the family cannot cope or if the older person's care needs exceed the limits of home care services.

Families can also choose to institutionalize an older relative on a trial basis. Families may benefit from relief of their care responsibilities and then reevaluate their decision after two to three months. Throughout these decision-making processes, families need to realize that decisions are not irreversible and that frequent evaluation of decisions is desirable.

Sharing Care at a Geographic Distance

As described earlier, caregiving efforts are frequently complicated by geographic distance. Local siblings often resent out-of-town siblings for not doing more. The following chart suggests ways that out-of-town relatives can share in caregiving by maintaining supportive contact with an older person. Such contacts not only provide the older person with ongoing links with people seen infrequently, but also relieve pressure on local caregivers.

Suggestions for Long-Distance Contact

Establishing routines for long-distance phone calls.	Calls are most effective as an emotional lifeline if they occur on a regular basis, such as the first Sunday of every month. Allows the older person to anticipate the contact.
Obtaining an extension phone for a couple.	An extension saves time by allowing both to participate in long-distance calls simultaneously. Eliminates the need to repeat stories and gives equal time to each.
Exchanging phone numbers with the older person's neighbors.	Phone contact on an occasional basis with supportive neighbors can serve as a source of information about the person's functioning as well as an acknowledgment and thanks by the family. (See Chapter 4.)
Sending brief, newsy letters.	Letters are especially helpful for those who tend to forget the content of phone calls. An older person with memory loss can enjoy reading letters repeatedly and relish the sight of them on the kitchen table.
Providing the older person with return-address labels and preaddressed, stamped envelopes.	Many older people fear that their handwriting is not legible enough for the postal service. A stack of envelopes ready for mailing serves as an encouragement for notes to family members.
Sending clippings, photographs, books, etc.	These can be easier for family members who are not letter writers. Their receipt can make an older person feel as acknowledged and remembered as with lengthy letters.
Recording and sending cassette tapes back and forth.	Tapes are especially useful for low-vision people, as well as those with poor memory. Both family members and older people can express thoughts verbally through this means without the expense of long-distance calls.

Another way that out-of-town siblings can share the care is by having the older person visit them. Such a visit has the added advantages of providing them with a chance to make prolonged observations of their parent's care needs. It also can serve as a test of the feasibility of a long-distance move for both the older person and family members. The primary obstacle to such a visit, however, is often the older person's reluctance to fly alone. Constraints on money and time often prohibit family members from accompanying the older person, no matter how intensely their parent dreads the thought of coping with a flight. Older people unable to walk long distances may be relieved to learn that airline staff can transport them by wheelchair from the arrival area directly onto the plane. Family members can then meet the plane with an airline-supplied wheelchair, which eliminates virtually all walking. If a transfer of planes is necessary, airport personnel can notify the intermediary airport of the older person's need for wheelchair assistance.

Family members should explain the special needs of an older person with marked memory loss to a flight crew member. For example, assistance with locating the restroom may be needed at defined intervals. In such instances, a first-class seat often places the older person closer to the restroom and in a position to receive more flight staff attention. In addition, people with memory loss should carry legible cards in their wallets or purses for purposes of identification. These cards should state their name, their destination, and the names of family members to meet them. Such cards can be reassuring to the older person who needs a reminder of where the plane is going and who will be waiting at the arrival gate.

Flight crew members should also be informed of the special needs of older people with hearing or vision problems. Crew members can convey announcements directly to the older person and help with reading signs or locating needed items. It is helpful to remind older people that flight crew members are trained to assist with sensory difficulties and other special needs. Worries about incontinence can often be diminished through the use of protective clothing or obtaining a seat close to a restroom.

A further obstacle to flying may be the older person's reluctance to leave a private home unattended. Worry about break-ins, frozen pipes, mail, or plants and pets can postpone a vitally needed visit. In this regard, reliable neighbors can allay anxieties. An older person's resistance to leaving a pet in a neighbor's or kennel's care especially frustrates family members more concerned with the older person's needs than with the pet's. Yet, their pleas for a restructuring of priorities may be unconvincing. In situations of irrational reluctance to leave a home, families can sometimes send one of their members to live in the home while the older person visits out-of-town relatives.

Achieving Fairness in Task Distribution

An unequal division of care tasks tends to underlie most sibling conflicts. Families generally follow the path of least resistance, with tasks falling to those living closest to the older person, to those with the strongest emotional need, to the females expected to be caregivers, or to family members with unstructured time. Unequal and unrealistic routines of care thus develop, based on habit and implicit norms. If alert to this tendency, families and professionals can attempt to distribute tasks on the basis of fairness and family strengths. Successful task delegation among family members can produce long-term support in place of short-term exhaustion.

In some families, the division of tasks falls into place because an adult child, as mediator during previous family crises, resurrects this role. When a frail parent with a new set of dependency needs is to be discharged from the hospital, the unchallenged leader functions as the family's liaison with medical professionals and conveys vital information to the others in a timely manner. The leader eliminates the need for a hospital discharge planner to become acquainted with individual members' strengths and weaknesses.

If the leader or another member of the family happens to be a nurse, social worker, physician, or other health professional, siblings are likely to expect this person to apply their skills toward the care of the parents. A nurse may be told by her sister, "You know all about these medications and their side effects, so you drive over every morning to give Mom her pills." The family professional may need support from a nonfamily professional to resist assuming excessive care responsibilities. Family members who lack medical experience need to be encouraged to learn tasks, such as insulin injection and sterile dressing changes, which they would prefer to load onto a trained sibling. Unless fair task distribution is made paramount, families are likely to wear out the medical personnel in their midst.

Another form of skewed task distribution occurs when siblings' expectations of each other follow traditional sex roles. A daughter's efforts to involve her brothers with the physical aspects of caregiving may be resisted by claims of unfamiliarity with "women's work." Her brothers may willingly handle tasks such as paying bills or driving the parents to appointments, yet expect her to assume the daily housekeeping tasks. Sons also may resist helping with personal care tasks, such as toiletry or bathing, in part because of their discomfort with intimate contact with a parent, which violates most norms about parent–son contact. Parents may also contribute to the maintenance of these roles; the parents may never ask a son to vacuum their living room rug but harangue a daughter for doing it infrequently. If the daughter is employed full time in additon to maintaining her own home and child care, she may need a professional's help in redressing this imbalance in familial expectations.

Unfairness in caregiving situations can also stem from occupational differences among siblings. Adult children who are unemployed or engaged in homemaking will often be expected by siblings to shoulder the bulk of the care tasks. Similarly, siblings whose jobs are flexible, through self-employment or part-time work, can be vulnerable to claims on their time by those whose work is more structured. In some instances, a sibling will view another's employment as expendable or adaptable to intrusions, expecting that person to help the parents with unexpected needs during work hours. A bank executive may repeatedly prevail upon his brother, a self-employed house painter, to help their mother with daytime needs. If the house painter feels his own employment being implicitly disparaged by his brother's expectations, his resentment may translate into reduced accessibility to his mother.

An especially painful obstacle to task distribution arises when siblings believe that parents favor one of them. As if to rectify the inequity, they may try to "dump" the majority of the care tasks on the perceived favorite. Remarks such as "Mom always gave you the best deal, so now you help her out" may spur arguments rooted in early life experiences. In instances where the parents praise one of their adult children more than others, professionals can prod them to become more aware of how they distribute their verbal appreciation. Otherwise, emotional weariness from feeling that their care efforts are insufficiently acknowledged can cause adult children to lose motivation for helping, for example, "I do so much for Dad, and yet he still lives for Jeff's phone calls from Colorado."

As noted in the earlier discussion of inheritances, money can be a prime deterrent to consensus about the way tasks are to be distributed among siblings. Particularly difficult problems arise when a sibling who has more money than the others prefers to purchase services rather than provide them. Siblings who lack spare money may feel it is unfair that they invest time and effort while another sibling merely writes out a check. The wealthier sibling may also try to grant rewards to family members in exchange for tasks, such as, "I'll let you keep our extra car if you take Mom to her appointments with the doctor." Similarly, a financially successful sibling may take the parent out to dinner once a week whereas a financially strapped sibling may scrub the parent's bathroom and kitchen weekly. Although the same number of hours may be devoted to the dinner outing as to the household scouring, the sibling who performs the physical labor is likely to resent the other's ability to make a more glamorous and enjoyable contribution to the parent's life. The fact that financial differences produce an inequity of options can be accepted as a wider social reality, but within the context of family caregiving it may be resented: "It's because Dad put you through school that you have more money than the rest of us." Although at first caregiving can seem to be divided by the number of hours or dollars contributed, this example demonstrates that the value of certain tasks may not be quantifiable in these readily objective terms.

The following list depicts the major factors, in addition to money, which create differences among family members. It can be used to match family members with the care tasks which emphasize their strengths and minimize their limitations, especially if reviewed prior to a family meeting in which tasks are to be distributed.

Building on Strengths for Task Distribution Among Family Members

Skills and preferences: A handy person in the family may prefer to be responsible for the upkeep of the parent's home, just as an accountant in the family may find paying the parent's bills a comfortable form of contribution.

Location: Tasks which involve the delivery of vital items to the person's home, such as groceries and medications, may be easiest for the person who lives the closest. Those who live further away may take on tasks to be done in their own home, such as preparing meals to be frozen or making phone calls.

Physical health: Those with back injuries or other impediments to physical helping may need to confine themselves to nonphysical tasks, such as telephone checkups and functioning as a phone liaison with professionals involved in the older person's care.

Motivations and emotions: An adult child who has had a close, warm relationship with a parent may be able to perform tasks requiring intimate contact more easily than an emotionally distant sibling. Those who fall into conflict when they are around the older person may need to contribute in ways that do not require contact.

Other dependents: Those who have young children dependent on them or who are responsible for in-laws needing their care may already be overloaded. Rather than regularly scheduled tasks, they may be able to take on special projects which can be fit into their other responsibilities.

Blocks of time versus intermittence: Some find it less intrusive on their lives to provide help in blocks of time on a regular schedule than to give it in sporadic forms of assistance. If they take on tasks such as yardwork and laundry which require blocks of time, those who cannot provide blocks of time can be responsible for other types of needs which crop up intermittently, such as various transportation needs.

Degree of psychological burden or vigilance: Although certain tasks involve minimal time and effort, they may weigh on the mind of the person responsible for them. Someone who volunteers to "stay available" in case the older person falls may find that the requirement of telephone accessibility becomes more burdensome over time.

In-Laws

Relationships with in-laws generally arouse an array of conflicting emotions. These conflicts become detrimental when a couple is unable to agree on strategies for coping with them, or when gulfs in their relationship are thereby widened. This section explores the basis of such conflicts and how they can affect caregiving. If professionals and couples understand the source of such differences, potential problems can be anticipated and addressed before they affect the provision of care.

Value differences frequently impede the negotiation of in-law relationships. A son raised in a traditional family may believe that care for his parents is his wife's duty. She, on the other hand, may give priority to her personal goals, her immediate family, and her own parents. If her husband attempts to pressure her into providing care, she is likely to feel that he respects his parent's needs over hers. In turn, he may interpret her order of priorities as disrespect for his parents and him.

Whether her husband's family includes other female relatives may strongly influence the pressures felt by a daughter-in-law when care needs arise. A woman whose husband has two unmarried brothers is more likely to be targeted as caregiver than one whose husband has sisters. In the absence of other female relatives, her in-laws may insist on the traditional view of women as care providers, irrespective of her employment or other personal goals. If the daughter-in-law in such a situation refuses to be the primary caregiver, her male relatives may resent her for challenging their expectations and values.

Divergent perceptions of a parent's actions and words can further separate a couple. Early life conflicts fuel adult children's reactions to their parents. A son's wife, only having known his father in the cooler atmosphere of adulthood, may interpret his father's behavior differently. No matter how rightfully, her claim to greater objectivity in her interpretations may set off defensiveness, such as, "He's *my* father, not yours, so stay out of it." In this process, she may become more aware of traits she dislikes in both her husband and in-laws, thereby heightening latent conflicts with her husband.

When perspectives diverge, watching one spouse suffer parental manipulation is often extremely frustrating to the other spouse. Unresolved parent–child issues can provide a parent with a powerful emotional hold over an adult child. A husband may observe his wife making excessive personal sacrifices to attempt to win her mother's long-withheld respect and affection. As her caregiving efforts multiply, her mother's demands may also. Her husband may feel increasingly frustrated by his wife's submitting herself to a quest he perceives as futile. Similar versions of this dynamic occur when one spouse watches the other permit the parent to dominate conversations, exact frequent long-distance calls, or prolong intrusive visits no one in the family enjoys.

Ironically, close relationships between parents and adult children can also complicate caregiving. A mother and son may maintain such a deep intimacy that his wife feels as if she were an outsider when mother and son are reunited during visits. Geographic distance may have enabled wife and mother to tolerate each other's claims to his attention over the years. As the mother-in-law's care needs increase, the daughter-in-law may regard the prospect of her moving to their household or community as the ultimate intrusion on their married life. Accordingly, her husband may feel that her jealousy and guardedness are unwarranted, insisting he can balance his loyalty to his mother and his wife. In such instances, the way in which the son handled past conflicts between these primary women in his life critically influences how threatened his wife feels when her mother-in-law's care needs warrant increased contact.

Antagonism toward the care effort, by a spouse who does not regard in-laws with affection, can place a great strain on an adult child. Although some couples approach the care needs of both sets of parents with a spirit of partnership, others evolve an adversarial stance which interferes with a rational consideration of care options. Returning home exhausted from a difficult morning with her mother, a daughter may encounter her husband's complaints about her "spending so much time" away from him. Negotiating this tug-of-war between her desire to please her mother and her husband can cause a daughter to feel she is failing in both relationships. The conflict between an adult child who prefers to maintain the parent in the community and a spouse who insists on nursing-home placement is a particularly painful one.

With divorce and remarriage rates increasing, loyalty to former in-laws can add yet another dimension to negotiating in-law relationships. A woman leaving a thirty-year marriage may find that divorce does not lessen her affection for her in-laws. Grandchildren and years of shared experiences may tie them together. Should she remarry, her relationship with her new in-laws may seem superficial in its recency compared with the depth of this longer-term bond. Assisting her former in-laws may feel more natural than helping her current in-laws, leading to conflict with her present husband. Few models exist from previous generations for approaching dilemmas created by remarriage.

Competition between in-laws over holiday visits, time with grandchildren, and caregiving sacrifices can exist in long-term marriages, as well as in situations in which divorce has created multiple sets of in-laws. For example, if a daughter prefers contact with her in-laws more than with her own parents, she may need to conceal the frequency of her calls and visits to her in-laws in order to prevent her parents' making hurtful comparisons. Holidays can be especially stressful in this regard, when both sets of parents want contact simultaneously and a couple confronts the impossibility of being two places at once. Alternating holiday visits may achieve fairness but sacrifice preference. Fairness also emerges as a major issue when a couple wishes to invite one set of parents to live with them, yet fears the other set will interpret this invitation as a sign of greater love. A couple may worry generally about setting precedents by including one relative in their lives in ways they would not replicate later for another.

Stepparents

Relationships between stepparents and adult stepchildren can also pose distinctive problems. As an increasing number of older persons remarry, more adult children acquire stepparents and stepsiblings later in life. Although there are success stories of later-life marriages and stepparenting, these new relationships can be extremely complex. Few societal norms exist about how middle-aged children are to relate to older stepparents. First, this section examines stresses which can arise while a parent is courting prospective mates. It then explores the impact of later-life stepparent and stepsibling relationships on caregiving.

Family members with lives rich in companionship may be unable to comprehend the power loneliness has to engender changes in a parent's social behavior and compromises in choice of mates. Divorcing from a spouse of many years can result in an intensity of bereavement comparable with becoming widowed. For newly alone older people, the need to fill the gap in companionship can assume an urgency which motivates startling changes. For example, a previously reserved and conservative parent may join a club for older singles, purchase a new wardrobe, and begin keeping late hours. These behaviors may disrupt long-held parental images and dismay family members. A change in hairstyle and a dramatic weight loss may also accompany the new attire and social style, transforming the parent in ways that barely resemble the previous appearance.

Coping with bereavement and new social pressures, the parent may also start drinking excessively.

The difficult remarriage odds faced by older women compared with older men strongly affect later-life social behavior. Since women outlive men by an average of nine years[1], the relative scarcity of men increases as women grow older. A man searching for a new spouse in later life is likely to encounter a wide assortment of choices among his age peers as well as among younger women. In contrast, the scarcity of available men may force an older woman to lower her standards so that she takes on a mate with unattractive qualities "just to have someone." Among the current generation of older women, many moved directly from their families of origin into marriage; thus, their need "to have someone" may be made more intense by their prior socialization to depend on a man and their limited experience in living alone.

Financial considerations also frequently force older women to compromise in their choice of mates. For example, a woman who is widowed or divorced in her fifties must wait several years until she receives a monthly Social Security check. If she has spent her adult years as a homemaker, she may possess few skills to give her an advantage in the job market and may face age discrimination for the low-paying unskilled jobs usually held by younger adults. Under these economically strained circumstances, marrying a man who has a reliable income becomes an act of survival more than a quest for companionship. To a woman faced with little or no income, these pragmatic concerns can be far more important than personal freedom or the desire for a mate with a pleasing personality.

Although women in later life tend to seek economic protection, older men generally want someone to take care of them. A man who has never learned to cook or clean house may value a woman's housekeeping skills more than her conversation or affection. Similarly, a man with a progressively disabling condition, primarily concerned about his future care needs, may hope to find a nurturant woman who will spare his children the demands of caring for him. Since it is socially acceptable for men to marry younger women, men's chances of finding women healthy enough to be caregivers are enhanced.

As indicated previously, choices motivated by loneliness or economics may yield a mate who seems unattractive by other criteria. This becomes a problem when adult children react with incredulity upon meeting their parent's new companion and wonder how their parent could possibly be attracted to this person. Adult children may be unable to comprehend the parent's joyful obliviousness to faults in the prospective partner. During courtship, adult children's efforts to point out faults or urge caution are likely to provoke their parent's defensiveness ("You just don't know what he's really like"). When pressured to explain her happiness, the parent may pragmatically reply that "it is better than being alone." Most likely, the parent already has made unconscious tradeoffs before introducing the mate to adult children; the disadvantages have been blocked out in order to enjoy the prospect of companionship, financial security, or physical assistance.

Adult children's unhappiness with the parent's decision may be further complicated by their belief that the prospective partner is taking advantage of the parent's loneliness for unsavory motives. A son may believe that his father's fiancée is "marrying him for his money," fearing that her spending habits will drain his father's finances. He may plead, "Dad, don't you see what she's after," only to instill mistrust in the affection which his father has found emotionally rewarding. Similarly, a woman's adult children may urge her to reconsider by asking, "Don't you see that he just wants a woman to take care of him?" Such comments can be hurtful and counterproductive in dissuading a parent from planning a new marriage.

Adult children need to recognize that they are spectators with a vested interest, rather than objective observers to a parent's remarriage choice. Prior to advising a parent or voicing strong objections concerning a prospective partner, they should examine the underlying sources of their discomfort. For example, a future stepparent's physical frailties may be the chief focus of the family's wish to prevent the marriage. Their worry that the stepparent's care needs will become their burden, as well as strain their parent's health, may interfere with their ability to give the person a fair chance for their affection. Similarly, anxiety may arise from fears that the future stepparent will squander their inheritance; honest discussions with the parent can often alleviate such concerns. For instance, the parent may already have established trust accounts or provisions in a will to ensure leaving an intact inheritance.

Another source of resentment or discomfort is the perception that the new spouse will intrude upon the adult children's access to time alone with the parent. For example, after her mother's death, a daughter may have enjoyed one-to-one contact with her father. With the long-awaited closeness that had developed, the daughter may perceive the father's approaching remarriage as a second loss. If she does not identify this concern at the root of her dislike of her father's new companion, she may focus instead on the woman's less attractive personality traits or how poorly she measures up to her mother. Identifying such underlying feelings before making a negative pronouncement can be crucial to achieving a satisfying relationship with the stepparent, as well as preventing unnecessary hurt for the parent.

After weighing the personal sources of their discomfort, adult children may still believe that a parent is becoming entangled in a relationship that will prove detrimental. For example, a father in his seventies may rush too quickly into a marriage as an antidote to his grief upon the recent loss of his lifelong spouse. He may seize upon someone who bears a physical resemblance to the deceased, irrespective of the new acquaintance's fundamental dissimilarities or the length of time he has known her. Children may rightly fear that after the grief has subsided their father may be sorely disappointed by these dissimilarities. In such instances, family members might suggest that a choice of such magnitude be delayed until at least a year after the bereavement. Since active grief often interferes with adult children's perceptions of a potential stepparent's merits, they could request a delay out of respect for their feelings.

The financial disincentives to marriage are a final problem often confronted during the courtship. A woman receiving a deceased husband's veteran's pension may wrestle with the fact that she forfeits this income upon remarriage and cannot resume receiving it if she becomes divorced or widowed. If her companion has medical problems that could abruptly take his life, she may regard marriage to him as a financial risk. A similar dilemma occurs when a divorced woman is receiving sizable alimony payments, which she must forgo if she remarries. As a result, some couples may consider living together rather than marrying in order to minimize financial disincentives.

This option, however, may conflict with the couple's traditional values or religious beliefs. In other instances, the older couple may be comfortable with this alternative, but fear their families' reactions. If they have previously harassed their own children for cohabiting instead of marrying, they may now be embarrassed by this choice as a practical arrangement for themselves. Ironically, adult children who accept such arrangements among their peers may feel irrational discomfort with their parent's doing so. For many adult children, the suggestion of an older parent's sexual activity is the root of their discomfort with cohabitation, a possibility which they were able to ignore while the couple was dating.

Marriage contracts are a way to resolve both adult children's anxieties about their inheritance and a spouse's financial worries about losing income by marrying. For example, a woman who forfeits a sizable alimony check can be guaranteed an equivalent monthly payment from the spouse's estate in the event of his death. If she also fears being asked to leave a house that one of her spouse's children will inherit, a living trust can be included which grants her the right to remain in the home after her spouse dies. Adult children concerned about financial exploitation by the stepparent can suggest a marriage contract that protects against this possibility, without needing to inject this mistrust into their parent's happiness.

Stepparent relationships may become even more emotionally difficult when the stepparent comes to require care. Giving care as an expression of an emotional bond differs widely from providing help out of a sense of obligation. Prior to the emergence of major care needs, geographic distance may prevent adult children from developing a close relationship with a later-life stepparent. In other situations, closeness may fail to develop due to personality clashes or unresolved resentments from the courtship period. If their parent dies first, adult children may be linked to the stepparent not by affection but only by obligation to the parent's memory. When a stepparent needs care, however, some adult children discover an emotional bond with this person. Others withdraw all contact, expecting the stepparent's family to assume primary responsibility.

Watching their parent become emotionally stressed and physically exhausted from caring for an ill stepparent can intensify existing resentments. Even if an amicable relationship has been achieved, adult children may feel angry at the stepparent whose needs are tiring the person they most want to protect. They may increase their own assistance to relieve pressures on their parent, but find their resentment increases proportionately to the sacrifices made for the stepparent's care. In situations where the care needs become extreme, they may reach the point of pleading with their parent to permit nursing home placement for that parent's own self-protection.

A further aspect of such resentment can be adult children's perception that their stepsiblings are not "doing their share" to help the stepparent. Arguing, "It's your parent who's sick," they may expect the stepparent's children to provide support to protect their parent's health. The pressures of the caregiving period are likely to intensify unresolved conflicts with the stepsiblings, such as adult children's bitterness about their stepsiblings' receipt of extensive financial handouts. Opportunities to know the stepsiblings as people and therefore to have empathy for their life situations may have been limited prior to this stressful period. Stepsiblings can often benefit from family meetings in which conflicts are negotiated and responsibilities divided as fairly as possible.

In divorce situations in which both parents have remarried, adult children may have to deal with two sets of stepsiblings as well as two stepparents. The complexities can increase exponentially if care needs emerge simultaneously from both sides. A daughter providing care to her father's wife may find that her mother resents sharing her caregiving time with a woman who is not a blood relation ("Let her own family take care of her"). If the daughter avoids helping with her stepmother's care, she may then evoke her father's hurt as well as resentment from stepsiblings. With the increasing divorce and remarriage rate, along with the trend toward smaller families, such complex situations are likely to become more common.

In contrast to these difficult scenarios, some adult children develop affectionate ties with their later-life stepparents and are able to negotiate these complexities successfully. Some of the most bonding experiences between stepparents and adult children occur during the caregiving period, when they have to work together to ensure the parent's comfort. During this time, the adult children may witness self-sacrificing and dedicated acts by the stepparent and stepsiblings, giving them a deeper appreciation of the family into which their parent married.

Grandchildren

Two generations removed, grandchildren often possess greater tolerance for their grandparents' idiosyncracies and generational differences than do their parents. One reason is that grandparent relationships are generally not complicated by past authority conflicts. When childhood memories of grandparents are positive, special bonds of affection often exist. This affection, coupled with greater acceptance of generational differences, may enable grandchildren to approach caregiving responsibilities with an energy and optimism not possible with their parents.

A number of demographic and social trends, however, are complicating the grandparent–grandchild relationship. As noted earlier, the growth of four- and five-generation families is a profound demographic shift. As a result, some middle-aged grandchildren may be caring for both parents and grandparents. Although most grandparents tend to see at least one grandchild regularly, a growing number are separated by their children's geographic mobility and visit their grandchildren only infrequently. They may barely know one another, until the stage at which the grandparent is forced to move to the grandchild's community or home and frequent interaction becomes necessary. Alternatively, grandparents among some ethnic groups may have raised the grandchildren while their parents worked, creating intensely affectionate bonds between them. In such instances, grandchildren are more prone to care willingly for grandparents later in life.

Relationships with grandparents may be further complicated by divorce and serial remarriages, creating multiple sets of grandparents and stepgrandparents and competing responsibilities and loyalties. Due to custody conflicts, some grandchildren may be denied opportunities to visit one set of grandparents. Later in life, they may seek out or be contacted by these grandparents, only to find themselves faced with the care needs of virtual strangers.

The timing of a grandparent's care needs in relation to a parent's needs is another crucial aspect of the grandparent–grandchild relationship. A middle-aged daughter may be fortunate to have parents in good health, eagerly pursuing their retirement plans. While her parents travel, she may be faced with caring for her grandparents, as well as her own dependent children. An even more problematic situation for the middle generation is when their parents and grandparents both become ill at the same time, necessitating multiple care arrangements. For example, a fifty-year-old granddaughter may be caring for her seventy-year-old parents in her home and responsible for her ninety-year-old grandmother in a nursing home.

Even though young grandchildren are unable to assist directly with grandparent care, their naturalness and spontaneity may bring pleasure to the grandparents and some relief to their burdened parents. For instance, young children tend to be uninhibited by cognitive impairments or the sight of amputated or paralyzed limbs. The physical affection given readily by infants and toddlers can fulfill grandparents' needs, especially when physical or cognitive changes have made others less willing to touch them. In addition, the simplicity of games enjoyed by young children may fall within a severely impaired grandparent's range of abilities.

School-age grandchildren often feel self-conscious around chronically ill grandparents, and resist spending time with them. Such resistance is a problem for families whose time is stretched between grandparents and children. Families who attempt to devise outings to include children and grandparents often face difficulties identifying common activities. Going out to eat tends to pose numerous obstacles to shared enjoyment. Families first face the logistics of maneuvering both young and old from the parked car to the restaurant entrance, while the children impatiently run ahead or bump into their slower-moving grandparents. Children usually prefer fast-food restaurants, whereas their grandparents may be unable to tolerate the noise level and pace of activity in such establishments. If a restaurant is chosen with an atmosphere and menu preferable to the grandparents, the grandchildren's complaining and wiggling in their seats may result in no one enjoying the meal. Due to these generational differences in mobility, activity level, and noise tolerance, the parents often remain conflicted and forgo efforts to include both generations. Both grandchildren and their grandparents may actually prefer to stay home, playing a board game or working on a puzzle together rather than sharing outings which heighten the differences between them.

Grandchildren left alone with their grandparents are often fearful of their dying in their presence, without being able to express this fear directly. Unaware of what death looks like, young grandchildren become especially apprehensive when they see their grandparents asleep. Grandchildren who are the grandparents' companions for short time periods need their parents to explain, "When Grandma is asleep, it may look as if she's not breathing even though she is." Books written for children which discuss death can help them verbalize their fears. Some families find it helpful to play a game of "what if something happened" or to rehearse how to handle different types of emergencies. Children should never be left alone with a grandparent without a list of phone numbers of reliable people who can be reached to talk with them when they are worried or afraid.

As grandchildren approach the teenage years, they are frequently embarrassed or anxious about their grandparents' behavior. A grandson may laugh nervously and make a face of disgust when his grandfather removes his dentures at the dinner table. The parents may angrily dismiss the son from the meal, adding to all family members' tension and embarrassment. Grandchildren of a person with Alzheimer's disease may not want their peers to see their "crazy" grandparent, refusing to invite friends over or spending a disproportionate amount of time at their friends' homes. Preteen and teenage children should be informed about the physical and mental changes that cause the behaviors that embarrass them. Parents should model the appropriate responses toward people with memory, vision, or hearing losses, in addition to describing them.

Particularly frustrating interactions for grandchildren can develop around grandparents' hearing impairments. A grandson's excitement as he tells his grandfather about his first home run may turn to dismay and then sullen silence when his hearing-impaired grandfather does not respond with commensurate enthusiasm. After an accumulation of such interactions, the grandson may cease trying to tell his grandfather about events important to him, thus closing off what could otherwise have been a time of close communication. Some children's disappointment and embarrassment in relation to a grandparent's hearing impairments lead them to avoid interaction altogether. Prior to a buildup of frustration, grandchildren need to be instructed about speaking slowly and distinctly, positioning themselves where their grandparents can clearly see their lips, and using hand gestures and simple drawings to supplement their spoken messages.

Preteen and teenage children frequently compete with their grandparents for their parents' listening time and for transportation to favorite activities. A woman returning from work may be greeted by her teenage daughter anxious to talk about her boyfriend and asking for a ride to a basketball game. In the meantime, her mother may call with a request for a ride to her doctor's office. Unable to manage simultaneously these conflicting claims on her time, she may react harshly toward both her daughter and mother. Her eruption of anger can leave her feeling guilty, the teenager resentful, and the grandparent bitter over a sense of being neglected.

In such instances, parents need to set aside separate periods for listening to their children and for receiving phone calls from their parents. Unplugging the phone is a helpful strategy when their children need blocks of listening time, as long as their grandparents have alternative phone numbers for emergencies. Transportation conflicts can be partially resolved by a car pool, taxis, or occasionally paying someone else to drive. Driving services have developed in some communities to relieve working parents of conflicting transportation demands. Using paid transportation services is often preferable to making a forced choice between these types of conflicting needs.

Preteen and teenage children often resent being excluded from decisions about their grandparents that impinge on their living space. Giving up a private room for a grandparent is a particularly sensitive issue, especially if this decision is made without the grandchild's involvement. Preoccupied with their worry about their older relative, families may inadvertently exclude grandchildren from decisions about household routines, such as the noise level from the television and stereo, common space for guests, or length of phone calls. When grandchildren are involved in the process of making decisions about difficult choices, rather than learning of decisions after the fact, they are less likely to resent changes affecting them, such as missed vacations or staying off the phone "in case Grandma needs to reach us." A teenager who will be asked to forgo having friends over and listening to loud stereo music on the weekends when his grandmother visits should be permitted to participate in the planning of particular visits.

Some parents may try to protect their children from the work of caregiving. Working parents who feel guilty that their children are deprived of their support and contact during the day may attempt to assume all the tasks rather than infringe on their children. They may rationalize that children should be free to play and enjoy their childhood. Such protectiveness, however, overlooks the possibility of the grandchildren having special times while helping their grandparents, as well as a sense of contributing to the family. A better strategy would be to involve the children in family meetings or individual discussions about caregiving tasks. Teenage grandchildren can generate lists of tasks they want to contribute, such as reading and visiting with their grandparents, daily phone checkups, providing transportation for appointments, or doing yard work. Younger grandchildren can engage in crafts projects, telling riddles, or taking walks with their grandparents. Grandchildren who sit quietly listening to their grandparents' stories of the past also perform an important function, which can be included on a list of contributions.

In contrast to their parents' highly structured time, grandchildren are more likely to be available after school or on weekends, or to have time just to sit and talk with their grandparents. An important function that takes advantage of grandchildren's greater flexibility is for a grandchild to stop in after school to care for a grandparent's incidental needs until parents arrive after work to manage the early evening tasks. This arrangement significantly shortens the number of hours that the grandparent is alone during the day. When a grandchild is assigned such a primary responsibility, however, parents should pay the child commensurate with the care tasks and extent of time forfeited from other activities. Allowing the grandchild to share this assignment with neighborhood friends or cousins can make it more pleasurable, as well as lend status to the grandchild's role in helping to keep the grandparent out of a nursing home.

The grandparent–grandchild bond can be a powerful and intensely satisfying one. The opportunity for a child to contribute to a grandparent's comfort can be a valuable learning experience as well as create positive memories of their relationship. Parents exhausted by working and caregiving should not disregard the benefits for their children from participating in the daily care tasks. Such involvements can also make grandchildren acutely aware of the dilemmas their parents face and make them less prone to criticize their parents if nursing home placement becomes necessary.

Family Meetings

Professionals increasingly utilize family meetings to dispense information and assist families in their problem-solving. A physician may call for a family meeting in order to explain complex medical choices, hoping thereby to minimize misunderstandings and avoid the need to repeat information. When the need for a medical decision is urgent, this ability to gather and dispense information efficiently can be crucial. Other types of family meetings tend to focus on delegating tasks and resolving conflicts that have arisen during the caregiving effort.

Family meetings often seem desirable to family members for reasons beyond their obvious functions. A daughter overburdened by her mother's care may use an informational meeting as an indirect way to get her brothers to pool funds for the hiring of extra help in her mother's home. Since covert purposes may not be readily apparent to professionals, those who conduct family meetings need to be alert to the private agendas which almost always underlie a family meeting's ostensible purpose. Professionals may find it helpful to acknowledge openly to families this tendency toward covert purposes, but emphasize their need to steer around private agendas in order to provide a helpful neutrality.

Meetings are not beneficial for all families. Since families differ widely in their reactions toward such meetings, professionals intending to dispense information or facilitate decision-making should assess a family's relationships prior to arranging a meeting. When the members of some families gather together, group explosions erupt which would not have occurred in more scattered discussions. Fragile forms of cooperation may be harmed, at the same time that the professional's ability to remain unaligned may be impaired. With such families, professionals may be more effective conducting behind-the-scenes bargaining or conveying messages between family members who cannot converse without arguing.

Once a meeting is deemed beneficial, the choice of its time and location may be fraught with divisive potential. Although the professional's time constraints may be the chief determinants of when and where the meeting can be held, family members may try to use these arrangements to exclude certain members of the family. If the meeting is held at the home of a family leader, the others may resent this implicit reinforcement of their existing power structure. Those who would be able to attend if given sufficient notice may resent impromptu arrangements.

Since a frequent motivation for family meetings is to correct an uneven distribution of tasks, professionals may find that their primary role is to encourage the attendance of family members who have been least involved in the care. Unless behind-the-scenes effort is exerted, a task-delegation meeting could consist, ironically, of a gathering of those who are already fully contributing. Professionals who contact these peripheral family members may hear explanations of their noninvolvement that illuminate the family's dynamic in new ways. A professional's willingness to listen to their concerns, along with providing assurances that the meeting's objective is some degree of fairness, may make it safe for such family members to attend. Those who prefer to remain detached may nevertheless appreciate the acknowledgment implicit in the phone call; they may also be receptive to learning ways to contribute without coming into direct contact with the rest of the family.

A question which often stymies family members and professionals is whether or not to include the older person in the meeting. The answer essentially depends on both the meeting's announced purpose and the nature of the private agendas likely to underlie the discussions. If the primary need of the caregivers is to ventilate their weariness, the older person's presence might inhibit the release of such feelings. Besides, hearing only ventilation of grievances is not likely to help the older person. On the other hand, a discussion of the physical and emotional strains of caregiving, which includes the older person, can be structured to help the older person recognize the family's limits. The older person could then become involved in joint problem-solving to find ways to reduce the strain. Among siblings still competing for a parent's affection, the parent's presence could replace unrealistic contests over who can offer the most help with more realistic negotiations.

When the older person is not to be included in the meeting, some family members may ask professionals to conceal the fact that it took place: "She'll think we're ganging up on her." Although such concealment may be convenient in the shortrun, professionals expecting to have further contact with the older person can spare themselves and family members later awkwardness by advising against a secret meeting. Instead, a family meeting can usually be explained in terms that make an older person's nonparticipation acceptable, especially if the professional offers to summarize the content and to represent the older person's point of view during the meeting.

The outline below highlights a structure for family meetings that can be employed with or without professional leadership. Although some families may need a professional to conduct only the initial meeting, others may find that they continue to need a neutral third party at subsequent meetings. In other instances where a natural family leader exists, the professional's assistance may be confined to training the techniques inherent in the model. Family members comfortable with this style of negotiation may find it suitable for resolving other care dilemmas, such as conflicts between the older person and nonfamily caregivers.

A Structure for Family Meetings

I. *Identify the problems.* Each family member writes out a wish list of ways the situation could be improved. Lists are compared and disagreements identified.
II. *Exchange solutions.* Family members engage in a bartering process in which favors are traded back and forth until some semblance of fairness is achieved.
III. *Write out a time-limited plan.* Successful trades are recorded with specific measures of content and frequency, and a date is set for revising the plan based on experiences during the trial period.

Prior to a family meeting, individual members need to be aware of the obstacles to fairness described in the preceding section. The notion of fairness is particularly susceptible to distortion by the kinds of emotional issues which predominate in families; reviewing these obstacles, however, may help family members separate relevant concerns from those which should be resolved in other contexts. A son who realizes that an urge to retaliate for boyhood rivalry lies behind his tendency to load his brother with excessive tasks may be able to restrain that impulse in the interest of finding a workable solution to the immediate problems.

Reviewing the factors which build upon family members' strengths and minimize their limits may also set the stage for a reasonable approach to fairness. For instance, a career-oriented daughter-in-law who wants to maintain distance from assisting her in-laws may agree to a task that does not require sustained or frequent contact. Her spouse who has pressured her for more involvement could then value this contribution toward his parents' care. Grandchildren may check in on their grandparents in exchange for a block of time alone with their parents on weekends. In-laws, stepchildren, siblings, and grandchildren should all be involved in generating ideas about how they can be of assistance, while also meeting some of their own needs.

Beginning the meeting by writing wish lists immediately focuses on concrete statements rather than vague feelings. The leader should instruct family members to describe their suggestions in terms of observable and measurable actions. Instead of writing a statement such as, "I wish I could be relieved of doing Mom's housework once in a while," a child could write, "I wish we had a rotating system so I could take a week off from Mom's chores once a month." This pinpointing process moves family members away from generalizations which can feed conflicts toward specific details which allow for constructive discussion.

During the process of passing the lists around or reading them aloud, some problems may be spontaneously resolved. Preferences not previously expressed may receive concessions as soon as they are made known. For example, a brother may offer to his sister, "I didn't know you felt badly about my taking Mom out to dinner. Why don't you come along with us on my tab, since you do work so hard on her housework?" In some instances, the simple recognition of disparities in effort, added to a voluntary compensation, eases resentment more than structured solutions. In the relief of expressing themselves and resolving pent-up conflicts, however, family members may offer to do more than is practical on a day-to-day basis or may seize on solutions that only partially address their concerns. Warning participants of this tendency can help them be realistic.

The leader's primary role during a discussion of wish lists is to maintain the family's focus on identifying problem areas, and to keep track of emerging problems. A large piece of paper tacked on a wall can serve as a map for aspects of caregiving which are surrounded by differing points of view. Tasks which family members want reassigned should be posted, as well as the terms of spontaneous agreements which may be exchanged. The leader may need to stop conversations on the side and draw attention back to the wish lists, an arduous responsibility in talkative families. Most importantly, the leader should halt negotiations which are not producing immediate solutions, deferring their discussion to the second part of the meeting. Once each wish list has been examined, the first phase can conclude.

In guiding the meeting into the second stage, the leader first selects the most resolvable items for discussion in order to allow the family to achieve a few simple successes. Practicing the negotiation process on the easier issues permits skeptical participants to feel confident and gives the family a sense of unity on which to base more difficult negotiations. The strategy to be emphasized is that compromise is a give-and-take process in which favors are traded, for example, "What can you offer Jim, if he takes on the housework for a week each month to give you a week off?" His sister may volunteer, "I'll stop complaining that he isn't helping out. I won't nag him to do anything else." Weary of the nagging, Jim may regard her offer as a satisfying trade.

As the bartering proceeds, the leader should scrutinize each exchange to ensure that both parties gain something tangible, making it a win-win situation. Since the cessation of complaining can be observed and measured, it is an item that can be legitimately traded if it is adequately valued by the receiving party. When accustomed to assigning tasks a value other than money and time, families can achieve forms of barter which maximize their collective convenience. For example, a brother may pledge to mow his sister's lawn every Thursday night while he babysits for her children, if she agrees to take his shift of staying with their mother each weekend.

The third phase, writing out the plan, can be carried out while the bartering winds down. Time constraints or the family members' impatience during one sitting may necessitate that the leader end negotiations and postpone unresolved problems to the next meeting. Each family member can be given a copy of the written agreement; participants may then feel secure that the terms of the trades cannot later be denied. In addition, the plan's power can be enhanced by each family member signing it. The blank chart which follows is a possible format, but family members may prefer simply to list the individual trades.

Setting a date for a meeting to consider revisions is a crucial last step, since this defines the interim as a trial period for tolerating impractical compromises until they can be altered. When it is emphasized throughout the meeting that the goal is to produce a tentative plan to be tested, more trades may be offered than if they were regarded as unretractable. Skep-

FAMILY PLAN FOR TASK DELEGATION			
	Who Helps	How Often	Notes on Trades
Grocery Shopping			
Laundry			
Bill-paying			
Check-up Calls			
Yard work			
Transportation to the Doctor			
Meal Preparation			
House-Cleaning			
Miscellaneous Errands			
Signatures:			

From Nancy R. Hooyman and Wendy Lustbader, Taking Care: Supporting Older People and Their Families *(New York: The Free Press, 1986). Copyright © 1986 by The Free Press.*

tical family members may want to "try on" tasks portrayed to them as difficult in order to experience those aspects firsthand. A log book can be established in the older person's home to record the completion of pledged actions in order to minimize conflict from selective forgetting. For those inclined not to follow through with commitments, the date for a family meeting to discuss progress and revisions is a critical deadline.

Only Children

Adult only children experience caregiving relationships differently than those with siblings to share the responsibilities. Their feeling of being alone can be pervasive—of being solely responsible to meet parents' needs with no one else to help, to complain to, to share worries, or even to resent for not doing more. They may have more difficulty coping with their aging parents' physical changes and mortality, because of their realization that with their parents' deaths, they will be totally alone, without immediate family. This awareness of being alone in the face of performing difficult caregiving tasks can result in the unrealistic expectations to attempt to be all things to their parents.

This sense of responsibility may be even greater for individuals who become only children later in their lives, due to the siblings' deaths, or whose siblings have little or no contact with the parents, because of mental incapacity, imprisonment, or alienation from the family. Frequently siblings may refuse to help, thereby creating dilemmas similar to those faced by adult children without siblings. In such instances, adult children may be motivated not only by an obligation to meet all their parents' needs, but also by a sense that they must compensate for the missing siblings. Filling in for this kind of absence can feel especially relentless when the child feels guilt from having survived, or maintained the bond with the parents.

Regardless of the stage of life or circumstances for becoming only children, parental relationships are particularly intense without siblings as buffers. In many instances, the intensity of the relationships can function as a positive force in the lives of adult only children, with care of parents viewed as an opportunity to express gratitude for support and closeness. The paradox may be that adult only children feel bound by their devotion to defer their own needs while considering care options for their parents. For example, they may agree to their parents' moving near them at retirement, even when they prefer the privacy afforded by geographical distance. The very warmth of these relationships can make adult only children feel that they do not have a right to maintain boundaries when their parents need their contact in later life.

Adult only children who maintain boundaries may feel especially unappreciative of their parents if a sizable inheritance awaits them, which will not be passed on to anyone else. The prospect of the inheritance may dominate their relationships with their parents. Knowing that they will be sole heirs, adult only children often feel that their sacrifices must be commensurate with the size of these resources. If other siblings have died or been disinherited, the inheritance can be colored with guilt ("Why should I be the lucky one?"). In an effort to stave off such guilt, adult only children may feel compelled to avoid their parents' institutionalization at all costs, perhaps bringing them into their homes against their families' wishes or pursuing other options stressful to them.

When adult only children are married, their spouses may be more involved in caregiving than typical of spouses of adult children with siblings. In recognition of intense parental relationships, spouses occasionally make special efforts to become close to their in-laws. In the most fortunate instances, their in-law relationships approximate those of biological children. The adult only children and their spouses can then collaborate on caregiving decisions and responsibilities much as siblings do, taking turns with the time-consuming tasks and offering each other ongoing emotional support.

More frequently, spouses of adult only children do not develop relationships of equivalent intensity with the parents, but instead resent the closeness, time, and energy devoted to them. A husband may insist, "I married you, not your parents," disliking his wife's desire for frequent contact with her parents. He feels intruded upon by lengthy visits, especially at holidays and vacations. Anger with his wife's failure to maintain comparable interactions with his parents can become an additional source of conflict between them.

Grandchildren can also be drawn into the fray. Contacts with them often are asymmetrical, with expectations that they write, call, or visit this one set of grandparents more than the set who have other grandchildren. Grandchildren can find themselves in intensified roles that approximate those of only children, even if they have siblings with whom to share the additional expectations. Although they may feel equivalent affection for each set of grandparents, circumstances may force them to extend themselves more frequently to one set, perhaps hurting the other grandparents' feelings.

Efforts to compensate for the absence of other children and grandchildren in their parents' lives and to be fair in interactions with in-laws produce overwhelming pressures. Adult only children's free time may be filled with obligations to relatives, which leave them feeling that they cannot do enough for either side of the family. These conflicts are heightened if the parents move nearby at retirement or into the home after a medical crisis. Resentful of this encroachment on their private lives, their spouses may withdraw, making little effort to relate to the parents or to assist with extra work. As a result, adult only children can be left feeling even more alone.

In contrast to these competing pressures, adult only children who have never married may have devoted their lives to their parents and developed few outside relationships of equivalent intensity. Some adult only children have continued to live with their parents, despite employment which would have enabled them to live independently. While providing physical care for their parents in later life, they may remain emotionally dependent. When one or both parents is hospitalized, institutionalized, or dies, they often are at loss for ways to develop other supports or skills for pursuing their own lives. In addition to the loneliness from losing the organizing focus of their lives, those who assisted their parents rather than be employed face underemployment and the absence of reserves for retirement.

Adult only children providing care at the expense of their own needs can benefit from professional encouragement to use community resources and to accept assistance from outside helpers. Professionals can also work with adult only children to help them identify realistic responsibilities and to develop or maintain interests outside the care relationship. Individual counseling sessions may be the best way to assist them with feelings about their parents' aging, inheritance pressures, and the absence of immediate family ties. Similarly, efforts to mediate marital disputes around these issues may require sessions with marital counselors, especially if the caregiving conflicts reflect deep-seated divisions about parental relationships.

Adult only children may also need to build familylike relationships among friends, neighbors, and acquaintances. These familylike networks can assist them in caring for their older relative as well as give them support and respite. The strategy of building and utilizing ties with natural helpers for older people and their families is discussed at length in the next chapter.

Note

1. Elizabeth Markson. *Older Women*, (Lexington, Mass.: Lexington Books, 1983).

Suggested Resources

Cicirelli, Victor. "A Comparison of Helping Behavior to Elderly Parents of Adult Children with Intact and Disrupted Marriages," *The Gerontologist* 23 (1983): 619.

Compared help given by adult children with disrupted marriages (divorced, widowed, remarried) with that given by those with intact marriages. Those of disrupted marriages gave less help, perceived lower parental needs, had fewer filial obligations, and were more limited in helping, primarily due to job responsibilities.

Elder Link, 1-800-435-7666.

A service available to grown children outside New York who have aging parents in the New York metropolitan area. For a fee, will develop a service plan, including an evaluation of benefits, a weekly check-in phone call, and a monthly consultation with the adult children. Run by the nonprofit agency Selfhelp.

Foundation for Grandparents, 10 W. Hyatt Ave., Mt. Kisco, NY 10549.

A national organization that offers advice and assistance on grandparents' visitation rights.

SILVERSTONE, BARBARA, and HELEN KANDEL HYMAN. *You and Your Aging Parent* (New York: Pantheon, 1982).

An overview of the interpersonal, medical, economic, and psychological factors associated with aging and tips on how to cope with a variety of situations. See especially the section on family meetings.

WEAVER, DORIS. "Tapping Strength: A Support Group for Children and Grandchildren," *Generations* (Fall 1985): 5.

Presents a support group model for grandchildren, who were found to become more tolerant, accepting, and willing to assist in caregiver role.

CHAPTER 4

Natural Helping Networks

Natural helpers are vital for maintaining older people in the community. Based on decency, friendship, or a perception of mutual benefit, some individuals offer special assistance to older people while fulfilling their prescribed employment roles. These natural helpers provide informal services that are more familiar and acceptable to older people than formal agency services. In most instances, the link between their employment role and their spontaneous caring generally becomes blurred. Neighbors also help by observing older people's needs and providing spontaneous support.

Identifying and supporting natural helping networks ensures support for older people in the community and reduces the burdens on families. For older people alienated from their families or without relatives, natural networks can perform familylike functions. Families unable to provide help because of geographic distance, full-time work, or child care responsibilities may rely heavily on informal helpers in the community. Such helpers can supplement families' caregiving in numerous ways, ranging from relieving their worry to performing concrete tasks, such as meal preparation and assistance with errands.

Professionals and families can strengthen these helpers by sharing information, affirming their crucial role, helping them set limits, and linking them with others. When natural networks are weak or nonexistent, the task is to build informal support systems for the older person through similar techniques. First, this chapter suggests ways to identify and support natural helping networks, and then it presents approaches for the creation of networks. Interventions to prevent natural helpers from abusing older people are suggested in conclusion.

The following chart depicts examples of natural helpers and the ways they assist older people. It can be used as a guide by professionals or family members to assess an older person's natural support network.

Examples of Services Performed by Natural Helpers

Nurses and receptionists at doctors' offices: assistance with medical bill-paying and completion of forms, arrangements for transportation to and from appointments, liaison with family members, friends, and other professionals

Bus drivers: help getting on and off the bus, reminders to get off at the right stop, directions to destinations, assistance with packages

Apartment managers: social introduction to others in the building, checkup if older person is not seen, networking for the exchange of help between residents

Grocery store clerks: watch food buys, remind about needed items, help carrying packages and reaching for items on shelves, cashing checks

Postal carriers: daily checkup, reading important items to low-vision people, drawing attention to mail needing immediate response.

Bartenders: social introductions to other patrons, relaying messages between patrons, lengthy listening, referral to other source of assistance, taking telephone messages for those lacking a personal telephone

Meter readers, fuel oil deliverers: periodic checkups, someone to talk with

Pharmacists: special deliveries to the home, leeway on bill payment, repetition of medical instructions to older people with memory loss, education about side effects of medications, talk about health concerns

Cab drivers: assistance getting up and down steps, help locating the correct office within a building, carrying packages into the older person's home, and finding the way home

Hairdressers and barbers: social introductions to other patrons, opportunities to be touched, referrals to other sources of help, lengthy listening

Restaurant staff: special food preparation, nutritional reminders and encouragement, social introductions, special discounts

Neighbors: telephone reassurance, meal preparation (perhaps preparing extra servings of their meals), neighborhood watch, car pool to doctor's office, grocery store, or for other errands, socialization, periodic checkups, assistance with housework

Home health aide: daily telephone calls, bring meals on weekends or evenings, stop by after work for checkup

Identifying and Supporting Networks

Natural Helpers in Employment Roles

Locating natural helpers is time-consuming for professionals and family members, but worth the effort in terms of the information and support gained. Natural helpers are akin to field anthropologists observing people in their natural context. A grocery clerk may notice that an older person wanders the aisles, repeatedly looking for certain items. A bus driver may find that an older person fails to get off at the stop nearest home unless reminded. Family members who see their older relative within the known and mastered environment of a lifelong home may be unaware of problems the person experiences in the outside world. For this reason, families find it valuable to introduce themselves to natural helpers in neighborhood businesses as a way to check on the older person's functioning within the local area.

Meeting natural helpers and gathering information from them also gives them recognition. Their help may assume added importance when family members point out its value within the overall helping effort ("Without your making sure she gets the right groceries, we'd have a much harder time keeping her in her own home"). When they sense collaboration from the older person's family, helpers are often further motivated to personalize their aid. For example, when their questions about the older person's health status are answered, they may feel more trusted and included. Family members can affirm the helpers' interest and support by offering their home phone numbers and inviting them to share future questions and concerns.

Asking an older person directly to identify natural helpers is likely to yield little information. Older people often do not recognize special assistance when it is a subtle extension of employment roles. In small communities or urban neighborhoods with stable businesses, customers' relationships with proprietors tend to resemble friendships more than functional contacts. The human instinct to avoid acknowledging dependency, combined with this subtlety and feelings of friendship, may prevent older customers at supermarkets or banks from recognizing their extensive reliance on the staff for help with transactions.

Family members who accompany an older person through a typical day are able to learn what help occurs, by whom, and how often. For example, a son going with his father to a frequented restaurant will be able to glimpse which customers and staff greet him by name. The son can also see how a waitress cajoles his father out of ordering foods which violate his restricted diet. Similarly, a daughter who witnesses her mother's conversations at a beauty salon may sense that a hairdresser's caring responses to her mother are based on an intimate knowledge of the family circumstances.

In the process of network exploration, family members also may discover that an older person has more social contacts and a more attractive public personality than they thought possible. A man who is relatively silent and contained around his wife may be boisterous among his cronies in the neighborhood tavern. His charm and congeniality in that setting may surprise his son, who accompanies him to become acquainted with his natural helping network. The son may discover that the bartender knows a host of people who would help his father during a time of need, out of affection formed during years of pool games.

Natural helpers are often pleased to learn about others in the community concerned with the older person's welfare. Linking natural helpers eliminates overlapping efforts as each becomes aware of the others' help. Cooperative problem-solving can occur when family members or professionals convey information between natural helpers. If a bus driver hears that a teenage grocery clerk is willing to walk an older person home during an afternoon break, he could cue the person to stop at the store as he drops her off, thus solving her problem of getting lost on the way home. A postal carrier may check with an apartment manager when he notices unopened mail, or is concerned as to whether or not an older person is able to read the mail. The potential of such linkages is limited only by the helpers' imagination and willingness to become involved.

Natural helpers' friendliness can motivate older people to venture out into potential hazards, such as slippery steps, uneven pavement, steep hills, and busy traffic. A bus driver who greets an older woman by name or notices when she resumes riding the bus after a long illness may give her sufficient reason to walk to the bus stop and brave these challenges. A waitress who automatically places an older man's order when he enters the restaurant acknowledges his existence and provides a feeling of belonging. A clinic receptionist who converses at length with older patients inspires compliance with follow-up appointments and personalizes the health care experience in a way that busy health professionals cannot.

By providing motivation against becoming homebound, natural

helpers can deter depression in older people. A woman may maintain her weekly visits to her beauty salon more for her beautician's listening and touching than for attractive hair. As she enacts her weekly ritual, the trip gives her the exercise of walking to the bus stop, the social contact of talking with others on the bus, the mental stimulation of varied sights and conversations, and the mood elevation inherent in a change of scene. Looking forward to this outing one day each week can make the rest of the week's monotony easier to bear. Without the draw of her beautician's friendliness, she might stay at home rather than face a threatening environment.

Families can acknowledge natural helpers' value by giving them gifts or sending letters of appreciation to their work supervisors. Inviting them to speak up when the older person's needs begin to exceed their time constraints is another form of acknowledgment. Some may need encouragement to set limits on their help, as in the case of a clerk who allows an older person to build up excessive debts to a pharmacy. Periodic checking with an older person's natural helping network functions both as a support to ongoing efforts and as a way to identify problems before they erode the helpers' good will.

Neighbors as Natural Helpers

As the most accessible natural helpers, neighbors provide more frequent assistance to older people than other helpers. Natural helpers in business or public service have defined work hours and private lives outside the context in which help occurs, but neighbors are within reach on a potentially unlimited basis. Not surprisingly, one of neighbors' chief problems in helping older people is finding ways to limit their involvement. Many who could offer specific help remain aloof out of their fear of being overwhelmed by an avalanche of needs if they make themselves available.

When they do become involved, neighbors are often the keystone of the support needed to keep older people in their own homes. A relationship that begins with dropping over for coffee can become the provision of indispensable services. A neighbor who first notices that her older friend has difficulty reading medication labels may respond by giving her the morning dosage. Recognizing next that her friend cannot prepare hot meals without help, the neighbor may begin preparing breakfast during their morning conversation. As the helping multiplies in response to the needs, a neighbor could eventually find herself assisting the older person with getting dressed in the morning and then returning to help with bedtime tasks.

Problems arise when this neighbor realizes how confined she has become as a result of her responsiveness. Contemplating a vacation, she may find no other neighbors willing to take over while she is gone. The older person may discourage her from contacting family members out of fear that nursing home placement would be discussed. Neighbors in such predicaments often hear "Go ahead on your trip; I can manage" as assurance from dependent older people. Knowing how precarious the older person's survival would be during their absence, most defer vacations indefinitely. The prohibition against contacting family members then leaves them in a bind between loyalty to the older person and their own needs for privacy and leisure.

Family members and professionals who assist older people may remain unaware of such "neighborly" captivity for long periods of time. Typically, an older person's hospitalization precipitates discovery of this type of situation. For example, the neighbor may disappear on an extended vacation during the hospitalization; upon hospital discharge, family members must confront the full extent of their relative's needs. Similarly, a hospital discharge planner may contact a neighbor while checking on the older person's support system, only to hear accounts of frustration and weariness: "Please don't send her home; I can't do it anymore." Discharge planners often encounter such pleas from neighbors who have been the silent, behind-the-scenes supports for an older person's remaining at home.

Professionals and family members must maintain an ongoing awareness of neighbors' help in order to prevent such untimely discoveries. By asking her mother to describe the people she knows in her apartment building, for example, a daughter can determine who is most involved in her mother's life. She could then ask to be introduced to them during their customary visits. Such contacts communicate to neighbors how vital they are to the older person's well-being. Affirming that neighbors will not be alone with future care tasks allows them to be innovative in the help they offer, rather than protective of their personal turf.

Another way to support neighbors' helping is for family members to incorporate neighbors' errands into those they do for their relative. Ringing a neighbor's doorbell to see if there is a need for extra groceries conveys a cooperative attitude. It also implicitly rewards the neighbor for taking an interest in the older person's welfare. These contacts with family members may fill older neighbors' practical and emotional needs unmet by their own families. The time added to errands by this extra contact is not substantial and tends to be well worth the good will it creates.

When family members sense that a neighbor is becoming weary of helping, an effective way to broach the subject is to ask, "How can we make it easier for you to help?" Hiring someone to do the tasks the neighbor least likes to do may be a possibility. Another strategy is for family members to offer to pay neighbors for their time. Neighbors who feel they should be compensated will accept it; those who do not want to be paid usually appreciate the chance to decline payment. Listening to neighbors' accounts of their efforts over the phone may be the best way to avert weariness; this is particularly the case for out-of-town relatives who cannot offer neighbors concrete support. If the acts of helping seem to be a neighbor's sole meaningful activity, family members can enhance the neighbor's satisfaction and willingness to continue by taking the time to listen to these stories.

Daily checkups is one of the most useful functions neighbors can perform, without a substantial commitment of time. A neighbor in the house across the street can check to see that the blinds are drawn by a certain time each morning. If they are not, he can use a house key to check on the older person's safety. In apartment buildings, a next-door neighbor can make sure that the daily newspaper is taken in by a certain hour and alert the manager if it is not. The knowledge that someone will check on them removes older people's dread of laying helpless for days because a sudden incapacitation prevents their reaching the telephone.

Building Networks

Most older people, no matter how isolated they feel, have some type of natural helping network which professionals and families can activate. Even if neighbors have only a nodding acquaintance with the widow in the upstairs apartment, they nevertheless tend to be aware of her routines and deviations from habit. Similarly, concerned people to whom others can turn exist in most neighborhoods, senior high rise buildings, and retirement homes.

Some older people do lack informal supports. By complaining excessively and berating those who help them, they alienate their incipient helping network. Others withdraw from neighbors' and friends' gestures of kindness out of pride and a desire to protect their independence. Professionals and family members are thus faced not only with creating a helping network, but with encouraging the older person to accept help.

Building networks essentially requires that families and professionals assume a community-development approach of visiting the older person's locale to talk informally with neighbors and area business personnel. An outreach worker, for example, may visit with others in the lobby of a senior high-rise building. By questioning and listening, the worker usually learns which neighbors have the reputation of helping. In many cases, simply mentioning that a fellow resident has a problem can spark spontaneous offers of assistance. Neighbors may have suspected another resident's illness, but not known that daily meal delivery would be useful. Natural helpers are generally sustained by the satisfaction derived from helping and the hope of future assistance for themselves. Nevertheless, the professional or family's information and emotional support legitimates their informally organized delivery of meals. In localities where natural helpers do not exist, professionals often use networks of volunteers, especially from churches and synagogues, to provide both concrete help and emotional reassurance.

Not all professionals are comfortable or skilled in working with natural helpers. To be effective, professionals must be committed to the concept that informal helpers can be a vital resource, a perspective sometimes contrary to their professional training. In addition, professionals and natural helpers may differ in how they define adequacy of care and the need for professional interventions. For example, staff and neighborhood helpers may disagree about the advisability of nursing home placement for an older man living alone and incapable of self-care. Neighborhood helpers may be more directive in their assistance and may violate norms of privacy more than professionals are trained to do. Alternatively, professionals may not be aware of cultural preferences and norms of helping within particular ethnic groups.

Confidentiality can also be a problem for professionals because of their ethical and legal responsibilities. Providing information to natural helpers may violate the older person's privacy, unless the professional has first obtained the person's permission. Gleaning information from natural helpers can usually be accomplished without confirming or denying their speculations about the older person's private affairs. Professionals should make these boundaries clear through statements such as "I appreciate any information you can give me, but I can't answer your questions without permission from your neighbor." In instances where older people might harm themselves or others, confidentiality can be waived in favor of the pragmatic delivery of services.

Natural Helpers as Abusers

Although natural helpers are a major support to older people and their families, abuse can arise in such helping relationships. For those who prey on others' weaknesses, older people with a constellation of needs are ideal targets. Such individuals find people who are in need and then use their helping as a vehicle of abuse. A common example is the enterprising resident of a senior high-rise building who assists visually impaired people with paying their bills and skims off a profit in the process. The drain on a person's account can be so gradual and cleverly disguised that it goes unnoticed. Some may help themselves to groceries while making purchases for the person they are assisting. Others may take a portion of the cash on the way back from an errand to the bank, relying on the fact that a person with poor vision will be unable to keep track of quantities of groceries or cash.

When vulnerable older people begin to offer gifts or cash to those who assist them, the line between legitimate payment and abuse becomes blurred. For example, a homebound person who gives a neighbor cash to retrieve her mail or pick up her groceries may be induced to pay more for the services than is warranted. Still more problematic are situations in which isolated older people attempt to buy friendship by taking others out to lunch, giving them presents, or responding to complaints of poverty with generous loans. Family members and professionals are often perplexed by how to react when older people derive convenience or pleasure from spending their money in these ways.

Loneliness can deprive people of the ability to approach others selectively. The accurate assessment of other people's motives depends upon not being blinded by need. A homebound woman may be so grateful for a neighbor's visits that she overlooks the fact that she provides her neighbor free meals daily. Family members, seeing abuse where the older person chooses to perceive friendship, may wonder how a formerly shrewd relative allows herself to be taken advantage of in this way. To prevent hasty confrontations in such situations, professionals can indicate to family members the ways that loneliness can impede judgment.

Sensory and memory deficits can also interfere with the detection of abuse. Hearing, vision, or memory loss combined with loneliness are warning signals for considering that someone in the vulnerable older person's environment may take advantage of the situation. Families and professionals should translate an alertness to this possibility into a scrutiny of the older person's natural helpers. For example, a useful starting point is to ask how long an older person has known the neighbor who helps with vital needs. A neighbor who became friendly only after the person's needs became severe compares poorly with someone who extended friendliness to the older person prior to the onset of vulnerability. As a general rule of thumb, friendships with a history of mutuality are more reliable than new friendships with little shared helping.

Acceptable motivations for helping tend to be visible. People with kindness as part of their nature usually demonstrate this inclination in most of their contacts with others. Those with religious reasons often show or readily explain how their acts of helping fit into their beliefs. Those who help with the hope of investing in the future and being helped in return tend to be obvious in their attitude of storing away good will.

Suspicions of abuse are generally worth exploring when such acceptable motivations are not apparent.

Family members and professionals who suspect abuse should make themselves known as widely as possible within the older person's support system. Phone calls can convey that family or professionals are ready to receive information from those who may have observed the abuse. Phone calls become an important means of moving from suspicion to evidence. Those who might have information about abuse need to be assured that their disclosures will be handled tactfully and constructively. For example, a neighbor possessing incriminating information about another neighbor may fear retaliation if her role in exposing the abuse is not kept confidential. Another potential informant may worry that the older person's feelings will be hurt if the illusion of friendship created by the abuser abruptly collapses. Acknowledging and demonstrating sensitivity to these issues can help people feel better about becoming involved in what they perceive as a "touchy" situation.

Many types of natural helpers can serve as watchful informants. A postal carrier on his normal route may happen to observe a neighbor leaving an older person's house with an antique chair. A few months later, he may glimpse the same neighbor carrying out a vase or an armful of china. Eventually, when family members remark to the postal carrier that household items are missing, he may choose to share his observations, if assured of anonymity. Similarly, a store clerk may note that since a neighbor began shopping for the older person, expensive items have been purchased on her behalf that do not fit her customary selections. Family members and professionals need to establish themselves as trustworthy advocates of the older person before natural helpers in business roles are likely to confide such observations.

Some of the most commonly occurring forms of abuse are those perpetrated by chore workers and other in-home workers. Natural helpers who can make unannounced visits to the home are especially crucial as observers in these instances. A neighbor who drops in unexpectedly may catch a chore worker watching television instead of cleaning, or walking out with a bagful of "gifts" from the older person. An apartment manager with an office near the lobby may notice that an aide leaves the building sooner than the conclusion of required hours, or that a live-in companion leaves the older person alone most of the day. Because victimized older people are often reluctant to report such abuse, natural helpers who are willing to report it for them can function as valuable safeguards (see pages 211–212).

The prevention of abuse by natural helpers depends on an effective network of observers. The more people who have access to and are concerned for an older person, the less chance for abuse to remain undetected. Abusers are less likely to prey on an older person who has a variety of visitors or seems well known to neighbors. Family members may want to emphasize the visibility of their visits more than the frequency. They can attend a building social event with their relative or take walks with their relative at times when they are likely to be observed. Establishing a routine of private contacts with neighbors, under the guise of dropping off groceries, can serve as a pipeline of information as well as a sign of involvement that might discourage potential abusers.

When abuse by a natural helper is detected, the payoffs which the older person gains from the relationship need to be weighed against the harm inflicted. If the social contact provided by a financial abuser cannot be replaced and if the drain on the older person's money is not threatening long-term survival, family members and professionals may decide against confrontation. The hurt that would follow from forcing the older person to recognize a helper's friendliness as insincere may also discourage direct action. Although it is demeaning for anyone to admit to being duped, it is especially true for someone who already feels powerless in response to a necessary dependence on others. In some instances, this reluctance to acknowledge evidence of abuse can make older people angry at those who insist on the acknowledgment ("You just don't understand my friendship with her").

Other than confrontation, strategies that reduce the abuser's access to the older person's vulnerable areas are most effective. Finding someone else to help with bill-paying or household tasks can remove an abuser's pretext for opening the checkbook or entering the residence's private areas. An extra measure of protection is to make the abuser aware of the discovery of the abuse when introducing an alternative helper; this indicates to the abuser that gracefully bowing out is the only viable option. This approach also avoids a tug-of-war in which the helper attempts to convince the older person that family members are "after the inheritance," since the family does not try to impugn the "friend's" credibility in the older person's eyes.

In situations of extreme memory loss, however, removal of the helper's access to vulnerable areas is usually not sufficient protection. Someone who is unable to recall day-to-day occurrences cannot block inappropriate actions, such as a helper insisting on cashing a check at the bank after a family member has already done so. In such situations, threats of legal action may be necessary to halt the abuse, with concerns for the older person's loyalty to the helper becoming less important. The memory loss itself can make it easier for family members to provide a painless explanation for the helper's disappearance, if the older person notices the disappearance at all. Since older people with this degree of cognitive impairment are in constant danger of abuse, additional protective measures may be needed to ensure their safety.

This chapter has focused on how professionals and family members can utilize and support older people's natural helping networks to enable them to remain in their own homes. Professionals can also help activate families' supportive networks in order to relieve their caregiving stress. Families need encouragement to recognize their networks and to learn to accept offers of support. Neighbors can be especially helpful in assisting with errands, providing child care during family members' visits to their relative's home, or helping caregivers with their household chores. The professional's role with regard to natural helpers, in the caregiver's and the older person's network, is to gather information from the natural helpers and provide them with facts concerning the family that will strengthen their helping efforts; to acknowledge their involvement; to assist in setting limits on their helping; and to link natural helpers with each other, when and where appropriate. As discussed in the next chapter, strengthening families' support networks is vital to taking care of family caregivers.

Suggested Resources

BIEGEL, DAVID, BARBARA SHORE, and ELIZABETH GORDON. *Building Support Networks for the Elderly* (Beverly Hills, Calif.: Sage Publications, 1984).
> Includes discussion of use of networks for clinical treatment, family caregiver enhancement, case management, neighborhood helping, and mutual aid/self-help. Geared toward professionals.

COLLINS, ALICE H., AND DIANE PANCOAST. *Natural Helping Networks: A Strategy for Prevention,* (New York: National Association of Social Workers, 1976).
> Although the book discusses how to build natural helping networks generally, it is applicable to working with older people. Excellent discussion of the professional or consultant's role toward natural helping networks.

EHRLICH, PHYLLIS. *The Mutual Help Model: Handbook for Developing a Neighborhood Group Program.* Available from Southern Illinois University, Carbondale, IL 62901.
> A how-to guide for developing neighborhood-based support networks in a rural area.

FROLAND, CHARLES, DIANE PANCOAST, NANCY CHAPMAN, AND PRISCILLA KIMBOKO. *Helping Networks in Human Services* (Beverly Hills, Calif.: Sage Publications, 1981).
> How to build and maintain natural helping networks with groups of all ages. Includes some examples of network building with older persons.

National Self-Help Clearinghouse, 33 West 42nd Street, Room 1222, New York, NY 10036.

Publishes a bimonthly newsletter, *The Self-Help Reporter,* as well as keeps a record of self-help clearinghouses throughout the country.

ZARIT, STEPHEN. "Relatives of the Impaired Elderly: Correlates of Feelings of Burden." *The Gerontologist* 20, 6 (1980): 649.

The extent of burden reported by primary caregivers was not related to the behavioral problems caused by the illness, but was associated with the available social supports, specifically the number of household visitors. Suggests the potential effectiveness of an intervention program that increases informal social supports.

CHAPTER 5

Taking Care of the Caregivers

The emotional burdens of providing care tend to be greater than the physical or financial costs, particularly since caregivers frequently lose access to their forms of personal renewal. Most caregivers sacrifice leisure time, vacations, and privacy. Their friends may question their sacrifices or drift away out of disinterest in their problems. Lacking supportive networks, their interactions may be confined primarily to their older relative. As a result of multiple responsibilities, caregiver stress and depression are central problems in efforts to keep older people in the community. In fact, the caregiver's exhaustion, illness, or death accounts for most instances of nursing home placement.[1] Given these stresses, caregivers need to develop ways to protect their own physical and mental health. Such self-care techniques do not represent selfishness, but rather are intimately connected with the effective provision of care to their older relatives.

This chapter identifies signs of stress and depression, sources of caregivers' self-neglect, and appropriate self-care and stress reduction techniques. Caregivers faced with excessive demands are vulnerable to alcohol misuse, and abuse and neglect of their older relative. Interventions to prevent or end different forms of abuse are presented. Support groups are then discussed as an effective way to reduce caregivers' emotional burdens and provide relief.

The Warning Signs of Stress and Depression

Difficulty falling asleep or remaining asleep at night

Waking up early in the morning, feeling anxious and irritable

Marked changes in appetite, either toward overeating or loss of appetite; substantial weight changes

Increased use of sleeping pills, other medications, alcohol, or caffeine

Uncharacteristic short-temperedness, crying, or agitation

Delay or neglect of vital physical needs

Decreased resistance to illness

Difficulties with concentration and attention

Loss of energy or fatigue

Subdued mood; expressionless face or flat tone of voice

Rough handling and other signs of impatience in giving care

Recurrent thoughts of death or suicide

Signs of Stress and Depression

Professionals and caregivers themselves need to be alert to signs that stress and depression are taking their toll on those providing care. The following chart depicts the most common signals that changes in the caregiver's situation are necessary.

These signs, developing gradually, can go unrecognized in family caregivers for long periods of time. For example, a daughter may be aware of waking early every morning and feeling reluctant to face the day. Yelling at her mother for seemingly trivial reasons, she may attribute her short temper to tiredness. She may realize that she has been gaining weight, feeling tense, sleeping poorly, and wishing that her care tasks would end, but her life may seem so out of control that she believes she is unable to change anything. During her waking hours, she may maintain a frenetic pace of activity which keeps her from thinking and dealing with other problems in her life, such as her husband's resentment or her teenager's school difficulties. At night, she may fall into bed exhausted, but lie awake, unable to get her worries out of her mind. If family or friends urge her to take time for herself, she may insist that she is too busy or that her mother would be upset by anyone else's care. Despite her good intentions, her refusal to take care of herself may eventually harm her mother and her family.

Unrealistic expectations about handling multiple demands, and resistance to accepting help and taking time off are common causes of stress and depression among caregivers. The next section discusses these causes and presents ways that caregivers can take care of themselves.

Techniques for Managing Stress

Setting Limits for Unrealistic Expectations

Family members frequently adopt the maxim "If I called or visited Mother more often, she'd be less lonely." Bearing a pervasive and unending sense of responsibility for the older person's needs, they impose burdensome requirements on themselves for calls and visits. The contrast between their busy lives and the older person's relatively empty hours evokes guilt, as if the fullness of their lives were a substance which should be shared.

They may reach a point at which they believe that they lose no matter what they do: doing less for the older person seems to yield nothing but guilt and worry, and doing more only seems to increase their weariness and stress. Imagining what lies ahead, they miss the gray areas of compromise in which workable solutions lie. Instead, all-or-nothing options seem to loom, such as, "It's my job or my mother; I can't do both."

The crux of the matter is that no amount of contact from family members can compensate for the deaths of lifelong friends, the reduction of meaningful activities, and the other losses which generally accompany aging. The recognition that their devotion has a considerable but limited value and that they do not need to assume total responsibility is one of the most liberating insights family members can have. A son may respond to his widowed mother's loneliness by taking her on outings more frequently and trying to devise added entertainments. Spending more time with her than his personal life can afford, he may find that the hours of diversion he provides pass quickly for her and that her empty hours still seem long to her. He may realize that he cannot take away his mother's loneliness only after his repeated efforts have failed.

When family members let go of unattainable goals, they open up the possibility of feeling satisfied with the help they can provide. Whereas guilt-inspired contacts inevitably communicate burdened feelings to the older person, enjoyable interactions convey relaxed and welcoming feelings. Families who set achievable goals can often comfortably fit time with their older relative into their routines, rather than imposing numerous, inconvenient visits on themselves. Since the feeling of being enjoyed by family members has the power to extend beyond the visit's duration, families can best help their relative cope with loneliness by creating routines which do not burden their lives.

Some wisdom can be drawn from the common situation in which a daughter feels pressured by her mother's phone calls at odd hours of the day. The more her mother phones, the less warmly and attentively the daughter responds to the calls. With her need for warm, attentive contact still unsatisfied, her mother may then phone more often and complain more urgently about her lonely hours. Feeling crowded by her mother's needs, the daughter may try to fend off the encroachment with curt statements and other distancing responses. A successful solution to this kind of conflict usually depends on both people making concrete concessions. In return for her mother's agreeing not to call her, the daughter could offer two calls per day at times chosen by her mother during which she would concentrate her warmth and attention. Similar to the strategy for visits, this approach with phone calls replaces frequency of contact with quality of contact as a measure of devotion.

Various forms of physical dependency can be as perplexing as emotional dependency. With some illnesses, it is difficult to determine if the refrain, "I could never manage without you," is an accurate statement, a self-fulfilling prophecy, or a manipulative ploy. Family members may suspect that an older person is exaggerating physical symptoms in order to gain extra contact from them, yet be uncertain how to gauge the person's actual level of need. Their relative may be employing the "benefits" of being sick. Health professionals can assist family members in examining the seemingly unnecessary forms of help in terms of the additional benefits the person gains along with the help. If these secondary gains can be detached from the helping tasks, the older person may discover that getting better will not result in losing the benefits acquired by the sick role.

The following vignette illustrates this process of identifying the varied motivations for staying physically dependent:

> An older man who has been living alone since the death of his wife has a stroke. After several weeks of posthospital recuperation, his daughter tries to decrease his dependency on her by urging him to master the last details of dressing independently. He insists that he cannot put on his socks and shoes, no matter how hard he tries, and becomes angry at his daughter when she demands that he try to do it.

If the daughter analyzed the situation in terms of secondary gains, she would realize that her father's mastering his shoes and socks would relieve her of the need to come over every morning. In addition, the physical contact entailed by her sitting near him and touching his feet to help him with his socks would also become unnecessary. To separate the gain of a daily visit from her father's mastery of the specific task, the daughter needs to make clear to him that she intends to continue visiting daily after he is more independent. The benefit of physical contact could be detached by the daughter establishing a routine of putting cream on his feet when she visits, thereby giving him a separate route to obtaining that kind of touching. Every instance of overdependency will not yield such a simple extraction of the secondary gains; nevertheless, this way of reducing unnecessary dependency is effective when the motivations can be accurately identified and alternative routes to satisfaction supplied.

93

Handling Multiple Demands and Adjusting Care Routines

Combining full-time work with caregiving responsibilities is another potent producer of stress. A son who prepares dinner for his mother on the way home from work every evening may feel increasingly exhausted as he prolongs his work hours, week after week. In addition, he may feel pressured on the job by needing to leave at a set time each day, thereby depriving himself of the option to stay late to cope with unfinished work. The costs of this kind of daily routine in fatigue and job stress can be high. Similarly, a daughter may repeatedly use her sick time to handle her father's incidental needs, such as driving him to the doctor. When she has a cold or other minor illness, she is likely to force herself to go to work instead of taking needed rest. Faced with conflicts between her career goals and assisting her father, she may feel pressured to refuse promotions which would increase her working hours.

Family members caught in a bind between their jobs and their care tasks may need professional assistance to help them reach realistic compromises. The son portrayed previously could cook for his mother on the weekends, letting her reheat these meals on weekday evenings. Instead of stopping by daily, he could phone her after arriving home. The reheated meals and phone contact may not be as satisfying to his mother as freshly cooked meals and face-to-face contact, yet may relieve the son's workday stress to enable him to assist his mother for a longer time. Likewise, the daughter could pay for a cab to take her father to the doctor, thereby conserving her sick days for her own illnesses. In addition to job satisfaction, accepting a promotion could give her the funds to afford other services.

Life problems unrelated to the older person's needs, often intensified by caregiving pressures, can detract from the quality of care. A daughter going through a divorce may be too distracted and disorganized to provide competent care. Trying to cope with her mother's needs and her own grief, she may inadvertently confuse medication dosages and forget to take her mother to medical appointments. When problems in the caregiver's life are of such intensity, professional assistance in arranging short-term nursing home placement may be preferable to keeping the older person at home. With these pressures removed, the family member can concentrate on her personal circumstances until ready to resume giving care.

Nature of Care Tasks and Interactions

The nature of the caregivers' interactions with their relative are affected by the type of care tasks they must perform. When their relative's decline occurs imperceptibly, families may not notice the shift from primarily social visits to those in which blocks of time are devoted to the tasks of daily life. The daughter who washes her mother's bathtub on Tuesday may need to do so again on Friday. Meals have to be prepared three times a day and urine-soaked sheets washed daily. Other tasks may not necessarily consume large blocks of time but require constant vigilance, such as daily phone reminders to take medications.

Compared with meeting their relative's social needs for companionship and entertainment, caregivers often find basic care tasks to be relentless and repetitious. The only observable result from their efforts may be the older person's further decline. Those who also care for dependent children are especially unlikely to feel a sense of accomplishment at the end of their busy days. In contrast to child care, however, efforts on behalf of older relatives are unlikely to be rewarded by signs of increasing independence, thereby disappointing the human desire to see improvement in response to effort.

Spending a portion of each visit on meaningful projects can help remedy this sense of futility. For example, mounting photos in a family album with their relative's assistance, sorting through old papers together, or taping reminiscences of family history can be accomplished in small increments. The time added to care routines may pay off in growing satisfaction as results become evident. The older person also gains by being able to focus on something other than physical decline. The memories evoked by such projects may stimulate more animated discussions than would occur if the family's contacts remained limited to meeting basic needs.

Caregiving is also affected by family members' sense of loss over their relative's personality changes. They may feel that the person to whom all this time is devoted has already been lost. A stroke's disabling effects may turn a previously talkative man inward, leaving a withdrawn facade bearing little resemblance to his former personality. A woman may respond to a diagnosis of cancer with exaggerated passivity, which contrasts markedly with her former vigor and assertiveness. She may allow intrusive forms of help without complaint, becoming a "good patient," but foregoing traits which made her beloved to her family. The wife of an Alzheimer's patient who no longer recognizes her may consider herself a "married widow." For some family members, this loss of the person they once knew is worse than actual death.

Encountering such changes in a relative's personality is deeply painful to family members. If unable to relieve their sorrow, family members may devise excuses to avoid personal care tasks. Witnessing this collapse of their strong parental image can leave some adult children feeling angry at their parent for seemingly deserting them. Reactions can vary widely among family members, with those less pained by the changes becoming impatient with the ones who avoid their responsibilities. Professionals can help by urging family members to talk about such feelings openly with each other and by encouraging those who find direct contact too painful to assist their relative in other ways.

Learning to Accept Help

Some family members turn down offers of help at the same time that they complain to professionals about their physical and mental exhaustion. When others try to assume some tasks, they find excuses to keep on doing them on their own. Socialized to be nurturing and responsible, female caregivers are especially prone to such behavior. Women often believe that they should be able to do everything themselves, as proof of their love, competence, or marriage vows. Accepting help is experienced as admission of weakness or failure. Some believe they should not have to ask for help, but that others should automatically know their needs and volunteer aid. Placing themselves in a "no-win" situation, they resist assistance, yet inwardly resent being left with the care.

Others believe that no one else can meet their standards and that their relative will suffer under someone else's care. They perceive help as intrusive. For example, a daughter may have difficulty sharing control with a hired worker, presuming that the worker would disrupt her way of organizing the household. She may reject her sister's offers of help, remembering childhood lapses in her sister's reliability and believing that inferior care would result from a joint effort. Family members caught in this bind often need suggestions from professionals in order to adopt a more flexible logic. When their feelings about being the best caregiver are acknowledged, they can sometimes see that disruptions or imperfections in care routines are worthwhile tradeoffs for the benefits of respite. They may then be able to establish a priority of care tasks requiring their personal attention, letting go of less important functions.

Professional guidance can also help caregivers perceive the long-range consequences, both to themselves and their relative, of refusing help. When prodded with, "What do you think will happen if you go along this way and get more and more tired?," the caregiver may realize that she is not serving her relative's needs by neglecting herself. A woman may be persuaded to allow her children to help with their father's care once the possible consequences of her sudden illness or death are made prominent to her. A professional may spur her to view such help as ensuring quality care for her husband, rather than an admission of inadequacy.

Hired assistance introduced on a trial basis assures the caregiver that the situation can be reevaluated if problems arise. Some caregivers are un-comfortable with the prospect of supervising an in-home worker and benefit from instruction in the skills depicted on page 211. Reviewing these supervisory skills can prevent problems before they arise.

Self-Care

Just as a jogger looks forward to the end of running a course, it is psychologically necessary for caregivers to anticipate a break in their routines. For example, knowing that an out-of-town sibling will visit next month and take over for two weeks allows the primary caregiver the inner prompting, "I just have to make it till August when Bob comes." By establishing intervals of coping, a seemingly endless amount of effort can be replaced by a defined period in which to pace emotional and physical output. When a difficult situation has a definite end point and each por-tion of effort brings the conclusion closer, caregivers can distribute their coping capacities in order to conserve for the final push toward the end.

Removal of pleasurable events, however small, from an individual's life can produce stress and low moods. Personal forms of renewal, whether a long walk, time with a supportive friend, watching a sunset, reading a novel, or having a leisurely bath, allow a person to focus on aspects of life other than those which are draining. Even when a weary caregiver cannot leave the house for blocks of time, visualization of a pleasant event, such as taking a few minutes to look at favorite vacation pictures and trying to recall the smells, sounds, and sensations, can be revitalizing. Pleasurable activities, however briefly enjoyed, can place sacrifices back into the con-text of life as a whole, from which they derive their meaning.

Caregivers can be supported in making contracts with themselves, such as setting the goal of at least one outing a week and designating its time and date. They should also be encouraged to pay attention to the en-joyable feelings derived from leisure activities. After plans are made, the older person's protests at being left often result in the caregiver canceling plans. Acknowledging both the relative's upset feelings and personal disappointment were the outing to be missed is an effective response in such instances. For example, the caregiver could say, "Mom, I know you hate being alone in the house, but I've got to get out or I'll be too irritable with you."

Out-of-town vacations are particularly effective for renewing caregivers' spirits, but are often the hardest kind of respite to enact. Families may repeatedly postpone their vacation plans because they feel guilty about having a good time while the older person stays home. Their guilt may be especially intense if the vacation is to a spot which their relative cherished or had planned to visit prior to becoming ill. Some families arrange to have neighbors check on their relative or they hire helpers through an agency, only to cancel their plans at the last minute out of worry that something might happen while they are absent. When families turn their lives over to caregiving, taking time for themselves on a vacation can seem frivolous compared with the reality of care needs.

The question, "What is the worst possible thing that can happen if you go away?," may help families recognize that the worst will probably not happen. Their anxieties can also be addressed by advance discussion of an emergency plan with the temporary helpers, thereby preparing for anything that might happen. An emergency plan includes a notebook listing critical phone numbers, medications, daily routines, and idiosyncratic needs. Caregivers can first be encouraged to try out minivacations, such as weekends away. Through such trial efforts, they may discover that both the actual experience of the vacation and the reservoir of memories can stimulate their patience and enthusiasm, thus prolonging their ability to provide care.

Caregivers need to pay careful attention to maintaining their physical health. Proper diet, exercise, sleep, and time for relaxation are essential. Unfortunately, most caregivers feel so busy preparing meals for their relative or assisting them with rehabilitative exercises that they neglect their own diet and fitness. A daughter exhausted from cooking for her father may grab highly caloric snacks rather than preparing meals for herself. A wife struggling on a limited income to develop a low-salt diet for her bedridden husband may so dislike eating meals alone that she goes for days without eating. Sharing meals at home and occasional dinners out with friends provides social contact as well as improved nutrition. Rather than purchasing frozen dinners that are high in salt but low in vitamins and roughage, caregivers should buy those containing essential nutrients and low in calories, such as Weight Watcher's dinners.

The benefits of exercise are well known: better sleep, increased energy, maintenance of the cardiovascular system, improved joint flexibility, and stimulation of the production of chemicals which alleviate stress. Despite these documented benefits, caregivers may regard exercising as one more demand to fit into their already crowded schedule. Incorporating exercise into daily routines is a practical way to address this problem. For example, the caregiver might walk on errands rather than drive, or exercise along with the older person. A caregiver who has difficulty getting out of the house can benefit from a stationary bike, aerobic tapes or records, and tension-releasing exercises which can be done at home, perhaps while the older person is sleeping. Many exercises can be performed while sitting in a chair, talking on the phone, or watching television (see Suggested Resources). After a caregiver begins to incorporate exercise as part of the daily routine, the benefits of feeling more energetic and less tense tend to outweigh the time taken from other responsibilities. As a word of caution, caregivers should consult a physician before undertaking a strenuous exercise routine.

A major health problem for many caregivers is interrupted sleep. Without adequate rest, caregivers can feel consistently exhausted, discouraged, and depressed. The older person's wandering or phone calls are often the cause of sleep interruptions. In such cases, finding someone to be on occasional night duty can assure a few restful nights. When the caregiver's worry prohibits sleeping through the night, changes in daily routines may be helpful. Exercising late in the afternoon, avoiding naps, drinking warm milk, and relaxing right before bedtime are small changes which busy caregivers can incorporate into their routine.

Relaxation techniques can be helpful whenever caregivers feel tense and overwhelmed. Pausing for five minutes to breathe deeply can provide quick relief. Counting breaths or focusing on pleasant images while sitting in a relaxed and quiet state can also be helpful. A gentle shoulder and neck massage can relax both the giver and receiver of the massage. Listening to music encourages physical movement, such as clapping and swaying, which are beneficial to the rest of the body. Professionals can encourage caregivers to list the ways they relax most effectively and to turn to these reminders when they feel overwhelmed.

Caregivers may find themselves becoming overly serious about life. They may discourage laughter for fear of disturbing the older person, without realizing that humor can be a powerful antidote to stress. Laughter stimulates the production of body chemicals which are natural anesthetics and relaxants, and thus counteract nervous tension.[2] Humorous television or radio programs can be enjoyed while performing care tasks. Grandchildren can be encouraged to share their riddles and jokes with both the caregiver and the older person. Recognizing the ludicrous aspects of the care situation and laughing at mistakes rather than feeling remorse can make the situation more manageable.

When the Stress Is Too Much

Setting limits, adjusting care routines, accepting help, and taking time for themselves can counter the stresses on the caregiver inherent in many care situations. Caregivers who lack such a repertoire may turn to ineffective ways of coping, such as alcohol misuse, and abusive or neglectful behavior.

Alcohol Misuse by Caregivers

Stressed by multiple responsibilities, caregivers may begin using alcohol to quell their anxiety or to forget their worries when they do manage to get away from their caregiving duties. Professionals who work with families must remain alert to the possibility that alcohol is playing a deleterious role in the care situation. Concerned family members may attribute signs of substance abuse to the caregiver's physical exhaustion, low mood, or inadequate sleep. Family members wanting to avoid helping may look the other way at the obvious signs of empty bottles in the liquor cabinet or dirty glasses in the sink. The caregiver may rationalize being entitled to a small nip in the morning to get going and a little enjoyment in an otherwise pleasureless day.

Caregivers' alcohol misuse not only negatively affects them, but also the person for whom they are responsible. Unable to think clearly or move steadily, family members who drink can inadvertently harm their older relative. Such negative effects are depicted in the following chart:

Negative Effects of Alcohol Use by Caregivers

- Oversleeping in the morning: neglecting early-morning care needs and medication dosages; leaving the older person in bed an excessive length of time; failing to change incontinent pads promptly
- Medication errors: miscounting dosages; mixing up medications; forgetting medication
- Risk of injury: impaired judgment and coordination during transfers
- Sleeping through the older person's cries for help: inability to be roused from a stupor during an emergency or other urgent need, such as assistance with toileting
- Loss of emotional inhibitions: releasing uncontrolled anger; making abusive remarks to the older person that would not be made while sober
- Keeping the older person awake at night: loud or boisterous conversations in proximity to the older person's sleeping area; the presence of disruptive guests who are also inebriated
- Neglect of the older person's personal hygiene and meal preparation
- Misuse of money: resulting in inadequate funds for food, medications, heat, and so forth—all of which affect the older person's daily comfort

---

The best ways to prevent alcohol misuse in response to the stresses of caregiving are the self-care techniques discussed throughout this chapter.

A caregiver who allows regular breaks and plans frequent pleasures will be less prone to resort to alcohol for the relief of stress. Those with lifelong alcohol problems should be urged to seek professional assistance, since stress reduction techniques do not address the problem of alcohol addiction.

Family Abuse of Older People

Types of Abuse

One of the most difficult consequences of caregivers' ineffective coping efforts is abuse of the person in their care. Most instances of abuse are not intentional, but result from the accumulation of stress and limited resources for providing care. In many cases, caregivers do not recognize their abusiveness; those who acknowledge it often are at a loss as to how to stop their harmful behavior. The following chart can be used by professionals to help families identify manifestations of uncontrolled stress and other forms of abuse.

Abuse of Older People by Family Caregivers

FINANCIAL	EMOTIONAL	PHYSICAL
• Spending the older person's funds for purposes other than his welfare	• Ignoring the older person except to provide physical care	• Withholding necessary personal or medical care
• Refusing to spend funds for the older person's welfare	• Delaying bathroom assistance, meals, changes of clothing, as a means of punishment	• Hitting, bruising, physically restraining, or sexually molesting the older person
• Depriving the older person of financial decision-making rights	• Verbally insulting, humiliating, or threatening the older person	• Depriving the older person of a quiet, safe, or private environment
• Mismanaging the person's funds such that necessary medications or nutritional needs cannot be met	• Blaming the older person for family stress; affirming the older person's feeling of being a burden	• Leaving the older person alone for long periods of time when it is not safe to do so

Overt forms of abuse, such as mismanaged funds, verbal harassment, or physical striking, more readily come to professional attention than subtler kinds. For example, the fact that an older person is left alone for long periods of time or deprived of a quiet environment at night may emerge only after a careful series of interviews in which the professional checks on these less visible areas. Similarly, family members may be unaware that they intensify their relative's fear of being a burden when they discuss care difficulties within the person's earshot. The following warning signs can alert professionals to situations in which they should be especially watchful for abuse.

Warning Signs of Abuse[3]

- Guarded caregivers who do not allow professionals to be alone with the older person
- Excessively stressed caregivers
- Signs of alcohol and drug abuse
- Resistance of caregivers to others having regular access to the older person
- Lack of continuity with health providers
- Severe emotional distress exhibited by the older person
- Unclean hair or clothing; signs of insufficient personal care
- Unexplained bruises, cuts, fractures

Caregivers who shadow visitors to the older person's home or who refuse to leave the examining room when health professionals request privacy with the older person usually have something to conceal. When encountering such resistance, professionals should become all the more determined to obtain time alone with the older person. One strategy is to enlist the help of a second professional who can occupy the caregiver long enough to allow the other privacy with the older person. Another is to state openly that private time is a necessary part of the health professional's service to the older person and to insist courteously but firmly upon obtaining it.

Assessment and Interventions

In instances of familial abuse, community-based care options are often lacking for both the older person and the family. Professionals encountering abuse within families need to recognize that they can easily make the situation worse if they cannot offer better alternatives. The most common professional error is to move too quickly from detecting the abuse to confronting the abuser. To be beneficial, interventions must be preceded by a careful effort to understand why the abuse is occurring, why it is tolerated, and what alternatives can be provided. Without such forethought, interventions tend to produce combinations of the following list of destructive consequences:

Destructive Consequences of Hurried Interventions in Situations of Familial Abuse

- Outside helpers are prevented by either family members or the older person from having further access to the household.
- The abuser's anger at being confronted translates into a worsening of the abuse.
- Family members and the older person feel embarrassed and demeaned by their awareness that people outside the family know about the abuse.
- The abuser fends off forms of help that might have led to cessation or lessening of the abuse.

Professionals frequently define evidence of poor care by family members as abusive. Poor care, however, can result from family members' ignorance or physical exhaustion rather than malicious intent. For example, an older man may refuse to get up at night to help his wife to the bathroom, reasoning that interrupting his sleep makes him too tired the next day. He may regret his wife's discomfort and humiliation from being forced to urinate into protective pads during the night, but regard it as a worthy tradeoff for his obtaining rest. Unable to meet all her needs, he may choose to overlook the fact that her bedsores become worse as a result of nightlong contact with urine.

Perceiving a situation as abusive often depends upon point of view. The wife in this example may feel that her husband is cruel in refusing to help her during the night, no matter what his explanation. She may complain to her visiting nurse that her bedsores "ache all night" after she urinates and that her husband is "insensitive and selfish." From a medical point of view, the nurse would be correct in informing the husband that his failure to assist his wife during the night is hastening the sores' deterioration. Unless the nurse also offered a solution to his need for rest, this information would only intensify his guilt over contributing to his wife's discomfort. Choosing to reject the nurse's services might then seem preferable to facing his guilt or to losing sleep, two equally negative options.

Similar to many situations of abuse, the lack of substitutes to provide relief to the primary caregiver is the cause of the harm in this example. The problem is not inherent in the husband as a caregiver, but rather in the nature of the demands on him and his lack of resources to cope with them. Another example of how limited options can result in abuse is a daughter who virtually drops her father into his wheelchair instead of transferring him smoothly. Her lack of training in transfer techniques and her suppressed anger at confinement by the care tasks may account for her rough handling of her father. If a visiting physical therapist provided her with training and a home health aide allowed her time off from care demands, the daughter would probably stop harming her father in this way.

The following list suggests questions for assessing situations where poor care is evident. To reduce families' resistance to questioning, professionals should convey an attitude of gathering information for the sake of improving care, rather than that of a detective uncovering weaknesses.

Assessment Areas

1. What has been the nature of the long-term relationship between family members and the older person? Were the adult children physically or sexually abused earlier in life? When forced to be caregivers, those with unresolved resentments may consciously or unwittingly use the situation to get back at the parent. The power to withhold needed help to a physically vulnerable parent offers adult children a position of superior strength which can play into past and current battles.

2 . What current life problems unrelated to the care needs are pressuring family members? Are financial constraints interfering with compliance with medical recommendations? Is the primary caregiver overwhelmed by demands from several dependent people at once? Job stresses, personal health limitations, and worries about their own children are examples of problems that may affect caregivers' capacities to meet care demands constructively.

3 . What difficulties are resulting directly from the older person's care needs? How much rest are caregivers getting? What personal sacrifices are caregivers making in order to serve the person's needs? How much constant surveillance is involved in the caregiving tasks? Is the care especially stressful or repugnant? How drastically has the older person's personality changed in response to illness? When difficult care needs are present, the availability of extra help and professional support become critical determinants of family members' ability to sustain nonabusive care.

Problems from each of these sources frequently intersect to contribute to an abusive situation. Past family conflicts, competing priorities, and complex medical needs can emerge to produce extreme stress and poor care. Professionals should devise an intervention for each causal area, aiming to reduce several sources of the stress simultaneously. A son may need weekly counseling to deal with unfinished business with his father; at the same time, he may require state-supported chore services to relieve him from some of the household tasks. Job pressures may be unavoidable, but a sibling could perhaps be persuaded to give him a weekend off per month. Increased medical support from a visiting nurse and home health aide, and training in techniques that simplify care tasks may also ease these tasks.

Professionals are often frustrated when mistreated older people do not perceive themselves as abused. In these instances, the older person's inclination to protect family members may translate into a refusal to acknowledge exploitation or neglect. A professional who tries to be the older person's advocate against the family may encounter vehement rejection of such adversarial helping strategies. The following vignette illustrates such a situation:

> A son and his family move into his father's home when the son is fired from his job. They begin to use the older man's social security income to fund their personal needs, as well as for household and grocery costs. Ongoing unemployment leads the son into severe alcohol use and eventual mismanagement of funds so that his father's nutritional needs are not met the last two weeks of every month. Also, the older man begins reducing his dosages of vital medicines in order to stretch his supply until the next social security check arrives.

By urging this older man to throw his son out of the house in order to protect his health, a professional might provoke an angry response. The older man may regard his running out of food and medicine as the government's fault for restricting unemployment benefits, rather than attributing these problems to his son's actions. Believing that he is helping with his family's survival during a time of need, he may derive considerable satisfaction from this role in their lives. The increased contact with his family may also be rewarding compared with the loneliness he felt prior to their moving in. A professional who tried to portray the son as an abuser would only offend this older man, closing off potentially effective interventions.

Interventions which do not violate this man's perception of being protector of his family are likely to be viewed more receptively. Offering the son referrals to alcohol treatment and job-training programs may address the older man's concerns for his son without challenging the nature of their relationship. Arranging for a monthly prepayment of pharmacy expenses to coincide with the arrival of the social security check could be presented as a budgetary tactic rather than a protective strategy. By first determining how an older person perceives the situation, professionals may be able to devise realistic interventions and avoid doing harm.

Situations in which severe memory loss has impaired an older person's ability to recognize abuse differ from those in which the older person can be consulted. For instance, an older woman may be too forgetful to detect that her family is spending her funds for purposes other than her welfare. Monetary abuse may come to a professional's attention through a phone call from a relative who is not benefiting from the financial gains. Unless the professional can gather enough evidence to threaten legal action, confrontation could lead to the family's rejection of further contact with outside helpers. If the family has been providing vital services while taking a cut from the older person's assets, blocking their method of self-payment might also result in a discontinuation of their services.

Professionals occasionally encounter the ethical paradox that the help of family members who gradually reduce ample funds may be superior to the nonabusive helping options that are available. The cost of replacing the family's services with hired help may equal or exceed the rate at which they had been draining the funds. In addition, a cognitively impaired older person, unable to believe or remember the reasons for the termination of the family's help, may feel only a sense of abandonment. As in the previous examples, professionals need to weigh the consequences of their proposed interventions against the effects of a continuation of the abuse. In spite of physical neglect, financial exploitation, or emotional conflict, older people generally prefer care from relatives and continued residence in familiar surroundings over placement in other settings. For most people, the known is preferable to the unknown, even if their present situation appears intolerable to outside observers.

Support Groups for Family Caregivers

Family caregivers often feel that no one except those in the same situation can understand the toll of caregiving on their daily lives and relationships. Such feelings are intensified when friends question their sacrifices or urge them to institutionalize their relative. At the most basic level, support groups composed of family caregivers provide an opportunity to socialize with others capable of comprehending their dilemmas. The chance to commiserate about the painful aspects of their lives and laugh at humorous incidents relieves what is often a deep sense of isolation. Support groups may be organized to focus on particular kinds of disabilities, such as Alzheimer's or lung disease, or oriented to family caregivers generally. Although most support groups are affiliated with social or health service agencies, some have arisen spontaneously among families. A trained facilitator usually helps start a group, but meetings often continue when professional assistance ends.

Support group members come to recognize the universality of their own experiences by listening to others tell their stories. When they offer each other suggestions of favorite physicians or information about financial benefits, their awareness of community options grows. Even when members do not know of appropriate community resources, collective problem-solving can generate creative solutions. Families share practical caregiving tips, equipment, and supplies. A wife who gives her husband's walker to another member also conveys the hope that conditions can improve. In this exchange process, members find giving help can be as beneficial as receiving it. Sharing their insights to help solve others' problems, they become more aware of their competence and the importance of their caregiver role.

Support groups encourage an active stance toward problems. Even if the difficulty cannot be eliminated, the caregiver's attitude usually changes. Simply being able to admit a problem's existence can ease the pain. For example, a woman upset about yelling at her husband for repeatedly forgetting information may feel relieved to hear others confess the same inclination. Another illustration is group members' reassurance to a son who is uncomfortable with his relief at institutionalizing his mother. Members' expectations of themselves and their relatives are thus modified as they come to recognize human weakness.

Although support groups are not conducted as therapy sessions, the process of sharing feelings facilitates therapeutic effects. Members can express emotions, such as anger and guilt, without others judging them. Since group members are not part of their regular circle of friends, participants are freed of the need to maintain a strong exterior for the sake of social niceties. By assuring confidentiality, support groups allow members to talk about issues not comfortably discussed elsewhere. A husband may be able to discuss the problem of his wife's incontinence within the group, having kept this information from his adult children out of embarrassment.

The sense of support and active mastery can extend beyond the group meetings. Members generally watch out for one another, expressing concern when individuals are absent and monitoring their weekly coping efforts. Sometimes members form phone reassurance networks, calling regularly to check on one another. Those able to get away may meet for lunch, share a potluck dinner, or provide respite and other forms of assistance for one another. Social gatherings may occasionally include their older relatives. Members may sponsor a newsletter as a way to provide information and strengthen their sense of belonging. Support groups also serve a consciousness-raising function, thereby increasing members' awareness of gaps in services to which family caregivers are entitled. Politicized by this group experience, caregivers may become involved in public education, advocacy, and legislative action. For example, families of Alzheimer's patients, cognizant of their potential as a voting block, engage in letter-writing, lobbying, and publicity campaigns to increase funding for research and services.

Despite these advantages of participation, a number of barriers can prevent family caregivers from attending support groups. The scarcity of respite programs is a major obstacle. Even when respite can be located, the older person may protest so strongly that the caregiver finds it easier to stay home. For exhausted caregivers, attendance at a support group meeting can seem to be one more demand on their time. They simply may not have the motivation to make the necessary arrangements, particularly if transportation is a barrier. Many caregivers, especially older spouses, may be unaccustomed to the idea of revealing their personal feelings and concerns to strangers. They may equate group participation with the stigma of "therapy" or "mental health services." Admitting problems to others may be perceived as a sign of weakness. When such caregivers do attend, they are likely to be reticent to share their feelings, at least until they trust the group leader and other members.

These barriers need to be addressed by support group facilitators. For instance, if a list of group members willing to supply rides is maintained, then rides can be offered to potential participants. Likewise, phone "trees" can be coordinated to remind members of meetings. The meeting place should be accessible for handicapped participants, have phones available, ample parking space, and access to bus routes. The meeting time may need to be renegotiated to reflect changing membership. Retired family members tend to prefer daytime meetings to avoid night travel, whereas employed caregivers may prefer the opposite. Saturday mornings may be an acceptable alternative. Procedures to welcome new members, the availability of refreshments, and meeting rituals such as inspirational thoughts at the opening and closing can enhance members' comfort with the group experience. Additional techniques for facilitating support groups are included in the Suggested Resources.

Perhaps the most fundamental barrier to caring for the caregiver is that our society does not value caring for dependent persons. Caregiving for dependents, whether children or elderly, is defined as "woman's work," separate from the real business of life and without monetary worth. This cultural denigration of the caregiving role underlies caregivers' difficulties with asking for help, taking time for themselves, or recognizing the importance of their role within the long-term care system.

Fundamental shifts in such attitudes are occurring through the long, arduous process of social change. The increasing recognition given to caregivers by health professionals and the legitimization of the values of caregiving by the women's movement are promising first steps. In the meantime, professionals can encourage individual caregivers to take care of themselves and can refer them to viable community options for relief. Within their own agencies, professionals can work toward organizing support groups and obtaining funding for respite services. Taking care of the caregiver needs to be viewed as a primary component of the long-term care system. When accorded such legitimacy, caregiving will move beyond the private sphere to a shared public responsibility.

Notes

1. A. J. Kraus with R. A. Sposoff, E. J. Beattie, D. E. W. Holden, J. S. Lawson, M. Rodenburg, and G. M. Woodcock, "Elderly Application Process: Placement and Care Needs," *Journal of the American Geriatrics Society* 24 (1976): 165–172; Jeanne A. Teresi with John A. Toner, Ruth G. Bennett, and David E. Wilder, "Factors Related to Family Attitudes Toward Institutionalizing Older Relatives," paper presented at the 33rd Annual Scientific Meeting of the Gerontological Society, San Diego, Calif. (November 1980), 19–22.
2. Norman Cousins, *Anatomy of an Illness* (New York and London: W. W. Norton and Company, 1979).
3. Adapted from S. Tomita et al., "Protocol for Elder Abuse and Neglect," unpublished paper developed at Harborview Medical Center, Seattle, Wash. (1981).

Suggested Resources

Stress Management and Exercises

BENDER, RUTH. *Gentle Relaxing and Strengthening Movements for People with Back Problems, Arthritis and MS* (1983). Available from the Center for the Study of Aging, 706 Madison Ave., Albany, NY 12208.
> Demonstrates that gentle movement of the body increases blood circulation and oxygenation to cells and therefore strengthens the muscles. Shows that it is not necessary to do vigorous exercises to get the body in better condition.

Exercise, National Institute on Aging (NIA), Building 31, Room 5C35, Bethesda, MD 20205.
> The NIA will provide a list of information sources and free or low-cost publications that describe exercise programs.

GARNET, EVA DESCA. *Chair Exercise Manual* (1982). Available from the Center for the Study of Aging, 706 Madison Ave., Albany, NY 12208.
> Transcripts of four cassette tapes. All exercises use the chair for support and are beneficial for people of impaired mobility.

GIVDANO, DANIEL, and GEORGE EVERLY. *Controlling Stress and Tension* (1979). Available from the Center for the Study of Aging, 706 Madison Ave. Albany, NY 12208.

> Explains what stress is, its causes, and its effect on the mind and body. Shows how to relax the mind and body, relieve frustration, increase positive energy, and stay calm under pressure.

FALL CREEK, STEPHANIE, and MOLLY METTLER. *A Healthy Old Age: A Sourcebook for Health Promotion with Older Adults* (New York: Hawthorn Press, 1983).

> A comprehensive manual on how to develop health promotion programs for older people. Includes content and examples of handouts in the areas of nutrition, exercise, stress management, and personal and community self-help. Materials could be adapted for use either with family caregivers or the older persons themselves.

Fifty Positive Vigor Exercises for Senior Citizens (1979). Available from the Center for the Study of Aging, 706 Madison Ave, Albany, NY 12208.

> Encourages flexing and continued use of each portion of the body to improve balance and maintain good health. Includes specialized exercises designed for key muscles.

FRANKEL, LAWRENCE, and BETTY RICHARDS. *Mobility Exercises for the Older Person* (1980). Available from the Center for the Study of Aging, 706 Madison Ave., Albany, NY 12208.

> Exercises for bedbound as well as ambulatory people.

HARRIS, RAYMOND, LAWRENCE FRANKEL, and SARA HARRIS. *Guide to Fitness after Fifty* (1977). Available from the Center for the Study of Aging, 706 Madison Ave., Albany, NY 12208.

> A comprehensive and basic guide of exercise research and practice which draws upon a wide range of disciplines. Valuable for professionals working with older people or people with limited mobility.

PARKER, BARBARA. *Sit Down and Shape Up* (1983). Available from the Center for the Study of Aging, 706 Madison Ave., Albany, NY 12208.

> Over 150 pictures illustrate simple exercises and movements which can be performed in a straightback chair, while cleaning, or in a wheelchair. Designed for self-help.

SPILMAN, CAROL. *Over 40 Women's Fitness Book* (1982). Available from the Center for the Study of Aging, 706 Madison Ave., Albany, NY 12208.

> Discusses diet, relaxation, holistic health, sex, and motivation. Includes exercises, photos, and instructions.

WALKER, C. C. *Learn to Relax—13 Ways to Reduce Tension* (Englewood Cliffs, N.J.: Prentice Hall, 1975).

> A brief and readable how-to book geared to the general public.

Elder Abuse

KOSBERG, J. Abuse and Maltreatment of The Elderly (Boston: John Wright, 1983).

QUINN, M. J., and S. K. TOMITA. *Elder Abuse and Neglect: Assessment and Intervention* (New York: Springer Publishing Co., Inc., 1986).

Support Groups

BONJEAN, MARILYN. *In Support of Caregivers: Materials for Planning and Conducting Educational Workshops for Caregivers of the Elderly* (Madison, Wis.: The Vocational Studies Center, School of Education, University of Wisconsin—Madison, 1983).

A useful handbook for those conducting workshops for family caregivers.

Children of Aging Parents, 2761 Trenton Road, Levittown, PA 19056, 215-547-1070.

A self-help group dedicated to the needs of family caregivers. Aims to match the needs of people who want to start support groups with the names of people interested in joining.

Family Seminars for Caregiving: Helping Families Help (1984), Project on Families and Long Term Care, Pacific Northwest Long Term Care Center, University of Washington, Seattle, WA 98195.

GWYTHER, LISA, and BEVERLY BROOKS. *Mobilizing Networks of Mutual Support: How to Develop Alzheimer Caregivers Support Groups*, Duke Family Support Network Chapter, Room 153, Civitan Bldg, Duke University Medical Center, Durham, NC 27710.

Not specific to Alzheimer support groups, but describes setting up support groups in general. Especially useful for rural areas.

MELLON, JOANNA. *Support Groups for Caregivers of the Aged: A Training Manual for Facilitators*, The Natural Supports Program, Community Service Society, 105 East 22nd Street, New York, NY 10010.

The Natural Supports Project focused on strengthening families' capabilities through individual counseling and group work. This manual grew out of their experiences with support groups for caregivers.

SILVERMAN, ALIDA, CARL BRAHCE, and CAROL ZIELINSKI. *As Parents Grow Older: A Manual for Program Replication*, (Ann Arbor, Mich.: Institute of Gerontology, The University of Michigan, 1981).

A useful guide for developing and implementing educational and support groups for caregivers.

Women Who Care, Marin Senior Day Services, Box 692, Mill Valley, CA 94941.

Founded by a group of wives who were caregivers to disabled husbands and who have developed a model of respite care and peer support.

CHAPTER 6

Coping with Physical and Mental Changes

For the majority of older people, chronic physical conditions do not affect their ability to live independently but can interfere with the satisfaction they get from life. An older person who cannot easily leave her home may find little meaning from watching television all day. Older people with hearing loss tend to feel isolated, even when able to get out to social events. An older woman with incontinence problems, fearful of coughing and leaving a wet spot on her neighbor's couch, may refuse invitations. Although individual changes in memory, hearing, vision, mobility, bowel and bladder control, and sexuality are not severe for most older people, the accumulation of their effects over time can become obstacles to pursuing even simple pleasures. This chapter presents techniques that both family members and their older relatives can use to compensate for such physical limitations.

Memory Loss

The dread of becoming "senile" is virtually universal, yet what is commonly meant by the word occurs in only seven percent of people over age sixty-five.[1] Fears may be heightened by the increasing publicity and visibility given to Alzheimer's disease. Noticing their slips in memory and worrying about them more, older people may inappropriately label normal forgetfulness as dementia. One way to diminish fears and inappropriate lay diagnoses is for professionals to emphasize to older people and their families that some loss of memory for recent events is normal, especially after age seventy-five.

When older people and their families ask physicians whether memory problems will worsen, the assessment is difficult because the early stages of progressive conditions, such as Alzheimer's disease with its gradual onset, are often indistinguishable from normal memory loss. The first step in assessment should be a thorough medical workup to rule out the potentially treatable causes of memory loss, such as medication toxicity, depression, malnutrition, body chemistry imbalances, infections, and brain masses. Although eliminating such causes can be time-consuming and costly, older people and families can be reassured that they are not neglecting a condition that would respond to medical treatment.

Unfortunately, even with a thorough assessment to rule out curable diseases, the best answer a physician may be able to give about future memory loss is, "We'll have to wait and see." The fact that time is often the only way to tell whether some memory problems will worsen can be intensely frustrating to family members who are worried about their relative's long-term care needs. This section discusses ways to assess a person's safety living alone. The protective strategies presented can be modified depending on whether the person is experiencing mild memory loss or a more severe degree of impairment. Responses to personality changes often associated with memory loss are then suggested. This section concludes with answers to questions frequently raised by families about how to interact with relatives with severe memory loss.

Safety Assessments and Interventions

A primary concern which families often bring to professionals is whether their relative can continue to live alone. The following questions can be used by professionals to determine which aspects of the older person's life need closer monitoring. Worried family members should not attempt to probe on their own, since their relative is likely to react to their anxiety by trying to cover up troubling problems. Professionals should begin by exchanging anecdotes and gradually working these questions into the flow of the conversation, rather than making the person feel tested by a list of questions. Direct questioning is reliable only when a person feels secure enough to answer honestly; thus, assessment techniques which do not include efforts to make the person comfortable are bound to be inaccurate.

Fear of being unable to answer an interviewer's questions and then being diagnosed with Alzheimer's disease can itself cause an older person to forget answers which would have emerged easily in a less stressful context.

Questions for Assessing Safety

1. Do you often put pots on the stove and then forget they're on?
2. Do you tend to buy items you don't need at the grocery store?
3. Do you ever find yourself wondering whether or not you've already had lunch?
4. Do you have trouble sometimes remembering when you last took your pills?
5. When you go out, is it hard to get on the right bus or find your way home? Do you often lose track of where you parked your car?
6. Do you sometimes have trouble figuring out if it's morning, afternoon, or evening? Can you say what time of day it is right now?
7. Has it been hard lately keeping track of your favorite television programs or concentrating when you read?
8. Does it seem you're always looking for things you've misplaced, such as your keys or your wallet?
9. Has it been embarrassing lately trying to remember names of people you know well?
10. Do you sometimes wake up in the morning not knowing who you are or where you are?

People of all ages have difficulty with burnt pots, lost keys, and remembering to take pills, but usually not on a daily basis. Mixing up grocery items and needing to search for cars in parking lots is also common, but people tend to compensate by taking a shopping list and making a mental note of where they park. The difference between normal forgetfulness and problems which threaten safety is one of frequency and degree rather than any clear demarcation. Among the problems these questions may reveal, uncertainty about time of day, whether a meal has been consumed, and the names of familiar people tend to be indicators of problems beyond the normal range.

During their visits, well-intentioned family members sometimes practice "checking" their relative's memory status, imitating medical personnel by asking their relative to name the month, day of the week, or current year. Although the older person may conceal her uneasiness, these questions can cause such intense embarrassment that visits by those family members are dreaded. Mockingly put on the spot each time or perhaps even teased about forgetfulness, the older person may feel attacked rather than supported. A more subtle and caring way to check a person's memory status is to refer back to the content of previous conversations to see how much has been retained. If the older person consistently needs a review, then it is better to provide the review pleasantly within the conversation rather than test specifically for its necessity.

Older people often devise diverse and creative strategies to compensate for memory loss. For example, those who consistently forget to mark off the passage of days on their calendars may substitute an electric clock with a digital display of the day of the week and the date. Some older people keep their daily newspaper on the kitchen table for a prominent reminder of the date. When their medications are not linked to mealtimes, some people take a dosage when they wake up in the morning and then set an alarm clock or stove timer to remind them of the next dosage. When cooking, some lay out all the ingredients at once and then put each item away after the required portion has been used. Families should avoid reacting to these efforts as a sign of their relative's increasing memory loss; instead, they should praise such coping and encourage experimentation with other practical responses to memory problems. The following chart can be used by family members to help their relative make use of memory aids and to support this attitude of creative coping. In devising aids, families may find it most effective to combine both written and spoken instructions, since memory for the written and spoken word differs. Because changes are especially disruptive to persons with memory loss, families should attempt to maintain simplified routines.

Memory Aids

Problem	Possible Solutions for Family Members
• Burning pots; leaving food in the oven too long	Leave written notes about simple safety measures. Keep an egg timer on the stove so that the older person learns to set the time when using the stove or oven. If the person repeatedly forgets to use the timer, it may be necessary to phone the person when food is to be put in the oven and again when it is to be removed.
• Forgetting to eat	Cue person to eat by phoning at mealtimes and giving verbal step-by-step instructions; leave nonperishable food items where the person is likely to see them. Written instructions about mealtimes can be posted on the refrigerator.
• Mismanaging medications	Set up a sequence of envelopes for each medication time per day; utilize a medication box with days of the week marked; phone at

(Cont.)

Memory Aids *(Continued)*

Problem	Possible Solutions for Family Members
	each dosage time to cue taking out the envelope or medication box; label medications. Check medication supplies frequently.
• Losing purse and keys within the home	Install a prominently placed hook near the door for hanging the purse and keys. If the person repeatedly forgets to use this system immediately upon entering the home, the front door key could be tied to a string and worn around the neck.
• Becoming disoriented regarding time of day and person's day of the week	Obtain a clock which portrays time of day and day of the week; a tear-off calendar beside person's bed with cueing at night to tear off top page; a radio set to turn on at midday to cue a mealtime or medication dose; a large wall calendar listing daily activities; a list of the day's activities in order of their occurrence posted on a bulletin board or written in large letters on a sheet of paper.
• Becoming confused while dressing	Lay out the next day's clothes for the person the night before, preferably in the sequence they will be put on; cue with phone call in the morning; place large objects, such as an umbrella and hat, by the door.
• Forgetting to bathe; insisting that they have bathed when it is clear that they haven't	Post a bath chart on the bathroom door or put a mark on the calendar after assisting the person with bathing. Establish a bath day on which a family member will come over to assist on a regular basis. Arrange implements (soap, towel, etc.) in order of use. Attempt only one task at a time.
• Misplacing and forgetting to pay household bills	Obtain a large, colorful shoebox that can be left on the kitchen table, with "Bills" marked on all sides. Repeatedly remind the older person to place mail in the box, to be sorted when helpers visit. All visitors should be informed of the system to help the older person learn the habit.
• Wandering	Install photoelectric device on floor (such as those used in stores) to make an alerting sound if an older person tries to leave. Install deadbolt locks; place a latch above the older person's reach (cannot be used when the older person lives alone because of fire danger). Have older person carry an ID card or wear ID bracelet with name, address, and phone number. Affix bell to outside door to alert others when door is opened.

Despite these coping strategies, families may have to tolerate an uncomfortable degree of danger while their relative continues to live alone. The family's willingness to accept risks, such as fire from food left on the stove or financial exploitation due to poor judgment, may depend on the intensity of their relative's insistence on remaining independent. Family members may need to make their peace with each possible disaster in order to permit a particularly insistent relative to live at home. They may reason, for example, that "The house may burn down, but until that actually happens, at least he gets to stay in a familiar place." Being called at all hours of the night by a disoriented older person, or contacted by the police each time their relative loses the way home, however, are examples of stresses which may become intolerable over time.

Responding to Personality Changes

Changes in a relative's personality and emotional responsiveness tend to be more painful for family members than coping with the practical problems. These changes may include loss of interest in others' lives, mood swings inconsistent with past personality patterns, and increasing negativism and episodes of depression as the older person becomes aware of cognitive losses.

Reactions to memory loss which resemble paranoid disorders are particularly disturbing to families. A woman may move her treasured diamond necklace from its customary location and then forget both that she moved it and where she put it. Groping for an explanation for its disappearance, she may blame her daughter, who often helps clean her home and therefore has access to her jewelry. In such situations, family members readily discover the futility of using rational argument or confrontation to attempt to prove the falsity of this kind of accusation. A more productive approach is to try to understand the ways that the false belief functions to protect the older person from a painful awareness. In this instance, mistrusting her daughter is less painful to the older woman than facing her memory loss. The admission, "I can't remember where I put my valuable necklace," may be unacceptable because it would undermine her confidence in her ability to manage her life, a belief which tends to be more vital than trusting in a family member's love.

In contrast to paranoid disorders which tend to affect several areas of life simultaneously, the delusions expressed by older people with memory loss are usually confined to an aspect of life affected by their memory loss. A woman who misplaces her keys when she returns home may assert that "little men" are coming through her window and hiding the keys when she turns her back. Her seemingly "paranoid" thought is better understood as confabulation, the covering up of gaps in memory with invented or imagined information. Similar to the previous example, the motivating force behind such delusions is the need to explain memory failure in a way which places blame outside the self. Another example is an older man who tells his family that his customary bus route has been discontinued, rather than admit that he can no longer find his bus stop. If his daughter were to present evidence that the route is still functioning, he would probably become even more insistent that the stop had been discontinued in order to defend himself against the implications of his daughter's information.

Serving a protective function, suspiciousness and confabulation diminish the awareness of memory loss and therefore also the sorrow from that awareness. Depression develops when an older person is unable to deny the awareness through such protective measures. The person may begin making such statements as "What's the use of being alive if I can't remember anything?" More than any physical limitation, the loss of mental ability can seem to remove the basis for continuing to live. In these instances, families should seek professional advice, since supportive counseling and attempts to structure their relative's daily life may alleviate the depression. When family members feel added stress in response to their relative's depression, attending support groups with other family caregivers can be especially helpful (see Chapter 5).

Devising activities to counteract the older person's cycle of depression is another helpful response. Embarrassed at being unable to keep up with others in conversations and with activities dependent on memory, the older person may refuse social invitations and recreational outings. The loss of stimulation caused by such isolation can increase disorientation, since clues to time of day and the sequence of days in the week are lost through the omission of outings. The isolation may, in turn, feed the depression. Eventually, the older person may display not only the typical symptoms of depression, but additional cognitive impairment hastened by the loss of stimulation.

Many activities provide mental stimulation and pleasure without requiring intact memory. People who can no longer follow the content of a sermon may nevertheless enjoy the rituals of a religious service. People in advanced stages of Alzheimer's disease often retain their skill at conversational banter, able to exchange pleasantries and superficial remarks at social gatherings. Similarly, activities such as musical events, long walks, window shopping, and drives in the car do not depend on memory to be enjoyed.

Becoming accustomed to a relationship limited by memory loss requires practice and emotional agility. Families may find that talking to a relative who cannot remember the content of their conversations seems useless. Similarly, their relative's lessened ability to express interest in their lives may discourage them from exchanging anecdotes. In such in-

118

stances, reading to their relative, singing songs, playing records, or engaging in simple projects can fill in awkward silences and provide a soothing way to spend time together. Physical contact, such as giving the older person a backrub or hand massage, can also take the place of conversations. Allowing the person to repeat stories that have been told and retold many times can be viewed as part of the visit's ritual, rather than a frustration. If the older person responds better to visual than spoken cues, reading reassuring letters, posting informational signs, and looking at magazines and photographs may be preferable ways to communicate.

Responding to Severe Memory Loss

Answers to questions frequently asked by relatives of older people with severe memory loss are provided below. The later stages of progressive conditions often include the breakdown of social inhibitions, failure to recognize family members, repetitive behavior, episodes of restlessness, minimal attention span, and extreme mood swings.

HANDLING REPEATED QUESTIONS. Answering the same question over and over again can be extremely frustrating to families. When her mother asks every five minutes, "What happened to my car?," a daughter may explain that the car was sold and the money from its sale deposited in the bank. This reasonable response may satisfy her mother only for the period of time during which she can retain the answer in her memory. Instead, the daughter could try to respond to the emotional tone behind the question, rather than to its content. After reassuring her mother with a touch on her shoulder that everything is fine, the daughter could distract her by switching the conversation to another topic. Similarly, if an older person repeatedly asks, "Where are you going?," or "When will you be back?," reassurance on an emotional level combined with a hug may be more effective than facts for soothing feelings of fear or loneliness.

PUTTING THE OLDER PERSON AT EASE DURING ANXIOUS TIMES. The nonverbal sensing ability in older people with severe memory loss is frequently as keen as that possessed by young children. For example, a worried daughter may verbally assure her father that nursing home placement will be a "good thing," while conveying anxiety and guilt through her tone of voice, body posture, and facial expression. Correspondingly, families can convey reassurance at these levels of communication. Focusing less on words of comfort and more on how the words are said, the family member who uses a calm voice, relaxed posture, and at-ease facial expression may be able to reduce the person's anxiety.

Distraction is another tactic for reducing anxiety in those with severe memory loss. Telling lively stories while accompanying the older person into the bathroom may help diminish fears of bathing. As the older person's clothes are removed, an exaggerated tone and gestures keep the older person from focusing on the reason for disrobing. If the stories are sufficiently animated, the moment of getting into the tub will be less difficult. As noted previously, this strategy can also be useful to reduce repetitive or anxious questions.

How to respond when the older person speaks as if deceased people are still alive or refers to untrue events.   It is usually not fruitful to try to force accurate information on someone whose thoughts are focused in another time and who is consequently uninterested in "reality" as known by family members. If, in the middle of otherwise rambling speech, an older person asks directly whether a deceased loved one is alive, then it is important to give accurate information. Families need to listen closely to distinguish this kind of reality testing from speech which moves back and forth in time without concern for current information.

How to respond when the older person is making no sense whatsoever.   With persons in the later stages of dementia, family members may need to introduce themselves at the beginning of each encounter, saying, for example, "I'm Mary, your daughter." To be mistaken for someone else or regarded as a stranger can be particularly painful to close family members. Those in contact with the older person need to learn to depersonalize this loss of recognition by viewing it as part of the disease process. For many families, however, an intellectual understanding of the disease may remove only a portion of what is a recurring hurt.

Obtaining answers to important questions.   General questions such as, "Where are you hurting?," tend to elicit confused responses; in contrast, a series of specific questions requiring only a shake of the head may yield more information. The most productive method may be to ask, "Does your head hurt? Does your neck hurt?," while touching each area of the body until the pained area elicits a nod. The request, "Show me where it hurts," may work for those who do not need this successive cueing. Another useful technique is to ask one question at a time and then to repeat what is understood for the older person to affirm or deny. Family members can note the particular questions and phrases which are especially effective for eliciting information from the older person. These personalized methods should then be conveyed to substitute caregivers or professionals who communicate with the older person.

Memory loss from Alzheimer's disease and other progressive conditions is often regarded as the most difficult change families can endure in an older relative. This section has presented only a few of the many strategies for coping with a relative's memory loss. Families wanting more detailed information should consult the Suggested Resources at the end of this chapter.

Hearing Impairments

The most harmful consequence of uncorrected hearing loss in later life is social isolation. Because they need to ask others to repeat themselves, or find that they miss pieces of conversation, older people with impaired hearing may eventually stay away from social situations in order to avoid feelings of impatience and awkwardness. Since approximately 30 percent of adults aged sixty-five through seventy-four and 50 percent of adults seventy-five through seventy-nine years suffer some degree of hearing loss,[2] many older people and their families need to develop effective coping strategies.

Unfortunately, some of the strategies that well-intentioned friends and relatives attempt may be rejected by older people. Efforts to give a hearing-impaired person the best seating, or to post someone alongside him to speak directly into his "good ear" may be turned down by a person who fears being "too much trouble to have around." Once this belief becomes established, a chain reaction of increasing isolation may ensue. Diminished contact with others results in a loss of the kinds of stimulation which maintain his mental alertness and orientation to daily events. The older person may find that he has less to say to others, even when someone takes the time to initiate a conversation. This seeming "dullness" and unresponsiveness can eventually cause family members to conclude that mental deterioration has occurred along with hearing loss.

Another problem, which often embarrasses family and friends and discourages them from including the person in social gatherings, is a hearing-impaired person's tendency to talk over others who have begun speaking. In such instances, the interrupted speaker typically stops talking and the person with hearing loss continues, unaware of having cut someone off. The visible embarrassment of participants in the group may occur too late to alert the older person and prevent him from feeling foolish or rude. Even when people are aware that the hearing-impaired person cannot help talking over others, they may feel annoyed, thinking, "He should look around before he speaks to make sure he's not interrupting." A simple coping strategy is a signal system, where someone sitting beside the older person nudges his foot when he inadvertently interrupts someone.

A further problem, which may add to the others, is the tendency for people with hearing impairments to speak more loudly than others. Particularly in a close setting, such as a restaurant, the loudness may embarrass family or friends who notice others' stares or who are sensitive to the broadcasting of private business. In addition, side conversations may be difficult to sustain, due to the person's loudness blocking the others' voices or being too distracting. As in the problem of interruptions, someone sitting close by can subtly remind the older person to speak less loudly.

Establishing such cues is preferable to withholding invitations out of anticipated embarrassment.

Family members may inadvertently cease trying to include an older relative in conversations during family gatherings and thus unwittingly compound the problem. This often happens unintentionally, as a consequence of their relative's lack of verbal participation. The older person may sit in a chair at the periphery of a gathering and participate only in greetings and partings. Although physically present, he is deprived of the content of what is happening around him. He may try to maintain a cheerful exterior to avoid appearing as despondent and isolated as he feels. His nodding and smiling at eye contact with others, whether or not appropriate to the inaudible conversation, is a protective reaction that may be misinterpreted as "senility."

The inability to hear what is being said can further lead a watchful older person to adopt suspicious beliefs about unheard conversations. Frequently, family members will use the presumed communication barrier as an opportunity to discuss their relative, despite his presence across the room, thereby confirming the person's worry that they are talking about him. Although specific words may not be audible, the content of a conversation is usually conveyed through body language, gestures, and occasional glances toward the subject of the conversation. The older person is then faced with a choice of feigning unawareness or tolerating possible dishonesty when he asks about what has been said. Even the most considerate family members and professionals may make this error, unaware of how easily the essence of a conversation can be visually discerned and how naturally suspicious feelings arise in these situations.

To avoid these problems, a standard practice at family gatherings can be to position someone beside the older person to give periodic summaries of what is being discussed. The interpreter role, requiring a great deal of patience and attentiveness, can be rotated among family members. The interpreter needs only to give the gist of what is being said, for example: "Mom is telling John about Billy's car accident. Dad's telling his usual jokes." When stories are too complex to be summarized, the expectation can be established that specific details will be provided later. With practice, family members can become skilled at this role and may be rewarded by their relative's more animated facial expression and rekindled interest in others' lives.

In caregiving situations, particularly between spouses, a personal sign language often evolves, which speeds simple communications and reduces the frustration of both the hearing-impaired person and those with whom there is regular interaction. Although the hand signals and facial cues do not permit complex forms of expression, this personal language may convey simple information effectively. As a result, the

122

hearing-impaired person may feel at ease only in the presence of those who can provide this communication link. The person may refuse to accept help from substitute caregivers because of this dependence on a personal language, putting primary caregivers in the position of feeling guilty when they insist on obtaining respite.

Professionals can help such caregivers by pointing out the disadvantages of allowing this dependence to continue. If a sudden illness forced them to leave the older person in others' care, the emotional impact of the crisis on their relative would be worsened by this lack of practice with substitutes. In addition, if the primary caregivers become exhausted by their lack of respite, their conversations with the older person are likely to shrink to a minimum of questions necessary for communicating physical needs, for example: "What do you want for dinner?" or "Where did you put your red shirt?" Respite tends to renew caregivers' patience for sustaining deeper conversations, especially when hearing loss is a barrier. The older person's discomfort with substitute helpers is a small price for the psychological gains that rested caregivers can provide.

The phenomenon of selective hearing may be particularly annoying to family members: ("He hears what he wants to hear.") They may notice that their relative manages to understand the content of conversations they try to conceal and then misses information directly conveyed. Closing off contact with others at will is a powerful way to express anger, frustration, and the need for control. Family members' irritation often reflects the reality that their relative is effectively taking control in this way. Viewing selective hearing as an exercise of control is more helpful than reacting to it as a deliberate attempt to make life difficult for family members. Restoring other areas of control in the older person's daily life is a strategy which may reduce the person's use of this means (see Chapter 7).

The combination of hearing deficits with memory loss can be a particularly difficult mix, especially when a constantly misplaced hearing aid results. Many older people with moderate-to-severe memory loss remove their hearing aid when ringing or some other annoyance occurs; when they need to put it back on, they cannot remember where they placed it. This practice can be especially frustrating to family members who phone to check up and find that their relative does not hear the phone ring or cannot hear what is being said. A phone can be installed with a volume control which amplifies the speaker's voice enough to be heard without a hearing aid. Blinking lights on lamps which are triggered when the phone rings may be vital for hearing-impaired people who need phone cues to overcome memory problems.

One of the most difficult problems faced by families is the older person's denial that a significant loss of hearing has occurred. The person may complain that "people aren't speaking loudly enough" as a way to avoid facing the need for adaptation. Some refuse to wear hearing aids obtained for them by family members. Similar to a cane, hearing aids are often regarded as symbols of old age and thus rejected, despite the isolating consequences of doing so. Many who overcome initial resistance to a hearing aid will give up during the adjustment period, claiming that ringing sounds or distortions make it "impossible" for them to tolerate the devices. Expected annoyances are used as excuses for wearing hearing aids only intermittently. Those who continue to drive without aids and without acknowledging the need for extra caution may be in danger of missing signals such as horns and sirens.

Family members may feel less frustrated by recognizing that their relative's refusal to wear a hearing aid may be an expression of anger at aging. A helpful response is to emphasize the positive aspects of being able to hear conversations more clearly. Another is to encourage the person to practice using the hearing aid with family members rather than strangers. Family members' participation in the adjustment process can serve as a crucial inducement; for example, they can offer to reduce competing sounds in the environment while their relative attempts a conversation with one person at a time. Photographs of famous people with hearing aids and contact with peers who use them can also help remove the stigma.

A summary of adaptive strategies for common hearing changes is provided in the following list:

Adaptive Strategies for Hearing Changes

IN THE HOME

Flashing lights on appliances, doorbell and telephone
Telephone with amplification devices and large push button adapter
Hard floor surfaces covered to eliminate reverberations

BY THE SPEAKER

Cues to the older person to lower his voice and not interrupt
Summaries of missed conversations
Encouragement to the older person to practice communicating with strangers
Support for practice with a hearing aid
Before speaking, gaining the older person's attention
Speaking with lips, gestures and facial expression visible to the older person
Speaking at a distance of three to six feet

Not eating, chewing or covering the mouth when speaking

Not speaking directly into the older person's ear, which eliminates
   visual cues

Enunciating slowly and clearly

Speaking slightly louder than normal, but not shouting

Using short, simple sentences

Using multiple approaches, such as gestures and objects, to illustrate
   messages

Checking for understanding

Using low tones, which tend to be more audible than high tones

Admitting their frustration and feelings of loss from attempts to talk
with a relative who cannot hear them is an important first step for family
members. The quality of the conversations they are able to achieve may
repeatedly disappoint them, gradually eroding their willingness to keep
trying. The blank stare of someone who has not heard a third or fourth attempt at rephrasing can make the speaker feel like a failure or produce
guilt about not trying harder to keep the conversation going. Writing
notes to their relative may be less frustrating, since the written word tends
to permit deeper levels of conversation that are no longer possible orally.
A willingness on the part of both family members and their older relative
to experiment with adaptive strategies is crucial for maintaining the
motivation to keep talking to one another.

Vision Changes

Although changes in vision do not affect social interactions as profoundly
as hearing loss, they restrict older people's social worlds, often causing
them to feel vulnerable and isolated. Vision is relatively constant until
ages forty to fifty and then it slowly declines due to physiologic changes
that affect approximately two-thirds of the people sixty-five and over.[3]
This chapter discusses how these changes can negatively affect older people's daily functioning. Examples of adaptive strategies which enable the
maintenance of normal activities are then presented.

As the eye's lens thickens and loses elasticity, flexibility declines,
resulting in a decreased ability to focus on near objects. Frustrated by difficulties in threading a needle or seeing the stitches, a woman who
previously derived enjoyment and pride from her needlework may stop
trying all forms of handicraft. Unable to read favorite recipes, she may
become disinterested in meal preparation and eating. As reading and
writing letters become more taxing, she may sit staring out the window, to

the distress of her family accustomed to a mother who was always busy. Even phone contacts may be curtailed by the blurriness of the phone directory.

Although able to see distant objects, most older people have difficulty shifting their vision to near ones. The risk of accidents from missing a step or a half-inch threshold thereby increases. Previously proud of her meticulous appearance, an older woman may not see food stains on her dress or wrinkles in her stockings. Her children may attribute her apparent slovenliness to "senility." She may not be able to read the dates on food packages or see the condition of perishable items well enough to avoid cooking spoiled food. Medication misuse may also result from inability to read label directions.

Loss of the eyes' flexibility also reduces the size of the visual field and depth perception. After an older person fails to see a truck approaching from the left and damages her car, she may be too shaken to drive again. As she has more difficulty seeing potential dangers from her periphery, she may feel less safe walking on her errands. Fearful of both driving and walking, her life space becomes increasingly circumscribed.

A second normal change is a decline in the function of the lens and iris, and in the pupil's diameter. A six to eightfold increase in time is needed to adapt to darkness. Levels of brightness become difficult to distinguish, with more light required to perform routine tasks.[4] Night blindness, or momentary blindness from the lights of oncoming traffic, frequently occurs. Some older people with vision problems need help accepting limitations on their driving and may benefit from the suggestions offered in Chapter 10.

Misunderstandings frequently result when family members do not recognize the occurrence of vision changes. For example, a daughter who treats her father to dinner at an expensive restaurant may be dismayed by his silence and apparent displeasure. She may fail to realize that the restaurant's dim light makes it hard for her father to read the menu and see what he is eating. He may want to hurry home rather than linger in the shadowy spot. Perceiving his behavior as lack of appreciation, his daughter may stop taking her father to special places.

The eye's sensitivity to glare also increases, making reading or watching television difficult. While her father reads the newspaper, a daughter may open the shades, which he then sullenly closes, leaving her puzzled by his desire to block out the pleasant sunlight.

With age, the eye's lens yellows and becomes opaque, filtering out dark colors and producing confusion about colors of similar intensity, brightness, or grayness. Confused by the red and green of a traffic signal, a man may face the humiliation of his first traffic summons from unknowingly running a red light. A woman who has always dressed stylishly may appear in outfits of poorly coordinated blues, which to her appear the same. Her family may interpret her changed appearance as an inability to dress herself and the need for more supervision.

Relatively minor adaptations, along with order and organization, can generally allow a person with declining vision to remain at home. Adaptive strategies to compensate for changes in vision are outlined in the list which follows. Since they involve primarily the use of light, implementing them is not costly or difficult. Techniques that are simple, economical, and designed in accordance with the older person's preferences are most likely to be used successfully.

Adaptive Strategies to Compensate for Vision Problems Common Among Older People

LIGHTING

- Multiple light sources evenly distributed in a room
- Consistent lighting throughout the house to minimize shadows
- Increased bulb wattage (except for people with cataracts)
- Three-way bulbs and dimmer switches to control light intensity
- Horizontal window coverings such as blinds to control light
- More intense light over work areas and at top and bottom of stairs
- Night lights placed throughout the house
- Lights within easy reach of bed
- Sheer curtains over windows to eliminate glare, drinking glasses with painted rims, Polaroid eyeglasses, nonskid wax on floors.
- Fluorescent or brightly colored tape around electrical outlets, light switches, keyholes, and doorknobs

COLORS

- Bright warm colors as cues and to make rooms pleasant
- Contrasting colors (between doorways and walls, dishes and tablecloth, risers and flat surfaces of steps; mark edge of step with paint or nonskid material in a color that contrasts with the rest of the steps)
- Light objects on dark surfaces
- Colors as a coding system, such as with medications and food items

127

PLACEMENT OF OBJECTS

- Simplifying the visual field, avoiding clutter
- Keeping objects in the same place and informing the older person if any object is moved

MAGNIFICATION OF OBJECTS AND LETTERING

- Large-print books, instructions, signs, playing cards
- Placing a collar with large numbers on the telephone; utilizing raised-number templates for dial and push-button phones; bright stickers on the phone
- Needle threaders or spread-edge needles
- Coding schemes of large numbers, dots of glue, nail polish, or raised markings on stove, iron, washing machine, and refrigerator dials; rubber bands or adhesive tape on medicine bottles and food items
- Hand-, stand-, or chest-held magnifiers or battery-lighted magnifiers; attachments to glasses for close-up activities; telescopic aids for watching television
- Adapted chess, checkers, and other games

USE OF AUDIO

- Timers, alarm clocks, cutoff timer for electrical appliances
- Radio stations that read the newspaper or provide dramatic performances
- Audio cassettes, talking books

In addition to these normal changes, some older people lose useful vision. The causes of their blindness are often treatable or preventable, however. Glaucoma, a buildup of fluid causing high pressure within the eye, can generally be treated, but not cured, with medicated drops or surgery. Families and their older relatives need to be alert to the warning signs of glaucoma: loss of side vision, severe headaches, nausea, blurred vision, tearing, dull eye pain, and halos around light objects. An eyeball pressure test can detect glaucoma before vision is damaged and should be performed every two years.

Cataracts, a clouding of the lens, is the most common disability of the aging eye. Corrective lenses or an implanted lens can generally replace the damaged lens. Senile macular degeneration, the primary cause of blindness among older people, damages central vision. Since side vision is not affected, the person is usually mobile but unable to read, enjoy television, or identify people at a distance. Since laser therapy may be helpful, families should encourage their older relative to check frequently for macular degeneration. A simple test is to cover one eye and look with the other at the words on a page and then at a straight-line object; if blurring or waviness is noticed, an ophthalmologist should be consulted.[5]

Late-life blindness can be profoundly isolating, such that getting through each day becomes exhausting and worrisome. An older person who is alone in her home without adequate stimulation may become confused, depressed, and noncommunicative. Family members may act as if all her senses have declined, talking about her as if she were not present or failing to tell her when they enter or leave the room. They may not recognize how her vision fluctuates along with her ability to detect the presence, absence, or direction of light or the outline of objects—all of which can aid her in learning adaptive skills.

With technological advances in visual aids and the growing number of public and voluntary organizations providing equipment, numerous adaptations can support blind older persons in their own homes. The following list of adaptive techniques can be combined with the suggestions to compensate for vision changes. More specific resources are identified in the Suggested Resources. These techniques are most effective when the older person helps to choose them.

Techniques to Adapt for Low Vision or Blindness

- Talking books operated through the Library of Congress
- Computer-operated voice synthesizers which read aloud from printed or typed pages
- Braille watches and talking clocks (when a button is pushed, a voice announces the time)
- Machines that translate printed words into Braille
- Audiotape cassettes for correspondence, reminders, and instructions to the older person, and for storing information, such as recipes
- Adaptive clothing, such as Velcro openers and zippers and large buttons
- Placement of furniture to allow an uncluttered circulation area; removal of loose throw rugs and small objects; rug corners and edges tacked down
- Establishment of coding systems, such as textured paper on medication bottles

Families dissatisfied with their interactions with a blind relative can experiment with a variety of communication techniques. Touching their relative's elbow gently and announcing their names in greeting may spark his attention. Rather than taking their relative's arm, they can put his free hand around an upper arm and have him walk a step behind to anticipate their movements. When entering their relative's room, they can explain who is present and where each person is located to help put him at ease. On outings to restaurants, family members can offer to read the menu and help locate the items on his plate by referring to their positions according to clock number. These are only some of the ways families and their older relatives can work together to generate creative and personalized solutions to vision problems (see Suggested Resources).

Arthritis

Arthritis is so common among older people and the symptoms so closely identified with the normal aging process that older people and their families often accept arthritis as an inevitable accompaniment to a long life. Physical evidence of arthritis is present in virtually all people over age sixty, with 80 percent having noticeable symptoms. Accepting arthritis as inevitable can lead to the unfortunate consequence of failing to seek treatment or learn about strategies that reduce pain and support independent functioning.

Families may not recognize how the unpredictable nature of arthritis pain can dominate their relative's life. Even on "good days" when pain subsides, the older person may live with the fear of the inevitable "bad day." Daily activities may become structured by strategies to avoid pain. Concentrating on coping with one obstacle after another in the completion of tasks can be exhausting, even when the amount of physical exertion involved in each task is minimal.

Rheumatoid arthritis is a chronic inflammation of the membranes lining joints and tendons. Osteoarthritis is a gradual wearing away of joints, especially those which bear weight, such as in the knees and hips. Pain and disfigurement in the fingers can be manifestations of either type of arthritis. An array of medications and surgical procedures have been developed to treat these and the other over one hundred forms of arthritis. This section concentrates on suggestions for helping older people and family members cope with chronic pain, loss of independence, and other psychosocial consequences of arthritis.

The prime danger for people with arthritis is reducing their physical activity in response to pain. The saying "move it or lose it" summarizes the essence of the problem. Movement stimulates the secretion of synovial fluid, the substance which lubricates the surfaces between joints, and increases blood flow to joint areas. Movement tones the muscles which hold joints in place and which shield joints from excessive stress. When someone tries to avoid pain by sitting still as much as possible, the losses in lubricating fluid and muscular protection make movement still more painful. Eventually, the muscles surrounding immobilized areas lose their flexibility and affected joints freeze into rigid positions called contractures.

For these reasons, older people almost always benefit from repeated encouragement to maintain physical activity in spite of pain. Professionals should provide them with vivid reasons for putting themselves through the discomfort of activity. Family members need similarly explicit reminders that performing tasks for their relative can be detrimental. Their ability to refrain from giving too much help often depends on their awareness of the ways that contractures and deformities evolve, saying, for example, "Mom, if I keep washing those dishes for you, you'll lose all that good function of your hands and arms."

Keeping track of progress through exercise charts and other measurement strategies is a particularly valuable form of encouragement for older people with arthritis. The exercise chart in Chapter 7 can be adapted to fit individual needs, as can the accompanying suggestions for family members. By exercising along with their older relative and putting on background music, family members can provide distraction from pain as well as motivation to complete the regimen. Another technique for measuring progress is placing a piece of tape on the wall to mark the height an older person is able to reach with his arm over his head, and to record the date this height was attained. As shoulder and arm exercises gradually improve his range of motion, the successive markers of achieved heights provide a dramatic demonstration of the benefits. In the absence of ways to see progress, daily repetitions of painful movements can seem futile next to the immediate comfort of giving up.

A dilemma for overweight older people stems from the fact that bearing excessive body weight puts stress on joints, yet exercises involving walking and standing burn the most calories. When the option is available, exercises in water reduce the risk of injury and allow greater freedom of movement. Water supports most of the body's weight, making exercise more pleasurable for someone coping with both joint pain and the impediment of heavy limbs. Family members can check with community pools for times scheduled for older people, or contact senior centers that reserve pool time for participants in their programs. Adult day care centers may also offer pool access, including van transportation to and from the center as part of their rehabilitation services.

For people with arthritis, each day may seem to consist of a succession of obstacles, from getting out of bed and fastening clothing to opening mail, dialing the telephone, and handling utensils for meals. In contrast to those with more visible impediments, people with arthritis can seem to move more slowly, become more tired, or complain more than their condition warrants. Conflicts can develop between older people who feel their situation has been inadequately comprehended or supported and family members who feel manipulated by relatives' requests for help or refusals to accomplish more on their own.

In such instances, it is helpful to establish advance agreements regarding specific tasks which the person with arthritis will complete on his own each day. Tasks selected should be those most central to long-term independence, such as getting dressed and cooking. Advance expectations permit the person to pace himself through the day to control the pain, alternating periods of activity with intervals of rest. For someone coping with chronic pain, family members should try to incorporate pleasurable events, such as planning to take him out to dinner after he manages to do his own wash. The arthritic person can anticipate these pleasures as he surmounts obstacles. A spirit of exchange may eventually replace conflict as the older person feels his coping efforts are acknowledged and family members feel relieved by his continuing to accomplish tasks of daily living on his own.

Physical therapists can be especially helpful in recommending appropriate types of activity and teaching older people how to find the correct balance between exercise and rest. People with arthritis often need professional guidance to learn to distinguish pain which can be safely tolerated from pain which is a cue that the optimal level of activity has been exceeded. In addition, family members can learn to perform passive exercises with their relative's arthritic joints, such as bending the person's knee up and down with gentle repetitions as he lies on a bed. Therapists can teach warm-up techniques for preparing muscles and joints for movement that relieve early-morning stiffness and serve as a prelude to exercise sequences.

An occupational therapist can be enlisted to assist with specific aspects of independent functioning. In addition to surveying the home for helpful modifications, such professionals can suggest adaptive devices to compensate for reduced joint flexibility. For instance, someone with advanced deformities in hand joints would benefit from a therapist's installing plastic extensions on lamp switches, making them a length and size more easily gripped. Other useful adaptations include built-up handles on cups, utensils, faucets, stove controls, and doorknobs. Someone with shoulder stiffness can be taught the use of a grasping device for reaching overhead items and for picking up things off the floor. To supplement the equipment for household safety listed in Chapter 9, occupational therapists are trained to devise creative solutions to individual problems, such as substituting a wall dispenser of liquid soap and shampoo for someone who is unable to grasp slippery bars of soap and containers of shampoo.

The following list provides descriptions of other practical aids that can make daily life more manageable for older people with arthritis. To obtain items that are unavailable in local stores, families can write for the catalogs of medical supply companies or consult with the rehabilitation departments of local hospitals and home-care agencies. The local chapter of the Arthritis Foundation can also be contacted for information about adaptive devices and for obtaining their useful publication, the *Self-Help Manual for Patients with Arthritis*.

Practical Aids for Coping with Arthritis

EATING AND FOOD PREPARATION

Jar opener: A piece of rubber with a nonskid surface that provides a better grip of jar covers; a metal opener, inserted under the kitchen counter, that turns the lid while the person holds the jar steady

Electric can opener: Experimenting with different brands prior to purchase is advisable, since some are easier to use than others

Food processor: Those which can chop food without the need first to cut it up into small pieces are preferable.

MANEUVERING COMMON OBJECTS

Page turners: Mechanical or electric

Playing-card holders: These are devices which enable players to view their cards without having to grasp them.

Handling cash and coins: A small jar of the sticky substance used by bank tellers can be kept in a purse or pocket. Fingertips dipped into the substance eases picking up bills and coins.

Key extenders: Household keys can be attached to large plastic handles.

Portable cup and utensil handles: These can be attached for use in restaurants.

GETTING DRESSED AND GROOMED

Zipper pulls: A device for grasping and pulling hard-to-reach zippers

Shoe horns with long extensions: These are for people who are unable to bend far enough to reach their feet. Gripping devices are also available for pulling on socks.

Brushes with long handles: These provide for an easier grip.

Velcro fasteners: These can be sewed onto clothing to take the place of hooks and buttons.

Enlarged-handle toothbrushes: These provide for easier gripping.

Products on the market promising instant remedies for arthritis cause confusion for older people and their families. Numerous advertisements promote diets, vitamins, and special devices as "cures" and "miracle treatments." For example, the effectiveness of dimethyl sulfoxide

(DMSO) in treating arthritis is unknown, although many older people strongly believe in its efficacy. Filtered seawater, alfalfa tablets, vibrators, and magnetic bandages are further examples of advertised remedies whose usefulness has not been scientifically demonstrated. Books which detail useful strategies, such as relaxation techniques for coping with pain, are included in the Suggested Resources.

Relief of pain and improvement of function are the main goals of most arthritis interventions. Among researchers and service providers, the consensus is growing that joint deformities can be prevented in most arthritic patients and that the degenerative course of the disease process can be slowed or arrested through three avenues: (1) teaching methods of protecting joints from preventable damage; (2) prescribing and encouraging exercise regimens; and (3) promoting the independent accomplishment of activities and chores through the use of adaptive equipment and techniques for minimizing pain and fatigue. Patients whose reaction to pain takes the form of self-prescribed immobility for the sake of immediate comfort are likely to become increasingly disabled. Those who are helped to accept controlled amounts of pain during activity can usually maintain an independent life.

Incontinence

Although incontinence is one of the most threatening and humiliating changes associated with aging, it is one of the least discussed among older people and their families. Urinary incontinence can range from the discomfort of slight losses of urine to the shame of severe, frequent wetting. Fecal incontinence may begin with stains on underclothing and eventually become a total loss of bowel control. Families and their older relatives tend to be unaware of coping methods and treatment options, believing that nursing home care is the only alternative if incontinence becomes severe. Many older people, too embarrassed to inform their families or medical personnel of the problem, isolate themselves through their worry and sense of humiliation.

The first sign of an older person's eliminative control problems is often her beginning to restrict her lifestyle, without revealing the reason. For example, she may refuse invitations which involve long trips in a bus or car or other activities with limited restroom access. Family and friends may attribute her inhibited activity to other causes, or may be reluctant to embarrass her by asking about a suspected problem.

Although some older people will eventually confide the difficulty to a trusted family member or friend, others will respond to increasing problems in this area by going to even greater lengths to conceal their occurrence. Many rinse out underclothes and sheets by hand to hide stains from family members who help with the laundry. Despite numerous steps to a basement washing machine or a mattress which is heavy to lift at the corners, some refuse laundry help altogether to conceal telltale stains on clothing and bedding. Families may then mistake these refusals for assertions of a stubborn, foolhardy independence. In other instances, people with incontinence suffer sleep deprivation through their efforts to maintain control during the night.

Since the problem in its adult form tends to be handled silently, the extent to which incontinence is imprisoning is usually not appreciated by those who have not had to cope with it. Some older people avoid all social gatherings out of fear of leaving stains on couches or chairs. They may decline car rides to the doctor out of the dread of an accident on the upholstery, limiting themselves to the stressful alternative of a long bus ride or the expensive option of a cab trip. Some give up grocery shopping because of the absence of public restrooms in the stores or because of worry about getting caught in a long line at the check-out counter. Rather than face such predicaments, many choose to omit all outings except getting their mail. For a person living in an apartment building, the elevator ride to the lobby mailboxes may have to be carefully timed and may include the dread of being detained in a conversation with a friendly neighbor.

Fear of the consequences of detection by others can assume many forms. Some older people do not confide the extent of their difficulty to a physician because of worry about the expense and discomfort of complex tests, the possibility of hospitalization for these tests, or fear that a serious illness such as cancer may be causing the problem. Others may dread being asked to move from senior apartments or retirement homes, having heard of fellow residents leaving for this reason. Many worry that family members will question the feasibility of their continuing to live independently. They fear that nursing home placement will result once their relatives are aware of the problem.

The older person living with a partner faces more pressured versions of these same dilemmas. Couples often have a taboo against discussing incontinence, despite their mutual awareness of the problem. A partner may be repelled by the stench on clothing and upholstery, yet say nothing in order to avoid humiliating the other. He may respond to occasional wetness on sheets during the night by beginning to sleep in a separate bed. If the partner's smell sensitivity is keen, he may cease all affectionate contact, adding yet another negative consequence to an already painful situation.

An older person's denial of incontinence is one of the most troubling reactions that families face. Many older women experience a type of incontinence in which small quantities of urine dribble out during the day. Acclimated to the smell or having lost a degree of olfactory sensitivity due to aging, some block the problem's occurrence from their awareness and thus defend against its implications. Family members may be offered a dampened easy chair when they visit, finding themselves in an awkward position once they sit down and discover the problem. Using confrontation to try to break down such denial, family members may encounter hostility or hurt feelings; yet the alternative of saying nothing may become untenable because of a stench in the home which impedes social contact and essential forms of assistance. A partner who refuses to join in maintaining the person's denial and confides in family members may feel guilty for violating marital trust.

As an immediate way to reduce the older person's embarrassment about the topic, family members and professionals can explain that incontinence has been estimated to occur among up to 25 percent of men and 42 percent of women over age sixty-five living in the community.[7] An older person living in a senior high-rise building may become more open after hearing statements such as, "In this building alone, it's likely that at least twenty other people have problems with controlling their bladders." Since few feel comfortable confiding to others in their social group, most older people have no way of knowing that others nearby share their humiliation. A fortunate side effect of increased television and magazine advertising about protective products is increased awareness among older people that incontinence is a common problem.

Once incontinence problems are revealed to a friend or relative, one of the most important interventions is to ensure that the older person also tells her physician. The older person should be informed that medical attention may alleviate or reduce these difficulties. Even when incontinence cannot be eliminated, the discomfort and inconvenience can usually be eased. Treatable instances of incontinence include those caused by bladder or urinary tract infections, which may be cured after a course of antibiotics. Sometimes prescribed medications cause urgent and frequent urination. If informed of a medication's detrimental effects on a patient's quality of life, the physician may adjust the dosage or prescribe a different medication. Chronic incontinence can result from neurologic conditions, such as Parkinson's disease and organic brain syndrome. Other physical causes which should be investigated medically are prostate problems, pernicious anemia, diabetic neuropathy, and various cancers.

Many older people are reluctant to use the protective devices which resemble diapers both in physical design and in their discomfort to the wearer. In recent years, an increasing number of products have become available which offer protection without these disadvantages. One product description states: "The lightweight, highly absorbent material and waterproof backing help prevent embarrassing accidents. Also, because of their unique form-fitting shape, they are virtually undetectable, even under tight-fitting clothes."[8] These disposable pads are sometimes attached to specially designed undergarments. If such products are not available locally, they can often be ordered by mail from health care companies.

Other methods for coping with incontinence are as numerous as they are creative. Practice with stopping and starting the flow of urine helps some older women regain control. This method strengthens the muscles around the opening to the urethra and increases the woman's psychological sense of control. Fluid intake can be restricted prior to bed or when bathroom access is limited. Some older people can habituate their bodies to scheduled times for elimination, using the intervals between these points for errands and outings. Others are helped by antidiarrheal agents which can be prescribed by physicians when looseness of stool contributes to their control problems. Bedside commodes and urinals are useful for nighttime urinary frequency, omitting the need for a caregiver's assistance with getting to the bathroom.

Older people and family members are often confused about various types of catheters and their effectiveness for urinary incontinence. Indwelling catheters, in which tubing carries the urine from the urethra to a catchment bag, require skilled nursing supervision, tend to be uncomfortable to wear, interfere with sexual activity, and often increase the older person's vulnerability to urinary tract infections. For men, externally worn condom catheters are available which have fewer of these disadvantages. Catchment bags designed to be worn on the person's leg are undetectable under loose pants and can be emptied easily. Unfortunately, externally worn catheters have not yet been developed for women.

As family members and their older relatives become more open about discussing this problem, creative solutions can become a collective effort. For example, the older person can be given a seat closest to the bathroom at family gatherings, and care can be exerted to keep the bathroom unoccupied as much as possible. On trips, frequent stops can be planned on the itinerary, omitting the need for the person to keep asking for them. Washable upholstery covers can be placed on the person's favorite chairs, both at home and at family members' homes. An attitude of acceptance and support by family can significantly reduce the older person's anxiety about the problem. Even the freedom to laugh wholeheartedly can return to an older person who restrained this expression from the fear that laughter would cause urinary release.

Sexuality

Psychological responses, particularly fears about declines in sexual functioning, tend to constrain sexual activities more than the physical changes that occur with age. An older man worried about insufficiently hard erections may avoid discussing this with his partner or his doctor, thereby isolating himself with his anxiety. An older woman facing a scarcity of partners may think she has become unattractive. In addition, both men and women may be deprived of touch from friends and family members, a poignant loss that is rarely acknowledged by professionals and families. This section begins by exploring ways to combat the pervasiveness of touch deprivation among older people. Common physical changes which affect sexual activity, as well as the myths and attitudes which are often obstacles to sexual expression, are then described. Throughout, sexuality is defined broadly to include touching and holding, in addition to the sexual exchange of energy that occurs between partners.

Touch Deprivation

The need to be touched is as basic as any other physical need. Adults of all ages enjoy being held as much as children do, but this need is much less acknowledged in adulthood. People often free themselves to satisfy this need within the sphere of sexual relationships, only to tolerate the absence of physical contact in other types of relationships. Initiating a hug from a friend or relative is especially difficult for older people socialized not to express physical affection or fearful that such gestures will be met with rejection. Touch deprivation is thus a significant issue for unpartnered older people, who may live for years without physical contact on a sustained basis.

Ways to be touched during everyday life become increasingly crucial when opportunities for intimacy decline. Weekly visits to her hairdresser may be a sacred ritual for an older woman who lacks anyone else in her life to touch her. The sensation of strong hands lathering the soap on her head and positioning her shoulders while combing out her hair may be the closest facsimile to physical affection available to her. In the same way, an older man may cherish the way his clinic nurse lets her hand linger on his wrist after taking his pulse. Service providers having physical contact with people as part of their work should remember to maximize opportunities to touch those who lack other means of receiving contact.

Home health aides have extensive opportunities to touch older people. Helping someone bathe provides virtually endless options for contact. Washing the person's hair, giving a back rub with soap, and toweling hair afterwards can be fundamentally satisfying to a homebound person whose contacts with others are limited on all dimensions. Many older men refuse the services of home health aides because they dread an erection from being touched in these ways while in a tub of hot water, especially if the aide is a young woman whom they fear will be embarrassed. Female aides encountering resistance from older men should allude to their prior experience with helping men bathe to reassure them that embarrassment will not be a problem.

Adult children frequently urge their parents to set up separate beds or bedrooms when one of them has an incapacitating illness. In these instances, the healthier parent's need for uninterrupted rest is assumed to take precedence over their sleeping together. More than at any other period of their marriage, however, the ill spouse may need to be cuddled during the night. People derive considerable comfort from being held, especially after disfiguring surgeries such as mastectomies, colostomies, and amputations. One strategy is to have the healthier spouse sleep elsewhere in the home once every few nights, rather than establishing separate beds or bedrooms. Family members can also help by allowing the healthier spouse to take an extended nap during the day while they tend to their ill parent's needs.

Pretexts for touching become particularly useful within families accustomed to limited forms of physical affection. Back rubs, haircuts or manicures are a few of the means by which family members can create opportunities to touch their parents. Care needs may open up a variety of previously unavailable arenas of contact, such as through assisting with rehabilitation exercises. Family members can use touch to relieve a parent's anxiety, placing a hand on the person's arm during medical examinations and other stressful situations. More powerful than words of assurance, touch is one of the most calming responses that can be offered to fear. Just as crucial is for family members to be attentive to ways they communicate impatience and anxiety through their touch, perhaps transferring the person too forcefully or hurriedly tugging at clothing.

During periods of physical and emotional pain, the need to be touched is often most acute and least available. Physicians and other health providers can help by prescribing touch as part of the treatment rendered by caregivers. For instance, the wife of a man paralyzed on one side by a stroke could be instructed to caress his paralyzed arm, both to stimulate a return of sensation and to help him accept this changed body part. His son could be encouraged to hold his father in a standing position for several minutes a day to relieve his wheelchair restlessness and to give him close physical contact. When cancer is the primary diagnosis, health professionals should be particularly attuned to caregivers' unconscious fears of contagion and explicitly encourage physical contact.

Age-Related Sexual Changes

Knowing about normal physical changes helps older people to maintain their sexual self-esteem. The following chart can be adapted into a simple brochure for older people to read as they wait in medical exam rooms, allowing them to gain information in a nonthreatening manner. The questions stimulated by these descriptions of normal, though not necessarily inevitable, sexual changes could then be raised with the health care provider if the person is comfortable doing so.

Common Age-Related Sexual Changes

CHANGES IN MEN

- The time needed to obtain an erection may increase, and the erection may be less firm.
- Ejaculation may decrease in force and volume.
- Achieving a second erection may take longer.
- The urgency to ejaculate may be reduced, along with a decreased capacity to delay ejaculation.
- Orgasm may not be experienced during intercourse.

SUGGESTIONS/ADAPTATIONS

- Long, leisurely foreplay reduces performance anxiety by removing the focus from erection and intercourse and allowing time for a slower physical response.
- When the erection is not hard enough, placing the penis into the vagina by hand can sometimes help increase hardness.
- Hormone levels may be higher in the morning, making this an optimal time for sexual activity.
- Medications with impotence as a side effect (antihypertensives, tranquilizers, and antidepressants) can sometimes be exchanged for those less likely to affect sexual functioning, if physicians are informed of this concern.
- Avoiding alcohol use prior to sexual activity can be helpful, since alcohol increases desire, but decreases sexual ability.

CHANGES IN WOMEN

- Thinning of the vaginal walls and reduced vaginal wetness and elasticity can make intercourse uncomfortable.
- The time needed to respond to sexual stimulation may increase.
- The intensity of sexual response may decrease, with the orgasm becoming shorter or less pronounced.
- Urinary tract infections may occur more frequently because of thinner vaginal walls which offer less protection to the bladder and urethra.

SUGGESTIONS/ADAPTATIONS

- Water-soluble lubricants, such as KY jelly and vaginal creams, can be purchased over the counter in drug stores.

- Long leisurely foreplay helps increase natural lubrication and allows time for a slower response.
- Consistent sexual activity, including masturbation, maintains vaginal lubricating ability and vaginal muscle tone, reducing discomfort during intercourse.
- Drinking more fluids, and urinating before and after intercourse, serves to prevent urinary tract infections.
- Changes in sexual positioning can also help, such as aiming the penis down toward the rectum rather than toward the upper part of the vagina near the bladder and urethra.

Health professionals need to integrate such information about age-related sexual changes into their interviews with older people. A physician could broach the topic in one or two sentences which would permit an older patient to vent her concerns and questions. For example, she might respond, "Now that you mention it, doctor, I was wondering. . . ." One opportunity to open the topic occurs when an older person refers to missing a deceased spouse. Feelings about lost sexual intimacy may lie just below the surface, easily triggered by questions such as "When do you miss him the most? Is it when you get into bed at night or some other point in the day?" When presented with the chance to express her grief at the loss of intimacy, an older person may talk more candidly.

Fear of failure rather than physiological incapacity accounts for most cases of impotence in older men. As they grow older, many men do not adjust their expectations of erectile performance. They misinterpret slowed responses as failures, and then try too hard on subsequent occasions to meet their performance expectations. This excess of effort makes failure more likely, setting up a cycle of anxiety and disappointment. Some abandon sexual activity entirely, due to a false belief that their impotence is physical in origin and irresolvable. Many become depressed in response to this belief, equating sexual potency with personal strength. They feel that they are "weak" individuals if their erections are no longer powerful nor immediate.

Some older men begin avoiding affectionate contact, unwilling to risk revealing the dreaded inadequacy. They stay up late or go to sleep early out of fear that snuggling in bed will be mistaken for initiating sexual activity. Their partners then feel unloved and responsible for what they interpret as personal rejection. A woman in this position may confide in her physician, "My husband's not interested anymore," hoping that the doctor will "have a talk with him" and bridge their noncommunication on this topic. Worry that his partner is "getting what she needs elsewhere" may begin to consume the man who believes he is sexually dysfunctional, to the point where his suspiciousness keeps his wife homebound.

Health providers who are comfortable talking about sexual concerns can help bridge an older couple's noncommunication in this regard. Encouraging them to focus on forms of contact other than intercouse is a useful first step. For instance, a physician could instruct an older man not to attempt intercourse for a set time period, urging him to hold and fondle his wife. Lying together in bed, sitting close and listening to music, dancing, and massages can all be substituted for genital sexuality. The psychological paradox is that relinquishing the belief that sex requires an erection often helps men have erections.

Finding varied forms of sexual affirmation is particularly important when joint pain and other aspects of chronic illness interfere with the kinds of sexual activity traditionally enjoyed by a couple. Professionals may unintentionally imply that older patients' disability negates their sexual desires or that their frailty makes it unsafe to act upon them. Instead, health professionals should indicate their willingness to help older patients cope with limitations created by medical conditions. For instance, problems of pain in the sexual sphere can be addressed through medications, protective devices such as pillows and knee pads, and experimentation with different positions and sexual activity at different times of the day. Professional reinforcement of the permissibility of sexual activity is often needed when people allow pain to limit them more than necessary.

Attitudes and Myths

For both women and men, societal myths and attitudes tend to constrain sexual activities more than age-related physical changes. Older women suffer from a societal double standard of aging, in which signs of aging in men are viewed as "distinguished" while a woman with gray hair and wrinkles is seen as a sexual "has-been." An older woman who internalizes such attitudes may withdraw from possibilities for sexual intimacy. In addition, she faces the numerical constraint of fewer available male partners her age, as well as social stigmas against pairing with younger men. With few models of sexually active older women, she may view breaking out of these constraints as deviance and may fear accusations that she is imitating youth ("You're not acting your age"). Many older women are eager and willing to be sexually active but are frustrated by the scarcity of suitable partners.

Professionals' and family members' asexual responses to older people also serve to desexualize them. A physician prescribing an antihypertensive medication to a man in his seventies may fail to discuss the common side effect of impotence, assuming that the man no longer engages in sexual activity. Similarly, adult children tend to be uncomfortable with the image of their parent as sexually active, changing the topic when a widowed or divorced parent alludes to a desire for a sexual partner. Comments such as "What do you expect at your age?" and "You're too old to be thinking about such things" convey strong neutering messages that can compromise an older person's view of herself as a sexual person. In addition, older people living with relatives or in a nursing home generally lack privacy conducive to intimacy. An older couple's desire to hold hands or cuddle in bed may be viewed by professionals and family members as unhealthy and inappropriate.

The misinformation contained in popular myths is another prime reason for the unnecessary cessation of sexual activity by older people. For instance, some women believe that female sexuality ends with menopause, or that a hysterectomy removes sexual responsiveness. In reality, the freedom from worry about unwanted pregnancy and the annoyance of contraceptives can allow women greater enjoyment of their sexuality. Similarly, men who have had heart attacks often believe that they will die if they get too excited during intercourse, acquiring a habit of abstinence that may not be medically justified. Physicians need to be explicit about the permissibility of resuming intercourse after moderate exercise can be successfully performed, usually six to eight weeks into the recovery period.

Masturbation is another area of sexual expression where health providers' permission may be helpful. Negative myths about masturbation are pervasive within present generations of older people. Fears that mental incapacity, withered hands or some other punishment will result should be countered with neutral, informative statements, such as, "Stimulating yourself helps maintain responsiveness, without harming you in any way." Rather than embarrassing someone unaccustomed to explicitness on these topics, information can be offered through printed materials and recommended books (see Suggested Resources).

Another attitudinal barrier is that the current generation of older people, especially women, grew up with clear-cut restrictive guidelines about sexual behavior. As a result, they may be ashamed of their sexual feelings. Alternatively, some older women, because of early sexual experiences, may dislike sex. Within the current permissive atmosphere, they interpret their lack of interest in sex as something wrong with them. For some older people, new standards of sexual freedom can be as uncomfortable as Victorian strictures against sexuality. Younger professionals, in particular, need to be sensitive about conveying an attitude that "sex is vital for everyone."

Pressured by survival needs, some low-income older people may place social contact and intimacy at the bottom of their priorities. Medication costs often absorb surplus money low-income people would have preferred to use to purchase attractive clothing and hair styling conducive to their sexual self-image. Social occasions for meeting potential partners tend to be severely restricted for low-income persons. Traveling on organized tours, one of the best ways to meet other people, is usually prohibitively expensive for people who depend solely on Social Security for their income.

As with any other physical capacity, sexual responsiveness can atrophy through disuse. Regular exposure to stimulation from a partner or through masturbation can help forestall some of the age-related physical changes. Rather than declining, sexual activity may improve after the stresses of child-rearing years have abated and time constraints have been removed. Professionals and family members may need to examine the subtle ways they communicate disapproval of an older person's continued expression of her sexuality. Those in contact with isolated or ill older people need to stay alert for opportunities to touch them, filling in for the absence of partners and responding to the basic needs intensified by illness. Even for a homebound older person, the sensuality of the home or sickroom can be enhanced through the use of warm colors, pleasant smells, flavorful foods and soft fabrics. Positive comments about the attractiveness of the person's hair or clothing can affirm her sexuality. Encouraging the person to share anecdotes and photographs of past experiences, especially those of a romantic nature, acknowledges her vitality.

The impact of physical changes on the way people live must be addressed on several levels by health care providers. Proper management of chronic physical conditions requires integrating various forms of supportive care with medical treatment. With cuts in home care and increased restrictions placed on hospital care, health care providers are likely to find themselves without the time or funds to adequately address the psychological consequences of common physical changes. Older people and their families may have fewer supports and strategies for effective coping, increasing their risk of stress, abusive behaviors, and depression. Ways to prevent and minimize such negative repercussions are discussed in the next chapter.

Notes

1. National Institute of Mental Health, "Fact Sheet: Senile Dementia (Alzheimer's Disease)," U.S. Department of Health and Human Services (1980).
2. National Institute on Aging, "*Help Yourself to Good Health*," U.S. Department of Health and Human Services (1984).

3. Irving Dickman, *Making Life More Livable* (New York: American Foundation for the Blind, 1983), 5.

4. Ibid., 16–21.

5. NIA, op. cit. (1984): 4–7.

6. Ibid., 7–9.

7. Joseph G. Ouslander, "Urinary Incontinence in the Elderly," *The Western Journal of Medicine* 136, 6 (December 1981): 482–483.

8. Kimberly–Clark Corporation, Neenah, Wis. (1984).

9. B. D. Weiss, "Unstable Bladder in Elderly Patients," *American Family Physician* 4 (1983): 243–247.

Suggested Resources

General Mental and Physical Changes

COMFORT, ALEX. *A Good Age* (New York: Mitchell Beazley, Pub., Ltd., 1976).
A readable and upbeat book on aging and its changes.

Hotflash: Newsletter for Midlife and Older Women, National Action Forum for Midlife and Older Women, SUNY, Stony Brook, NY 11794.
An excellent newsletter that covers a wide range of topics of interest to middle-aged and older women, such as arthritis, incontinence, diabetes, sexuality, and shared housing.

NATIONAL INSTITUTE ON AGING. *Help Yourself to Good Health* (Washington, D.C.: Department of Health and Human Services, 1984).
A compilation of fact sheets on various health issues faced by older people, normal age-related changes, and techniques of preventive care. Very readable and practical.

Memory Loss

Alzheimer's Disease and Related Disorders Association (ADRDA), 360 North Michigan Ave., Chicago, IL. 60601, 800-621-0379.
Publishes *The Alzheimer's Disease and Related Disorders Newsletter*, useful to both families and professionals. Provides research updates and news of Alzheimer's Support Information Service Team chapters from around the country. Information packet available for $6.

MACE, NANCY, and PETER RABINS. *The 36 Hour Day—A Family Guide to Caring for Persons with Alzheimer's Disease, Related Dementing Illness, and Memory Loss in Later Life* (Baltimore: John Hopkins University Press, 1981).
Considered the "Dr. Spock" of caregiving for patients with dementia. Theme of the book is that Alzheimer's touches all members of the family. Includes

chapters for young people who live with or know a person with dementing illness.

Managing the Person with Intellectual Loss (Dementia or Alzheimer's Disease) at Home, Burke Rehabilitation Center, 785 Mamaroneck Ave., White Plains, NY 10605.

Brief, concise, practical how-to's for memory aids, bathing, and grooming and dressing.

POWELL, LENORA S., and KATIE COUTRICE. *Alzheimer's Disease—A Guide for Families* (Reading, Mass.: Addison-Wesley, 1983).

Detailed descriptions of Alzheimer's disease and reactions of friends and relatives to those symptoms and behaviors. Emphasizes professional intervention over self-help, but still a very useful resource for families, especially the section entitled "Taking Care of Yourself."

REISBERG, BARRY. *A Guide to Alzheimer's Disease: For Families, Spouses, and Friends* (New York: Free Press, 1981).

Good introduction to the scientific research and medical information.

THORNTON, SUSAN, and VIRGINIA FRASER, *Understanding Senility: A Layperson's Guide*, Potentials Development Inc., 775 Main Street, Suite 325, Buffalo, NY 14203, $5.95.

Concise, clear explanations of techniques for coping with behavior changes in persons with Alzheimer's disease.

Update on Alzheimer's, Special Issue, *Generations*, IX, 2 (Winter 1984).

A readable multidisciplinary approach to Alzheimer's. Covers the latest research findings regarding treatment as well as programs and community resources.

Hearing

American Speech-Language Hearing Association, 10801 Rockville Pike, Dept. AP, Rockville, MD 20852.

Can answer questions or mail information on hearing aids or hearing loss and communication problems in older people. Can also provide a list of certified audiologists in each state.

The Better Hearing Institute, 1430 K Street N.W., Washington, DC 20005, 800-424-8576.

Maintains a toll-free Hearing Helpline that provides information about hearing aids, tinnitus, nerve deafness, special devices, and other problems related to hearing loss.

HEARSAY, Association of Radio Reading Services, 15 West 16th Street, New York, NY 10011.

Self-Help for Hard of Hearing People (Shhh), 4848 Battery Lane, Dept. E., Bethesda, MD 20814.

Shhh is a nationwide organization for the hard of hearing. Publishes a bimonthly journal reporting the experiences of those with hearing impairments as well as new developments in the field of hearing loss.

Vision

The Aging Eye: Facts on Eye Care for Older Persons, National Society to Prevent Blindness, 79 Madison Ave., New York, NY 10016.
Publishes several pamphlets on specific diseases affecting the eyes.

Aids and Appliances for the Blind and Visually Impaired, The American Foundation for the Blind, 15 West 16th Street, New York, NY 10011.
A free catalog of special clocks, watches, canes, lights, and games.

American Foundation for the Blind, Unit on Aging, 15 West 16th Street, New York, NY 10011, 212-620-2000.
A national clearing house for information about blindness and visual impairment. Updated list and designation of nationwide low-vision centers; series of self-help manuals; catalogs of low-vision aids, including clocks, watches, timers, games, medical aids, sewing and writing aids, tools, and measuring devices.

American Printing House for the Blind, 1839 Frankford Ave., Louisville, KY 40206, 502-895-2405.
Catalog of writing aids, tape recorders, and educational materials.

Check Writing Guide, Independent Living Aids, Inc., 11 Commercial Court, Plainview, NY 11803, 516-681-8288.
Publishes a catalog which includes other aids.

DICKMAN, IRVING. *Making Life More Livable* (New York: American Foundation for the Blind, 1983).
An excellent detailed guide to aids and home adaptations for the visually impaired. Many of the suggestions could be useful for older people with other types of sensory impairments.

The Library of Congress, Blind and Physically Handicapped Division, 1291 Taylor Street N.W., Washington, DC 20011.
Resource for talking books for the visually impaired.

Recordings for the Blind, Inc., 215 East 58th Street, New York, NY 10022.
Records and tapes available.

Vision Inventory List, Vision Foundation, 2 Mt. Auburn Street, Watertown, MA 02172.
Information on special products and services for visually impaired people.

YEADON, ANNE. *Living with Impaired Vision* (New York: American Foundation for the Blind, 1979).
Written for nonprofessionals who work with visually impaired persons; a brief nontechnical coverage of what it means to be visually impaired.

Arthritis

The Arthritis Foundation, 3400 Peachtree Road N.E., Atlanta, GA 30326.
Publications available from the national office or from local chapters of the foundation.

BERSON, DVERA, with SANDER ROY, *Pain Free Arthritis*, S & J Books, P.O. Box 31, Gravesend, Brooklyn, NY 11233.

> Written by women with arthritis, the book presents thirty water exercises, ways to eliminate drug use, and how to develop a positive attitude. The underlying theme is taking charge of one's own wellness program.

HANSON, ISABEL. *Outwitting Arthritis*, Creative Arts Book Co., 833 Bancroft Way, Berkeley, CA 94170.

> This book approximates a written support group for people with arthritis.

Independence Factory, P.O. Box 597, Middletown, OH 45042.

> Nonprofit organization that sells practical aids (zipper pulls, enlarged-handle toothbrushes, etc.) for those with hand and limb limitations.

Living and Loving, Arthritis Foundation, 3400 Peachtree Road N.E., Atlanta, GA 30326.

> Provides clear, frank explanations of the sexual possibilities for people with arthritis or other crippling diseases.

LORIG, KATE, and JAMES E. FRIES. *The Arthritis Helpbook* (Reading, Mass.: Addison-Wesley, 1980).

> Provides information to assist arthritics with developing their own self-treatment programs. Topics include diet and nutrition, exercise, drugs, self-help aids.

Self-Help Manual for Patients with Arthritis, Arthritis Foundation, 3400 Peachtree Road N.E., Atlanta, GA 30326.

> Lists equipment and devices that aid self-help for anyone with a crippling disease.

Incontinence

CAPE, R. "Incontinence," in *Aging, Its Complex Management* (New York: Harper & Row, 1978), pp. 137–157.

OUSLANDER, J. G. "Urinary Incontinence in the Elderly," *The Western Journal of Medicine* 136, 6 (December 1981): 482.

> Includes review of drugs used to treat urinary incontinence.

OVERSTALL, P. W., K. ROUNCE, and J. H. PALMER."Experience in an Incontinence Clinic," *Journal of the American Geriatric Society* 28 (1980): 535–538.

> Study of 300 older people.

Sexuality

BARBACH, L. G. *For Yourself: The Fulfillment of Female Sexuality* (New York: Doubleday/Anchor Books, 1976).

> Dispels myths and provides factual information to help women understand their sexuality.

BUTLER, ROBERT, and MYRNA LEWIS. *Love and Sex after Sixty* (New York: Harper & Row, 1976).
Comprehensive review of normal physical changes, common problems, and new patterns of intimacy.

BRECHER, EDWARD. *Love, Sex and Aging: A Consumer Union Report* (Boston: Little Brown, 1984).
This book is based on the responses of more than 4000 individuals, aged 50 to 93, about their sexuality.

CHAPTER 7

Depression in Homebound Older People

Periods of low moods occur normally throughout life. Younger people possess a variety of ways to make themselves feel better, such as vigorous exercise, conversations with supportive friends, and distracting activities. Those who overuse cigarettes, food, alcohol, and other palliative measures do not usually experience detrimental consequences until later. Health limitations in later life begin to disrupt coping methods at the same time that losses associated with aging accumulate. This combination of more losses with fewer ways to cope with them accounts for a large extent of the depression among older people.

The warning signs of depression among older people are similar to those found among caregivers (see Chapter 5). Distinguishing between depression and grief as a normal response to loss is difficult, however. A further assessment problem is that the side effects of many drugs mimic or induce depression, as do some physical conditions such as malnutrition. A complete medical workup is necessary to determine whether symptoms such as sleeplessness, weight loss, or lethargy have a physical basis. One of the most frequent assessment errors is to attribute confusion and listlessness to dementia rather than depression. Some older people become disoriented because depression has caused them to stop responding to cues in their surroundings. Such a reversible omission sharply contrasts with the irreversible physical causes of memory problems.

Depression is most common among homebound older people. While debilitating illness is the most frequent reason for confinement, environmental obstacles also can convince an older person to stay home day after day. Depression itself often leads to reduced motivation for venturing out, and sets up a negative cycle in which becoming homebound then reinforces the depression. This chapter presents strategies to counter the losses associated with becoming ill and homebound as well as depicts responses to an older person's alcohol misuse and abuse of caregivers. The ethical complexity of the dilemmas raised for professionals and family members by an older person's desire to die are then surveyed.

Losses Associated with Becoming Ill and Homebound

- Loss of contact with friends and acquaintances; added dependence on relatives for social contact
- Loss of roles; fewer ways to engage in purposeful activity
- Loss of independence in self-care; decreased privacy and control
- Loss of ambulation; fewer opportunities for exercise
- Loss of sensory ability; diminution of pleasures
- Loss of out-of-home activities; fewer distractions and provocations
- Loss of mental stimulation; lessened cues from the external environment

Preventing Depression

Numerous environmental and psychological obstacles can converge to make a physically capable older person homebound. Common images of homebound older people center around those with obvious disabilities which prevent their going out on their own. Yet many older people confine themselves to home for more subtle reasons, such as a fear of stumbling on uneven pavement, difficulty seeing street signs, inclement weather, steps leading out of the home, steep hills between destinations and bus stops, worry about crime, the fast pace of traffic signals at intersections, heavy doors at building entrances, high curbs, the absence of benches for resting, and the scarcity of public restrooms in shopping areas. Staying home can easily come to seem preferable to facing these inconveniences and dangers.

When a debilitating illness is added to these disincentives, an older person may omit all outings except for medical appointments. At this juncture, the number of people who populate the person's life drops dramatically. Contacts with random strangers and conversations with store clerks, bus drivers, and acquaintances in restaurants are lost. The older person's friends and relatives then become the recipients of a concentrated social need that was previously diluted by these other contacts.

This dependence on their visits and phone calls places pressure on family members, who previously may have felt free to come over or call at their convenience. As the older person tries to satisfy unmet social needs at each opportunity, visits and phone calls may be prolonged beyond family members' endurance.

An older person's excessive focus on bodily needs is a further change often exasperating to family members and friends. Preoccupation with the rhythms of hunger and satiation, bowel movements, and the nuances of pain is a common consequence of becoming homebound. Family members who must listen to repetitive descriptions of physical concerns often come to dread visits and calls as intensely as the older person desires them. Families with a surplus of external concerns find it difficult to accept or understand this narrowed scope of attention, particularly if their relative's former range of interests was much wider. Efforts to interest their relative in other aspects of life, such as political events and family affairs, may be met with remarks in which the older person draws the conversation back to her immediate reality.

A dullness of perception can also arise in someone who no longer confronts novel experiences. The sameness and safety of home, unless occasionally interrupted, can leave an older person with insufficient stimulation. Healthy levels of stress inherent in venturing out into the world are lost when an older person faces a known environment day after day and says to herself, for example, "If I have to look at these four walls another minute, I'll go crazy." Activities such as preparing meals and watching television do not demand the degree of mental engagement required by unpredictable situations, such as negotiating busy crosswalks or handling transactions in stores. A homebound person gradually adapts to the absence of stimulation and challenge by paying less attention to what happens around her.

A weekly change of scene can improve a person's ability to look beyond herself. The variety of sights and sounds during outings promotes alertness, encouraging the person to notice aspects of her surroundings which spark memories and fresh topics of conversation. Being able to anticipate an event that breaks up the week keeps someone motivated to stay oriented to the passage of days. For this reason, family members who want to make the most of limited time find that providing an assured weekly outing is better than several spontaneous visits to the home. An outing requires more effort than dropping in briefly, but pays off by expanding the older person's scope of interests and making conversations more rewarding. Even when transferring the person to the car is difficult, going for a drive and eating in the car are viable ways to provide a change of scene and diet with minimal exertion.

Some homebound older people adopt a dictatorial style toward helpers. To impose order and exert control are basic human needs frustrated by physical limitations that interfere with a person's functioning. For instance, a man feeling powerless as a result of a stroke may insist that his son return items to precise locations in his room. He may specify how he wants his laundry folded and how he is to be helped getting dressed. His son may feel irritated by this insistence on needless detail and by the effect that tasks take twice as long to complete. Attempts to hurry his father or dissuade him from his demands may be met with anger seemingly disproportionate to the situation.

In many senses, the sickroom or house becomes a world to the person confined within its limits; details previously dwarfed by larger events assume a new importance. Families need to realize that what resembles rigidity and noncooperation is often an expression of the need for empowerment within this immediate sphere. A helpful strategy is to ask the older person to choose a few areas of daily life over which he will maintain complete control in exchange for letting family members use their discretion in other areas, for example, "Dad, I can't do everything the way you would do it, but I'd like to do at least a few tasks exactly how you tell me." The older person in the above example may choose to have his son precisely manage his bill-paying, and then agree to eliminate detailed specifications about folding his socks. Such negotiations are most successful when the older person looks forward to exercising a portion of resumed control while family members feel freer about overriding his preferences on less important matters.

Using time purposefully is another basic need often impeded when an older person becomes ill and homebound. Family members are often perplexed by attempts to devise activities that are both within their relative's capability and fulfill the need for meaningful involvements. Past sources of meaning, such as volunteer work and club memberships, often are eliminated by transportation problems and physical limitations. Vision, hearing or dexterity problems may interfere with sedentary activities, such as reading, writing letters, and listening to music. Even the ability to participate in the household's functioning may be restricted for people with severe disabilities.

Standards for meaningful activity shift as the person's number of choices declines. Family members need to be careful not to overlook forms of contributing to the household or community that they perceive as trivial, but which would satisfy someone who fears having nothing left to give or produce. A woman with severe arthritic deformities in her hands may derive a sense of participation in the household by loading rinsed dishes into the dishwasher. The fact that she occasionally drops a dish is less significant than the confirmation provided by this task that she continues to be a functional adult. In the same way, a man disabled by a stroke may find that using his "one good hand" to stuff envelopes for a charity affirms his capacity to be useful and allows him to maintain a link with the wider community.

A problem family members may encounter when they suggest such contributions is that the older person has already developed self-defeating beliefs, for example, "I can't do anything anymore." Once such beliefs become established, people begin to see the details of their daily lives through this lens and notice only those occurrences which support these beliefs. For example, the woman portrayed above may break a dish while trying to help and view this accident as further evidence of her uselessness. Family members may point out that she successfully placed ten items in the dishwasher, only to find that she magnifies the accident and withdraws from any further effort to participate in the household.

To change such self-defeating beliefs, the tendency to overlook successes needs to be countered with a system which makes accomplishments readily observable. In this regard, a progress chart can be utilized as a record of objective reality that cannot be distorted by negative perceptions. The number of meals at which this woman successfully loads the dishes can be noted on a sheet taped on the refrigerator, and broken dishes can be summarily ignored. When she subsequently says, "It's no use. I'm not getting anywhere with this," family members can show her on the chart, "Look Mom, this week alone you've loaded the dishes at five meals." Any quantifiable household task can be incorporated into a progress chart to demonstrate successes and contributions in this graphic and undeniable fashion.

Progress with rehabilitative exercises often moves so slowly as to be easily overlooked by a depressed person. For instance, a man recovering from a stroke may do his exercises halfheartedly, and then cite his lack of progress as evidence of the futility of continuing. The exercise "Progress Chart" shown on the following page can be used to shift a person's focus to measures that are small enough to be observable. Through comments such as "I see that on Monday you were able to do only three sit-ups and now you can do six," family members reinforce both the continued effort and the perception of progress. As time goes by, they can take out charts from past weeks to remind the person how far he has progressed in his efforts. The family's interest in these increments of progress can make them more rewarding to someone who would otherwise focus only on the tedium and pain necessary for improvement. By making a practice of looking at the chart at each visit or asking about it during each long-distance phone call, family members can emphasize the scale within which achievements are made by their older relative.

Exercising with someone else enhances the pleasurable aspects while deflecting attention from the discomfort. Family members can add to this

Week _____

	MON	TUES	WED	THURS	FRI	SAT	SUN
Morning							
Afternoon							
Evening							

Exercises:

A _____   C _____

B _____   D _____

Progress Chart

From Nancy R. Hooyman and Wendy Lustbader, Taking Care: Supporting Older People and Their Families (New York: The Free Press, 1986). Copyright © 1986 by The Free Press.

enhancement at the same time they compensate for their own loss of outdoor activity due to caregiving. Simultaneous exercise allows for mutual
encouragement as each prompts the other to improve upon previous attainments. A side benefit is that the older person may experience satisfaction from helping family members toward their physical goals, perhaps by
marking their progress on similar exercise charts. Music can be played in
the background and furniture moved aside to promote an atmosphere
conducive to exercise.

Even without a specific rehabilitative program, exercises can be
designed as a context for achieving small successes. For example, a route
within the older person's home can be designated as a lap, and a chart
utilized to monitor number of laps walked each day. As an initial activity
for a person who has become immobile, houselaps have the advantages of
not requiring clothing changes, the negotiation of physical barriers such
as steps, nor coping with extremes in weather. A helper's presence is
usually not necessary to ensure safety since handholds and resting places
are easily available within a home. The first series can be structured to be
an easy success, for example, two laps before each meal. Encouraged by
family members' interest and commentary, older people often spontaneously increase the number of daily laps. They thus obtain the benefits
of both physical activity and the added interaction with caring witnesses
to their progress.

Maintaining access to regularly occurring pleasures is another difficulty for homebound older people. Family members can encourage their
relative to make a list of activities enjoyed in the past, with the goal of
finding ways to make them accessible in the present. Contact with nature
through a garden, opportunities to sit outside in the sun, and the ability to
look at the stars, clouds or moon are examples of outdoor experiences that
a homebound person may mourn. Older people confined to wheelchairs
often reject the idea of having a ramp built over their front steps, worrying
about the expense and their neighbors' reactions. Organizations which
will arrange for the donation of free labor, if the older person purchases
the lumber, exist in many communities. Ramps can be dismantled when
no longer needed, and the lumber sold. Backyards can often be used when
the front of the house does not permit room for a gradual grade in the
ramp. The resumed capacity to be outside at will can restore an older person's spirits to a degree well worth the expense of construction and the
disfigurement of a yard.

Indoor pleasures can be structured as part of everyday routines.
Recorded books can be obtained for people with vision loss, and letters
taped by those no longer able to write. People who miss being able to shop
may enjoy making purchases through mail order catalogs, with family
members assisting with the order forms. Moving the bed of a bedbound

person near a large picture window provides visual access to street activity. Encouraging the older person to dress in street clothes and use perfume or aftershave conveys a sense of wellness and a continued connection with the outside world. Grandchildren can spend satisfying times with homebound grandparents through reading letters or poems out loud, listening to grandparents' reminiscences, or enjoying treats together, such as an ice cream sundae. These changes can minimize the detrimental effects of being homebound without imposing excessive demands on family members.

Helping someone maintain motivation for living in the face of accumulated losses is a slow and sensitive enterprise not limited to the province of professionals. Family members are often in the best position to spur this motivation, if their own insights or those suggested by a professional provide clues for action. The following list summarizes the strategies presented in this section:

Ways to Maintain Motivation

1. Institute a weekly outing for the mental stimulation, sense of anticipation, and mood elevation inherent in a change of scene. A ride in the car may be enough to break up the monotony of remaining in a known environment.
2. Restore areas of control. Since many illnesses result in a loss of the ability to direct areas of life previously managed independently, an effective countering strategy is to find specific ways for an older person to exert control over as many choices as possible.
3. Refocus the person's perceptions on small successes as a way of changing self-defeating beliefs. As small, readily observable successes build on each other, feelings of powerlessness tend to recede.
4. Devise contributions to the household, the family, or the community that satisfy the need for purposeful activity. The older person's past sources of meaning can provide clues.
5. Establish regularly occurring pleasures. No matter how narrow in scope, such pleasures, identified by the older person, can give him reason to keep on living.

In response to time constraints or lack of skill in motivating older people, health care professionals often treat the symptoms of depression without addressing the underlying emotional causes. Sleeping pills facilitate necessary rest, antianxiety agents lessen feelings of agitation, and antidepressants may have an activating effect, but medications alone generally do not alleviate depression in older people. Some health professionals conclude that depression is an inevitable accompaniment of old age, rejecting the value of providing opportunities for older people to work through their reactions to losses within verbal therapeutic modalities. Others cite the current older generation's resistance to mental health services as the prime reason for their infrequent referrals of older people to individual counseling and support groups.

The need to devise and propose forms of help acceptable to older people is a responsibility with which an increasing number of health professionals are confronted. For instance, some medical clinics serving high proportions of older people retain mental health counselors on their staffs who can be introduced by name rather than by professional title. Some physicians customarily request the services of home care social workers when making referrals for Medicare-funded visiting nurses, knowing that these professionals can address the emotional concommitants of illness while arranging for community resources. Senior centers and self-help associations are beginning to sponsor educational programs and support groups led by professionals sensitive to this need to deliver services in an acceptable format (see Chapter 10).

Alcohol Misuse by Older People

Losses associated with later life, such as death of a long-term spouse, disfiguring surgeries, and various forms of chronic pain, frequently lead to alcohol misuse. Alcohol then functions as self-medication for the depression that arises in reaction to these circumstances. Health providers should be watchful for signs of alcohol misuse by vulnerable people, cautioning them against the detrimental effects of becoming dependent on alcohol as a source of relief ("You've been through alot, but alcohol will only give you other problems to deal with"). Detailing the dangers, such as an increased likelihood of being injured by falling, sometimes gives older people sufficient motivation to resist overusing alcohol. Treatment of depression should also be offered, along with supportive contact in groups with others facing similar circumstances.

When approaching an older person's alcohol use, it is important at the outset to distinguish between lifelong abusers and those who began drinking in reaction to later life losses. Lifelong abusers are deeply accustomed to evading difficulties by blotting out painful feelings. They may never have learned to tolerate anxiety, boredom, hurt, and frustration. In contrast, those who have not used alcohol as a coping mechanism until later life generally know how to manage disagreeable feelings. Having been able to endure life's normal hardships, most nonabusers arrive at old age with a repertoire of coping skills. Such people tend to turn to alcohol only after health limitations disrupt their coping skills or an event of sufficient magnitude overwhelms them.

Education about the physiological changes which make alcohol use more precarious in later life is valuable for both lifelong abusers as well as those with recently developed dependence. Many are unaware that aging affects the body's ability to dispose of alcohol, with the result that they do not compensate by decreasing their intake. Those who have lost a significant amount of weight during an illness may not realize that reduced body fat means less dilution of alcohol throughout the body, increasing the inebriating effects of small amounts of alcohol. Unless warned, some older people expect themselves to be able to "hold" alcohol the way they have earlier in their lives, endangering themselves through this mistaken belief. Knowledge that changes in alcohol tolerance are normal may help those embarrassed by the fact that one drink has the same effect on them that three drinks may have on a younger person.

Older people who insist on using alcohol may need repeated warnings against the hazards of mixing alcohol with medications. For example, over-the-counter products with aspirin as their main ingredient (Anacin, Bufferin, Excedrin, and Alka-Seltzer) should not be combined with alcohol. Both alcohol and aspirin irritate the stomach, and their combination can cause or worsen bleeding in the stomach lining. Similarly, sleeping aids with antihistamine as their chief ingredient, such as Sominex, Sleepeze and Nytol, can be oversedating mixed with alcohol. Tranquilizers such as Valium, Librium and Serax are even more dangerous in combination with alcohol, to the point of lethality if large enough quantities are consumed. Prescription sleeping pills, such as chloral hydrate, Seconal, Nembutal and Dalmane, can also be lethal in their interactions with alcohol.

Despite the increased risk of accidents and other health dangers, many older people persist in using alcohol. This can be especially frustrating to family members who perceive that their relative threatens the very independence which the family is working so hard to protect. The bind for older people is that at a point in life when other ways of coping with stress and depression are less available, the easily accessible means of alcohol becomes more destructive as a coping mechanism. For homebound older people in particular, alcohol often functions as a convenient means of escape from the tedium of their daily lives and their anxieties about their future.

Some older people use alcohol as a rebellious act, a way to assert personal freedom and bodily autonomy within constraining circumstances. Life can seem particularly devoid of physical pleasure when a person's diet is restricted, opportunities for exercise limited, and sexual activity nonexistent. Breaking out against multiple restraints can serve as an act of vitality, flaunting the potential for danger in exchange for a liberated feeling. The proclamation, "So what? I'm going to be dead soon, anyway," often accompanies defiant swigs of alcohol and other violations of medical prohibitions. Such people seem to seize upon a sense of entitlement to the last days of life, even if these actions serve to reduce the number of their remaining days.

Alcohol use generally has a detrimental effect on several dimensions of life at once. For example, a man on a fixed income may deploy such a large portion of his funds for the purchase of whiskey that he is left with insufficient money for food and utility bills. Family members may react with rage and resentment each time they have to rescue him from malnutrition or from having his lights cut off for nonpayment. In addition to depleting what would have been an adequate income, this man's alcohol use could eventually alienate his family and cause him to lose both their practical assistance and emotional support.

Family members exasperated by a relative's abuse of alcohol may nevertheless have difficulty removing themselves from the rescuer role. They may feel ethically compromised, both by continuing their implicit support of the person's alcohol abuse and by ending their assistance, for example, "We can't let him starve and freeze to death." One budgetary strategy is for family members to offer to hold a portion of the person's income until the last week of the month. Another option is to offer food or the direct payment of utility bills, rather than providing cash supplements which can be used to purchase alcohol. The effective strategy of refusing to protect the older person from the consequences of mismanaged funds is best carried out with professional support. Professionals can offer alcohol treatment and other interventions once the resulting stress motivates the older person to learn more constructive ways to cope.

Limit-Setting with Abusive Older People

Many older people react to their losses by trying to exert control in ways destructive to their relationships with the people who help them. Those who become depressed in response to losses sometimes focus exclusively on themselves, losing sight of how their behavior burdens or disturbs their caregivers. Others have had lifelong difficulties with being compassionate and adjusting their actions to reflect others' needs. This section explores ways that older people abuse their caregivers and suggests strategies for limiting such abuse. Abusive behavior can develop so gradually and subtly that caregivers may be unaware of its occurrence, but find themselves angry or frustrated with the older person.

Abuse of Caregivers

FINANCIAL	EMOTIONAL	PHYSICAL
• Demanding that family members pay for hired help that is a luxury rather than a necessity	• Berating family members for taking needed rest from caregiving or for setting reasonable limits on helping tasks	• Waking family members unnecessarily during the night
• Giving away money or possessions previously promised to family members; using this as a punitive tactic	• Complaining excessively about circumstances that cannot be changed	• Refusing medical equipment or adaptive devices that would make the care easier for the family
• Turning up the heat more than is necessary, to the point of unaffordable utility bills	• Finding fault with efforts made in good faith	• Pushing, scratching, hitting, or biting caregivers who try to assist them
• Demanding long-distance phone calls beyond the financial capacity of family members	• Prolonging visits through nonstop talking; ignoring cues that the other person is in a hurry	• Exacting so much time-consuming help that caregivers cease tending to their own physical needs
	• Feigning or exaggerating symptoms in order to exact extra services	
	• Blaming family members for problems not in their power to control	

The goal of limit-setting with abusive older people is to prevent caregivers from becoming resentful. Firmly holding to limits is an act of caring that protects the relationship between the giver and receiver of help. A daughter who succumbs to her mother's requests to run up and down stairs several times an hour for unnecessary care tasks will eventually detest the sound of her mother's voice. Similarly, a health professional who allows an older patient to prolong appointment times excessively will dread that person's visits. Familiarity with forms of abuse and techniques for responding constructively are vital for family members and professionals wanting to promote satisfying relationships with the people they assist.

The apparent powerlessness of physically fragile older people can be deceiving. Ways to inflict harm other than through physical strength are abundant in caregiving situations. The preceding chart depicts some of the most common forms of abuse of caregivers by older people.

Some of these forms of abuse are amenable to limit-setting techniques, while others require more immediate measures to protect caregivers from harm. For instance, a patient with Alzheimer's disease may scratch a home-health aide who tries to help her get dressed. Cotton mittens secured around her hands would solve the problem. The following discussion draws on examples of abuse in which behavioral techniques are effective, recognizing that these techniques may be less useful for more complex forms of abuse.

Belief in the right to and necessity of setting limits is a crucial first step for both family caregivers and professionals. For instance, a daughter who feels "cruel" when she stops running upstairs to wait on her mother's every request is likely to find that her resolve quickly wears down. If she instead told herself at each juncture, "It's more loving to stay downstairs and keep from resenting her," she might hold to reasonable limits on the number of trips she makes. In the same way, a health professional needs to believe that interrupting a nonstop talker in order to end appointments on time is a service rather than rudeness.

Defining clear and specific limits prior to enacting them is also important. The daughter in the above example could resolve that she will go upstairs only three times each morning. She can say to her mother, "Mom, be careful not to use up one of my trips on help you do not really need." This would be a caring way to convey a firm attitude toward this numerical limit. The daughter could also advise her mother to "save up" small tasks that can be delayed, grouping them along with a more urgent need later in the morning.

With nonstop talkers, it is helpful to announce at the beginning of a visit that it will end at a set time. Midway through the time period, a statement can be made such as, "We only have half our time left, so I hope you've gotten to the things you most want to tell me." Five minutes before the end, concluding phrases should be inserted, no matter how little space the older person leaves for commentary, for example, "We have

162

to end in five minutes, so I'd like to finish up this one piece of business with you." Talking over the person's voice may be necessary for those who literally do not pause between sentences. Finally, a minute before the ending, standing up and moving toward the door conveys that the conclusion is imminent. In many instances, it is necessary to say words of farewell and walk out the door while the person continues to talk.

The next phase of limit-setting is the most difficult. People subject to limits for the first time from those they are accustomed to manipulating tend to test the boundaries by acting out. In this regard, it is helpful to imagine in advance exactly how the person is likely to challenge the limit-setter's will. The daughter described above could reasonably anticipate that her mother will use up her three requests for relatively trivial purposes, and then will claim an "emergency" when she calls out the fourth time. After the second request, a preventive strategy is to predict this behavior, "Mom, you'd better save the last request in case some really urgent need comes up, because it's important that I not respond to you after the third time."

When nonstop talkers sense the approach of a firm conclusion during a conversation, they tend to test the limit by dramatically and urgently detouring from the immediate topic. Some begin crying near the end or suddenly bring up something of great emotional import, for example, "Doctor, I've never told this to anyone before." A helpful response in these instances is "I wish this hadn't come up just as we've run out of time because I want to talk about this in depth with you. Let's set our next appointment and be sure we start out with it then." Both parties' feelings of abruptness can be smoothed by using touch to convey caring, while urging the older person through the door.

During the acting-out phase, being candid with the person about the difficulties of adhering to the limits can sometimes reduce the intensity of the person's challenges, for example, "Mom, I really love you, so it's hard for me to resist coming upstairs every time you call." Such comments help break the person's habit of trying to obtain reassurance through excessive demands. Openness about the overall purpose of setting limits also helps halt this pattern: "Mom, to care for you is to say no to you sometimes. If I stay downstairs and get my other work done, I'll be able to come upstairs later and enjoy my time with you."

A caution for family members wanting to limit a relative's troublesome behaviors is to avoid trying to change too many at once. Holding to limits requires considerable mental energy, which is best applied to a few target behaviors at a time. Another wisdom is to integrate rewards into any limit-setting attempts, such as performing extra services when a person becomes less demanding. Asking the person to make a list of "luxuries" is helpful. Luxuries are tasks which are not necessary, but which the person would like accomplished when time allows. These tasks can then be used to thank the person for respecting the limits.

Professionals need to avoid the error of permitting themselves to be charmed by older people who are abusive to family members behind the scenes. A physician may transfer her positive feelings about her own parents to a superficially affable older person. Not bothering to seek verification of the older person's complaints about family members, she may allow stories of familial neglect to color her responses to family members during phone calls and conferences. Advising them against nursing home placement, she may trigger guilt in relatives who have already exerted considerable effort toward keeping their difficult relative at home.

A related error is for professionals to grasp at presumed sources of support without taking the time to investigate the family history. A hospital discharge planner may pressure a daughter to allow her father to stay in her home until he completes his recovery. If the discharge planner is unaware that the father sexually abused his daughter earlier in life, her attempt to tap a filial relationship scarred by this kind of pain can be severely detrimental to the daughter. As a standard precaution, professionals should heed hesitation or reluctance expressed by adult children. Nonfamilial sources of support are preferable to forcing adult children to tolerate emotional strain of this magnitude.

Some families are able to relinquish inappropriate care only after professionals label what they are experiencing as abuse. For this reason, professionals should be alert to families' need for the situation to be framed in these terms in order to help them get out of destructive caregiving situations. The word *abuse* is a powerful tool for professionals who need to present a person's behavior in this way. The word conveys the concept that behaviors are occurring which should not be tolerated, often freeing overly kind and generous people to recognize safer boundaries.

The Older Person Who Wants to Die

Of all medical choices, "doing nothing" is usually the most difficult. For instance, when a hospitalized older person announces that she has had enough of life and prefers to be left alone, she usually continues to be probed by strange hands and urged to undergo humiliating and uncomfortable procedures. She may also be handed antidepressant medication and questioned by mental health professionals. Expressing the desire to die rarely finds a receptive audience among those whose profession it is to promote life, or among family members who have an emotional need to encourage a loved person to accept "everything that can be done." To enact her desire to die, an older person can refuse treatment for natural causes of death, choose not to comply with medications and care instructions, or seek an active way to commit suicide. This section probes each of these strategies to hasten death as well as the ethical dilemmas for family members and health care professionals.

The Right to Refuse Treatment

The majority of the money spent on medical care in a person's lifetime tends to be paid out for services received during the last few months of life. On a societal level, this reality translates into major expenditures of funds for limited results. On a personal level, many people find that the medical technology which allows them extra time does not provide them pleasure or meaning. Neither does watching their family incur excessive financial and emotional costs from taking time off from work to give care and agonizing over medical decisions.

People of all ages are haunted by images of dying in an intensive care unit. However, respecting a relative's wish to die at home often requires family members' courage and stamina. Holding back from calling an ambulance can be an enormous act of devotion when a loved person goes into severe respiratory distress or begins any other frightening prelude to death. Instinct is to take rescuing measures, rather than allow a natural dying process to run its course. When the dying process moves slowly, sustaining a person's last weeks and days at home can be exhausting on several levels. Care tasks, such as waking in the middle of the night to administer pain medications, tend to be physically draining. Watching a spouse or parent's gradual deterioration can instill a deep emotional weariness.

When their relative pleads, "Promise me I can die in my own bed," family members need to realize that societal supports for carrying out such wishes are limited. Hospice programs to support the families of people who choose to die at home have only been developed in the past decade. Many communities continue to lack such services. Funding constraints limit the types of medical conditions that these programs are permitted to serve, as well as the frequency and duration of home visits by hospice nurses and aides. Although these agencies increasingly utilize volunteers to provide respite for family caregivers, such relief is generally not available to the extent needed.

When older people and families resort to hospitalization at the end stages of illnesses, they forfeit control over their medical options. For instance, a wife caring for her husband at home may decide, after private discussion with him, to stop administering antibiotics for his pneumonia in order to allow him to die of natural causes. If she hospitalizes him at the last minute in response to her fears or exhaustion, she is likely to encounter the medical and legal impetus against such choices. Hospital staff may ignore her request not to put him on oxygen and to withhold antibiotics, using the rationale that doing so constitutes murder. She and her husband become, in effect, captives of the health care system and of the legal establishment which judges its actions.

Legislative recognition of the right to refuse treatment at the end stages of terminal illness is on the books in thirty-five states. Individual cases are being brought to court for judicial rulings to resolve ambiguities in the laws. In a recent California case, a mentally competent seventy-year-old man completed the legal documents necessary for having his respirator turned off. The hospital refused, claiming that his medical condition did not fit the state's legal standard for such actions, that is, "terminally ill with death imminent." A Superior Court judge upheld the view that the man's condition was not "terminal" because death was not "imminent."[1] This case illustrates areas of conflict still faced by physicians, despite natural death legislation, because of the need to interpret the meanings of the key words *terminal* and *imminent*.

Omitting lifesaving procedures is risky for medical professionals even for those patients in the final stages of irreversible dementing illness who sometimes refuse to accept food and water by mouth. In 1982, a team of prominent physicians attempted to draw up criteria for choosing not to administer nutrition and fluids by artificial means. They hoped that their leadership would make it easier for other physicians to face such situations. Their report stated that it is ethically permissible to withhold artificially administered food and water, and that these patients need only be made comfortable in such instances.[2] Despite clear directives from these and other medical professionals, court decisions have not supported such choices consistently enough to establish the safety of legal precedent. As a result, considerable disagreement exists within the medical community about how to handle these dilemmas. Physicians and family members often find themselves handing options back and forth in decision-avoiding volleys.

Such decisions are made still more complicated by the general reluctance of family members and professionals to question older people in advance about their preferences for emergency interventions in life-threatening situations. Some assume that they already know that person's preferences, while others feel uncomfortable holding such discussions. For instance, researchers at a large Boston hospital found that a third of the patients who had been resuscitated after their hearts stopped beating later said they would have preferred to be allowed to die. Less than a quarter of all those resuscitated had been asked in advance by their physicians about how they felt with regard to this option. Among other concerns, the patients cited fear of further suffering and discontent with the limitations of chronic illness as reasons for their preferring to die.[3]

The reluctance to discuss death is shared by many older people. When an older person resists discussing his preferences, it is helpful to ask, "Are you afraid of dying or are you afraid of death?" Some will readily admit that their dread is focused on the suffering that may precede death, rather than on death itself, for example, "I don't mind my life ending, but I can't stand the thought of that ambulance ride and what they'll do to me in the hospital." Family members who find raising the topic too painful or awkward should ask a medical professional to conduct a discussion of these issues. Reviewing the situations in which they would not want an ambulance to be called can help older people reduce their anxiety about dying, while later relieving relatives faced with emergency choices. Using a living will as a format for such discussions frequently frees up all parties to venture into sensitive areas otherwise avoided.

Living wills are documents which direct physicians to withhold life-sustaining procedures in the event of an irreversible terminal illness. A sample will appears on the next page. (For information on living wills and the guidelines for their use, see the Suggested Resources at the end of this chapter.) Some older people make private compacts with their physicians not to have their lives prolonged by artificial means. Signing a written document, however, adds legal validity under circumstances when it is most necessary. Living wills are crucial for helping family members make decisions in the event that their relative becomes comatose or mentally incompetent. Declining "last ditch" measures is easier for families when they have a signed document on hand and remember discussing their relative's preferences when the living will was signed.

Another difficult juncture for family members is being called upon to give informed consent for life-prolonging surgeries. Time allotted to family conferences in hospitals tends to be filled with necessary explanations of the risks and mortality rates of proposed interventions. For instance, a physician responsible for twenty other acutely ill patients may not have the time to address a family's grief and fear, in addition to the medical aspects of their parent's impending leg amputation. Presented in clinical detail with the possibility of their parent's death, the family's feelings may interfere with their grasp of the information given by the physician. Such conferences are often concluded by a helpless abdication of choice: "Whatever you think is best, doctor."

Many of the surgeries and treatments undergone by older people in their last months of life would probably be omitted if medical professionals had the time to depict their expected aftermath in sufficient detail. Unless professionals provide such descriptions, family members are usu-

---

LIVING WILL DECLARATION

To My Family, Doctors, and All Those Concerned with My Care

I, _____, being of sound mind, make this statement as a directive to be followed if for any reason I become unable to participate in decisions regarding my medical care.

I direct that life-sustaining procedures should be withheld or withdrawn if I have an illness, disease or injury, or experience extreme mental deterioration, such that there is no reasonable expectation of recovering or regaining a meaningful quality of life.

These life-sustaining procedures that may be withheld or withdrawn include, but are not limited to:

SURGERY   ANTIBIOTICS   CARDIAC RESUSCITATION
RESPIRATORY SUPPORT   ARTIFICIALLY ADMINISTERED FEEDING AND FLUIDS

I further direct that treatment be limited to comfort measures only, even if they shorten my life.

You may delete any provision above by drawing a line through it and adding your initials.

Other personal instructions:

These directions express my legal right to refuse treatment. Therefore, I expect my family, doctors, and all those concerned with my care to regard themselves as legally and morally bound to act in accord with my wishes, and in so doing to be free from any liability for having followed my directions.

Signed _____ Date _____

Witness _____ Witness _____

PROXY DESIGNATION CLAUSE

If you wish, you may use this section to designate someone to make treatment decisions if you are unable to do so. Your Living Will Declaration will be in effect even if you have not designated a proxy.

I authorize the following person to implement my Living Will Declaration by accepting, refusing and/or making decisions about treatment and hospitalization:

Name _____

Address _____

If the person I have named above is unable to act on my behalf, I authorize the following person to do so:

Name _____

Address _____

I have discussed my wishes with these persons and trust their judgment on my behalf.

Signed _____ Date _____

Witness _____ Witness _____

Courtesy of Society for the Right to Die, 250 West 57 Street, New York, NY 10107.

Living Will Declaration

Courtesy of Society for the Right to Die, 250 West 57 Street, New York, NY 10107.

ally unable to imagine the implications of surgical options with respect to their relative's later quality of life. For instance, learning about the long hospital course necessary for healing their parent's amputation and the likelihood that she will need further rehabilitation in a nursing home may enable family members to respect her wish to forgo surgery. In contrast, if a hurried physician only cites the improved likelihood of survival in performing rather than omitting the amputation, family members may be left with the emotional impetus to prolong their parent's life and their ignorance of what it means to do so.

Medical Noncompliance

Older people often make decisions about their living situations which are equivalent to choosing to die. Some in dire need of extra help at home refuse to accept it; others insist on being discharged to home from the hospital in spite of needing nursing home care. By choosing to live with inadequate care, they accelerate their dying process or increase the likelihood that nonlethal conditions will result in death. A man requiring dressing changes twice daily on an infected wound may insist on returning to his apartment rather than entering a nursing home. He may then fail to comply with his visiting nurse's instruction to change his dressing in the evening, thereby lessening the chance that the wound care she provides every morning will slow the advance of his infection and promote healing.

In most states, involuntary treatment laws specify that a person can be placed in a protective setting against his will only if he presents an immediate danger to himself or others. As in the above example, older people who commit suicide through the gradual process of self-neglect often do not fall within the narrow confines of such laws. Passive suicide methods, such as omitting vital medications or failing to comply with dietary restrictions, are readily available to older people with chronic health problems. For them, life-prolonging actions such as changing dressings and doing exercises require effort, while self-harming actions only require the absence of effort. In instances when an older person's health is extremely fragile, merely the mental decision to give up on life can cause an abrupt physical decline.

Many family members intellectually agree with older people's right to determine their own choices about medical care. When a relative exercises this right, however, they may find themselves in an ethical and emotional bind. For instance, the man depicted above may be told by his daughter, "Dad, if you won't go to a nursing home to get the help you need, you've got to understand that I can't drive twenty miles every night to change your dressing." The fact that her father knowingly chooses to remain in a situation of insufficient care may not prevent her from feeling guilty and sick at heart as his wound's condition worsens. Eventually, she may begin driving over at night, despite her tiredness from a full-time job, in order not to remain a bystander to his slow suicide process.

Family members frequently perform such acts of rescue to the point of exhausting themselves. Their relative's self-neglect becomes a type of emotional blackmail which traps them into the very sacrifices they had decided not to carry out. In the above example, a professional could prompt the daughter and her father to directly confront the underlying issues between them. A question such as "Why do you want your father to stay alive?" might spur the daughter to tell the reasons to her father. Responses such as "There's still so much I want to talk about with you" or "I know life isn't great for you now, but I like knowing you're here" might reduce or eliminate the father's self-neglect. Passive suicide through the neglect of vital care frequently serves as an older person's plea to be convinced that his life continues to matter to others.

Home health care professionals often become caught in similar binds of rescue when their services are utilized in the absence of hospice programs or by older people with excessive care needs. For instance, a Medicare-funded visiting nurse may find that a patient who has chosen to remain at home rather than enter a nursing home needs more care than she can provide within her service constraints. She is faced with the choice of leaving his care incomplete after each visit, or staying a sufficient length of time to deliver care which meets her professional standards. If she extends her visit, she will have to prolong her workday into her personal time or shorten her visits to others' homes. Paralleling family caregivers, home care professionals in these situations often exhaust themselves in order to avoid feeling inhumane and unethical.

When an older person's neglect of care needs or choice of an inappropriate living situation results from impaired judgment, involuntary treatment laws can sometimes be used to move the older person to a protected setting. In Washington state, for example, a person can be deemed "gravely disabled" under the commitment laws if her mental incapacity results in a life-threatening failure to care for herself. If her "failure to care" is not immediately life-threatening, however, the person usually has to be allowed to deteriorate to that point before the force of the law can be used to compel treatment. Families often mistakenly believe that by obtaining legal guardianship of a mentally incompetent relative, they can then compel her to go to a nursing home. Professionals need to emphasize to families that the awarding of guardianship is a separate legal process from involuntary commitment and that becoming an older person's guardian does not include the power to force her into an institutional setting against her will (see Chapter 8).

Responding to a Relative's Suicide Wishes

Toward the end of life, death often becomes attractive as a release from suffering. A person's will to live, when it can be re-created, arises out of a voluntary response to external motivations and internal promptings. This area of the will is beyond the reach of therapeutic methods, unless the person admits the therapist into this most private region through open dialogue. In many instances, the balance between an older person's will to live and his longing for release is so tenuous that an apparently small loss tips the balance toward his wanting to die. The difficulty for family members and professionals lies in distinguishing between appropriate acceptance of death and situations which call for therapeutic intervention.

Some older people indicate their readiness for death through anticipatory actions. Such preparations include completing or updating a will, giving away treasured items, writing letters to distant friends and relatives, informing family members where vital documents are located, and initiating conversations about the significance of their life and relationships. These actions, when gradual, are practical responses to an awareness of life's approaching end. When carried out all at once or accompanied by extended depression, they can evoke family members' alarm that a suicide plan is in the early stages of enactment.

Families confronted with outright suicide threats or who suspect their relative is contemplating suicide usually feel stymied when trying to decide what to do. Failing to take preventive action seems irresponsible. Yet requesting a mental health commitment team and thereby violating the person's privacy and autonomy seems too intrusive. The stress and humiliation of the legal process of commitment makes families feel that they would be inflicting yet another form of suffering on an already pained person. Furthermore, those who feel sympathetic with their relative's desire for death may fear that the older person will misinterpret their inaction or their expression of sympathy as a wish to be free from care responsibilities.

When a relative with a debilitating disease requests assistance with committing suicide, family members tend to face still more intense internal conflict. Their compassion toward the person's suffering may be as deep as their ethical repugnance toward the idea of helping someone end her life. People with degenerative diseases sometimes make pacts with themselves or with family members to end their lives when they reach a certain stage of physical incapacity, for example, "When it gets to the point where I can't feed myself, that's it for me." When the self-assigned timetable for coping approaches its end, the older person may not have a means of committing suicide available to her. If family members then refuse to obtain pills or supply a lethal weapon, their relative may accuse them of cruelty or indifference, insisting, "If you love me, you'll help me stop suffering."

Removing a person's means to commit suicide is an immediate way to buy time for consideration of other options. Items not readily replaceable by a homebound older person, such as a loaded gun or accumulations of prescribed medications, can be moved to a family member's home. This intervention is usually difficult to enact because the older person has to be confronted directly about his suicidal feelings. For instance, a daughter may fear her father's anger if she removes his hunting rifles without his permission. She may need professional encouragement to remove his rifles as a dramatic statement of caring, along with telling him "Dad, I love you and don't want you to die, so I'm storing these guns at my house for a while."

Calling an involuntary treatment team can also be presented as a statement of caring, for example, "If we didn't love you so much, we wouldn't bother with all this." A mental health professional's arrival at the home tells the older person that his feelings are being taken seriously and that family members are not yet prepared to accept his dying. The professional can then assess the person's potential for implementing his plan. For instance, many people fantasize about ending their lives, but are actually frightened or repulsed by the methods available to them. Others express anger toward family members through their threats of harming themselves, but have no intention of taking their lives. Permitting a professional to make these distinctions often clears up family members' confusion about how to respond to future suicidal statements.

In most states, mental health professionals cannot come to the older person's home unless he has directly threatened suicide and possesses the means of carrying it out. The kinds of statements troubling to family members are often more subtle, for example, "I wish I could just stay asleep" and "I wish God would take me." If their relative is receiving home care from a visiting nurse, family members can request that the agency also send a social worker to evaluate the person's feelings of despair and to help him address his reasons for wanting to die.

The following questions can be used by professionals to assess an older person's suicidal feelings.

1. *Why do you want to die?*
   Why is life unbearable right now?
   Did something just happen, a "last straw?"
   What could be changed that would make you want to live?
2. *Who would care if you died?*
   Whose life would be easier if you died? In what ways?
   Who would be hurt by your dying?
   How do you think your son or daughter would react to news of your death?
3. *How would you end your life?*
   Can you think of a way to die that doesn't hurt?

Do you have (a gun, pills, etc.)?
What scares you when you think about doing it?

Airing these thoughts with a professional often diminishes their hold on an older person's mood. The opportunity to vent disgust with life, anger at relatives perceived to be neglectful, and weariness from chronic medical problems can facilitate a relieving change of attitude, even though external circumstances remain the same. Feelings sometimes emerge in these interviews which professionals can translate into suggestions for family members, such as "When you are telling your friends on the phone about hard days taking care of your mother, try to make sure that she's not overhearing you in the next room." Conveying messages between the older person and family members is often a prime component of a professional's intervention, especially around sensitive topics, for example, "Your mother feels she's ruining your marriage by living here with you. Maybe you should confide in her more about the real reasons you're thinking about a divorce."

Wanting life to end can be a rational response to accumulated losses. Older people usually prefer to die rather than prolong lives which have ceased to be meaningful to them. Unless losses can be replaced and new sources of meaning found, older people tend to become less and less attached to life. Those who are in chronic pain or whose medical situation restricts them to little more than a biological existence may assert their right to refuse life-promoting treatments or to seek other methods to hasten their dying process. Family members need professional support as they attempt to find ethically and emotionally acceptable responses to their relative's choices. In many instances, helping the older person obtain a good death is the most loving response that family members can offer and professionals can facilitate.

Notes

1. Andrew Malcolm, "Plaintiff is Dead, but Suit Goes On," *New York Times* (November 8, 1984).
2. Sidney Wanzer, S. J. Adelstein, Ronald Cranford, Daniel Federman, Edward Hook, Charles Moertel, Peter Safar, Alan Stone, Helen Taussig, and Jan van Eys, "The Physician's Responsibility toward Hopelessly Ill Patients," *The New England Journal of Medicine* 310, 15 (April 12, 1984): 955–959.
3. Susan E. Bedell, Thomas L. Delbanco, E. Frances Cook, and Franklin Epstein, "Survival After Cardiopulmonary Resuscitation in the Hospital," *The New England Journal of Medicine* 309, 70 (September 8, 1983): 569–576.

Suggested Resources

BECK, A. T., C. H. WARD, and M. MENDELSON et al. "An Inventory for Measuring Depression," *Archives of General Psychiatry* 4 (1961): 561–571.
> The Beck Inventory is one of the most widely used assessment tools for depression.

BUTLER, ROBERT, and MYRNA LEWIS. *Aging and Mental Health,* 3rd ed. (St. Louis, Mo: Mosby, 1982).
> A comprehensive review of the most common mental disorders among older people.

Concern for Dying—An Educational Council, 250 West 57th Street, New York, NY 10019, 212–246–6962.
> Distributes living wills in different states. Also publishes a quarterly newsletter with up-to-date information on living wills and current court cases.

HAMILTON, M. "A Rating Scale for Depression." *Journal of Neurology, Neurosurgery and Psychiatry* 23 (1960): 56–62.

Handbook of Living Will Laws, 1981–1984 (New York: Society for the Right to Die, 1984).
> Includes text and analysis of 13 new court statutes; the artificial feeding controversy; new trends in proxy appointments; checklist of 23 living wills. Available for $5 from 250 West 57th St., New York, NY 10019.

KANE, ROSALIE, and ROBERT KANE. *Assessing the Elderly: A Practical Guide to Measurement* (Lexington, Mass.: Lexington Books, 1981).
> Comprehensive review of the major assessment instruments for use with older people.

"Liquor May Be Quicker, But." *FDA Consumer,* Food and Drug Administration, HFE-88, 5600 Fishers Lane, Rockville, MD 20857.
> Discusses alcohol and drug interactions.

REISBERG, BARRY, and STEVEN FERRIS. "Diagnosis and Assessment of the Older Patient," *Hospital and Community Psychiatry* 33, 2 (February 1982): 104–110.

ROBERTSON, JOHN A. *The Rights of the Critically Ill.* Order from C.L.U.M., 47 Winter Street, Boston, MA 02108.
> Detailed guide, including hospices, relevant statutes and living wills.

Society for the Right to Die, 250 West 57th Street, New York, NY 10019
> Publishes a catalog of the living will laws in different states. Concern for Dying, same address, distributes living wills (see above).

WANZER, SIDNEY, JAMES ADELSTEIN, RONALD CRANFORD, DANIEL FEDERMAN, EDWARD HOOK, CHARLES MOERTEL, PETER SAFAR, ALAN STONE, HELEN TAUSSIG, and JAN VAN EYS. "The Physician's Responsibility toward Hopelessly Ill Patients, *The New England Journal of Medicine* 310, 15 (April 12, 1984): 955–959.
> Focus is on the patient's role in decision-making and that a decrease in aggressive treatment of the hopelessly ill patient is advisable when such treatment would only prolong a difficult and uncomfortable process of dying.

Money: The Bottom Line

With the cost of hospitalization and long-term care escalating, most older people fear health care expenses more than other factors in their lives. Even if they have not been faced with their own medical expenses, many have developed fears of costs through the stories in the media and tales retold by friends or acquaintances. The threat to financial security represented by medical expenses can be experienced so intensely by older people that they omit prescribed medications, put off needed hospitalizations, and refuse to hire extra help in their homes, despite the detrimental implications of these omissions.

The initial sections in this chapter explain the governmental programs which help older people pay for their medical expenses and those which provide supplementary income. The later sections detail the various options that older people and their families have for the management of finances. Finally, the costs of various long-term care options are compared and the psychological effects of depleting life savings to pay for these options are discussed from the perspective of both older people and their heirs.

Understanding Medicare and Medicaid

Confusion about the submission of paperwork and worry about the benefits to be paid by Medicare and Medicaid produce considerable anxiety for older people and their families. Hospitals and other medical pro-

	MEDICARE	MEDICAID
Eligibility	• Determined by reaching age 65 or remaining on Social Security Disability for two years	• Determined by income and financial assets, including bank accounts, stocks and bonds, and real estate
Dispensing Agency	• The Social Security Administration; monthly premiums are deducted from the social security check	• The local welfare office of the state; often accompanies other forms of assistance from the state
Common Attitudes of Older People	• Viewed as an insurance program	• Viewed as welfare
Sources of the Funds	• Federally-funded and uniformly administered from state-to-state	• Federal–state partnership, with reimbursement rates and eligibility requirements varying from state-to-state
Nursing Home Benefits	• Pays for limited forms of care in nursing homes, usually for brief periods of time	• Nursing home benefit covers the duration of the person's life, once eligibility is established
Home Health Care Benefits	• Covers the full range of professional services, including nurses, aides, physical and occupational therapists, social workers but limited to certain types of health conditions and specific time periods	• Covers a smaller range of home health services, but less limited in duration and in the types of conditions which qualify a person for service
Coverage of the Cost of Medicines	• Does not cover any type of pharmaceutical expense	• Can be used to pay for most prescription drugs
Deductibles/ Co-payments	• There is one annual deductible for all types of services, a hospital deductible, and a portion of each outpatient bill which must be paid by the older person	• Varies from state-to-state; for people under age 65, there is usually a large deductible along with eligibility requirements; for those over 65, eligibility depends on income and asset restrictions

viders generate computerized billing statements which bombard older people to the point that it can be difficult to persuade them that the bulk of their mail does not reflect their indebtedness. These sophisticated printouts are often needlessly complex and do not clarify the proportion of the expense likely to be covered by Medicare and the recipient's supplementary insurance. The long waiting period between the submission of forms to Medicare and the receipt of a statement reporting the covered amounts leaves low- and middle-income older people unable to gauge the impact of a major illness on their financial status. The charts and discussion in this section should instill order in the prevailing confusion. Ways that family members can help older people reduce their anxiety about medical expenses are also suggested.

The gap between the actual amount a physician or other provider charges for medical services and what Medicare deems allowable is the key to understanding the limits of Medicare reimbursement. At this writing, Medicare pays 80 percent of the allowable charges, not 80 percent of the actual charges. The following example illustrates this reimbursement gap. After submitting a bill to Medicare for $170 in physician's services, the older person in this example receives a check for $80 accompanied by the following explanation of Medicare benefits:

PROVIDER	DATE OF SERVICE	ORIGINAL CHARGE	ALLOWABLE CHARGE	MEDICARE PAYMENT
Dr. Smith	2/5/84	$170	$100	$80

The older person's reimbursement in this instance is less than half the actual cost of the service because the gap between the actual charge and the allowable is so wide.

The problem with most insurance policies claiming to be supplements to Medicare is that they pay the difference between the Medicare payment and the allowable charge, rather than the full amount which is left over after the Medicare payment. As in this example, the typical policy would pay $20, instead of the full $90 still owed to the doctor. Not realizing the limits of such insurance, many older people respond to general mailings from insurance companies and end up paying monthly premiums for policies which do not translate into significant protection against high medical costs. Since they can be cost-effective in certain circumstances, existing policies should be examined carefully before they are discontinued.

An option for containing medical costs is to find physicians and other providers of services who accept what Medicare calls assignment. In contrast to the reimbursement method described earlier, the assignment method requires that the provider submit the charges to Medicare and receive payment for 80 percent of the allowable directly. In addition, the provider agrees to consider the allowable as the full charge for the service. If the bill in the previous example had been accepted on assignment, Dr. Smith would have received the $80 payment directly from Medicare and would have been permitted to bill the older person only for the $20 remaining of the allowable charge. Another advantage of the assignment method is that the doctor handles all the initial paperwork. Families should encourage their relatives to check with providers before any treatments or services are rendered to determine whether they will accept Medicare assignment. In some parts of the country, medical referral services will supply the names of doctors who accept Medicare assignment. A senior center, senior information and referral hotline, or the local medical association may have information about such referral services.

The chart on page 179 depicts a simple system which older people and their family members can use to make sense of the Medicare forms, supplementary insurance statements, and itemized bills, which tend to confuse even those who are astute at bill-paying. Recording the date particular services were rendered is the only way to match Medicare statements with those from supplementary insurances and medical providers. The actual charge for each date of service, rather than Medicare's allowable charge, is also a key to the matching process. To prevent mistakes, it is helpful to circle the dates of service and the original charges on the forms received from providers. Otherwise, the eye easily travels to errors, such as writing down the date of the statement instead of the date of the service. When several charges from a single provider occur on the same date, they can be listed as one sum on the accounting record.

Since itemized statements from providers arrive before reports from Medicare, the original charges for each date of service can be noted and then the statements can be clipped behind the accounting sheet. When duplicate billings arrive each month, they can be discarded if no new information appears on them. Months may elapse before Medicare and supplementary insurances send a report of their payments. When reimbursement reports finally arrive, their information should be matched with the dates and charges on the accounting sheet and filled in the appropriate spaces. A frequent source of confusion is when reimbursement for services from different providers are included in one check from Medicare. For determining how much should be sent to each provider, the "Statement of Benefits" accompanying the check can be matched against the items listed in the accounting system.

The chief difficulty of this system is getting started. Older people and their financial helpers should choose a date four to five months previous, and then make a pile of Medicare statements containing reimbursement

Medical Bill Accounting System

Date(s) of Service	Provider	Amount of Original Bill	Amount Paid by Medicare	Supplementary Insurance	Actual Expense	Notes
2/5/84	Dr. Smith	$ 170	$80	$ 20	$70	Sent the Medicare check and a check for $70 on 3/25.
2/16/84	Crosstown Pharmacy	$ 56	-0-	-0-	$56	Paid cash for medications.
2/24/84– 2/28/84	General Hospital	$2800	all but $360 (the deductible set by Medicare)	$360	-0-	Sent the $360 insurance payment to the hospital on 4/1/84.
3/1/84– 3/31/84	Wheelchair Rental Agency	$ 58	$46	-0-	$12	Sent $12 rental payment on 4/12/84.

MEDICAL BILL ACCOUNTING SYSTEM

Wendy Brandts, MSW
Visiting Nurse Services

DATE	PROVIDER	AMOUNT OF ORIGINAL BILL	AMOUNT PAID BY MEDICARE		NOTES

Medical Bill Accounting System Form

From Nancy R. Hooyman and Wendy Lustbader, Taking Care: Supporting Older People and Their Families (New York: The Free Press, 1986). Copyright © 1986 by The Free Press.

information for dates of service within this period. The blank form shown on the preceding page can be enlarged before it is duplicated to ease its use by people with low vision or hand tremors. As information is gleaned from the forms, the statements should be clipped behind the accounting sheet. It is not necessary to record the dates of service consecutively, since scanning the date column is easy enough for finding particular dates. As itemized billing statements from providers are then matched to the Medicare statements, duplicate bills and original mailing envelopes can be discarded. Turning a threatening collection of envelopes into an orderly pile of statements, with a cover sheet, can do more to relieve anxiety than any amount of verbal reassurance. As the older person maintains this system month by month, it becomes possible to predict the Medicare reimbursements likely to be received for repeated services.

For those who are proud of having survived a lifetime without "handouts" from the government, this accounting system gives a graphic demonstration that they are contributing responsibly to their medical debt. Later discomfort from the need to apply for medical assistance through the "welfare" office can be reduced through this emphasis on their fair contribution. The accounting system can also be used as supporting documentation for a Medicaid application. The following questions and answers explain what older people and their families most often want to know about Medicaid.

Questions About Medicaid (State Medical Assistance)

1. *How is eligibility for Medicaid established?*

Each state determines its own income and asset limits for eligibility. At this writing, several states use $1500 for individuals and $2200 for couples as the cut-off point for assets. This means that a couple with $4,000 in the bank would be ineligible for assistance, no matter how low their monthly income and how severe their medical expenses. It is sometimes difficult to convince older people to spend the contents of their savings accounts to get them down to the eligible level, despite the financial help they would gain by doing so. Information about application procedures can be obtained by phoning the state's department of health and human services.

2. *What are the legal ways to spend the contents of a savings account to meet the state limit on assets for medical assistance?*

It is not legal for an older person to give away the contents of a savings account to relatives in order to qualify for medical assistance. A legitimate basis for achieving eligibility is depleting assets through the payment of household and medical expenses. When the need for state-funded assistance is anticipated, older people should be encouraged to record the cash they lay out for pharmaceutical costs, medical supplies, and other items not covered by Medicare. Receipts can be saved in an envelope and kept with the accounting system.

3. *What documents should be assembled in advance of a Medicaid application?*

Generally, all sources of income must be verified with documents, such as copies of Social Security, Veteran's or private pension checks and bank statements listing interest income. The cash value of all liquifiable assets must be similarly certified with bank statements, real estate assessments, letters from life insurance companies stating the cash value of policies, and brokerage statements regarding the value of stocks, bonds, and money market funds.

4. *If someone already has Medicare coverage, what is the benefit of assistance from the state?*

The state's assistance functions largely as a supplement to Medicare; it does not replace Medicare. In essence, the state pays what is left over after Medicare pays its portion of claims. The chief value of state assistance for most older people lies in its coverage of drugs and other health care expenses not covered at all by Medicare.

5. *Why do some medical providers refuse to accept patients with Medicaid coverage?*

Providers must accept assignment on Medicare claims when a patient is covered by state medical assistance. They are then reimbursed by the state for the difference between the allowable charge and the amount paid by Medicare, not for the full amount of their actual fees left over by Medicare. This means a significant loss of income from patients with Medicaid coverage compared to patients who can be billed for the full amount left by Medicare.

As the suggestions in this section imply, family members can employ many strategies to relieve their relative's worries about medical expenses. Their older relative may then be willing to consider accepting additional services that must be paid out of savings and to apply for state assistance when it becomes necessary. Relief from worry also facilitates compliance with prescribed medications, an area particularly vulnerable to cost-cutting measures by people concerned about their financial status. Keeping track of medical expenses through an accounting system also gives people a sense of control over an area of life that may seem less amenable to their influence than all the others.

Financial Assistance

Older people and their families are often confused by the distinctions among Social Security retirement benefits, Social Security disability benefits, and Supplemental Security Income (SSI). For instance, SSI is run by the Social Security administration, but funding for SSI comes from general U.S. Treasury funds. In contrast, Social Security retirement benefits are paid out of a fund from workers' and employers' contributions. Regardless of their income or assets, workers who have paid into the Social Security system are entitled to Social Security benefits. Eligibility for SSI, however, depends on whether an applicant's income and assets fall under the limits. It does not require a history of covered employment contributions. The following section presents some of the most frequently asked questions about each of these programs.

Questions About Social Security Retirement Benefits

1. *How does a widow qualify for Social Security?*

During the next few decades, most of the women in the generations reaching retirement age will collect on the basis of their husband's earnings records rather than their own, due to their discontinuous work histories and lower salaries. A widow may start to collect surviving dependent's benefits when she reaches age sixty, but she then loses 28.5 percent of what she would receive if she waited until age sixty-five. For a surviving spouse to collect benefits, the marriage must have lasted at least twelve months. Widows under age sixty who are not disabled and who do not have disabled or entitled children under age eighteen in their care cannot receive Social Security benefits.

2. *Can a divorced woman collect her ex-husband's benefits?*

A woman who is divorced after at least ten years of marriage and who reaches retirement age may collect up to 50 percent of her ex-husband's retirement benefits when he retires, if she remains single. If she has paid into Social Security and her benefits at retirement would be greater than the 50 percent, she will receive her own benefits instead. A widowed or divorced woman who remarries loses her former husband's Social Security benefits and cannot collect on her new spouse's benefits until married at least nine months.

3. *If a person collects Social Security benefits before the age of sixty-five, what are the consequences?*

At age sixty-two, 20 percent is deducted from the monthly entitlement that would have been received at age sixty-five. When a person reaches age sixty-five, this level of payment is not increased to what it would otherwise have been. A prorated formula is applied to calculate this deduction for each month nearer to the age of sixty-five that the person retires.

Questions About Supplemental Security Income (SSI)

1. *What is the difference between SSI and Social Security retirement benefits?*

As noted above, Social Security retirement benefits are based on a person's covered earnings record, while SSI eligibility is determined by meeting certain income and asset limits. Thus, SSI can be received as a supplement to retirement income that falls below the SSI standard.

2. *How much can a person have in the bank or own and still be eligible for SSI?*

The 1985 limit on assets is $1500 for individuals and $2200 for couples. Stocks, bonds, and any cashable assets are included in this limit, except for a home, the value of one car, and household goods with a total equity value of $2,000 or less. The cash surrender value of insurance policies and of any real estate beyond a primary residence also count.

3. *Can a person earn money and still collect SSI?*

The first $65 in earnings per month does not count against the SSI payment; half of the earnings beyond $64 are deducted from the monthly payment. Any other income above $20 a month, such as gifts received from relatives and Veteran's payments, counts against the SSI payment.

4. *At what income level is it possible to receive SSI in addition to Social Security?*

At this writing, the SSI standard is $352 a month for individuals and $372 a month for couples. Older people whose income is less than that amount can apply for a monthly SSI payment to bring them up to that income level. For instance, someone with a Social Security income of $330 could receive $22 from SSI monthly, as well as Medicaid, if that person's assets are low enough to fit eligibility requirements.

5. *Can a person give up income in order to qualify for SSI and automatic Medicaid?*

Many people receive a small pension check, such as Veteran's benefits, in addition to Social Security, which brings their total monthly income over the SSI limit. They are not permitted to decline this additional income in order to qualify for SSI, even if the extra pension payment brings them only a few dollars beyond the SSI standard.

6. *If a person goes to live in their son or daughter's house, will they lose their SSI?*

Whenever an older SSI recipient's living arrangements change, their SSI eligibility is reevaluated. This applies both to their moving in with relatives and to relatives' moving into their home. In reassessing eligibility, a number of factors in the living situation are considered, including the number of people in the household and household costs.

Older people with income below the SSI standard and savings only a few thousand above the asset limit may resist the idea of depleting their savings. They may skimp on medical expenses to protect their nest egg, rather than make themselves eligible for both Medicaid and SSI. The fact that they do not have to apply at the welfare office for either SSI or the accompanying Medicaid sometimes helps older people overcome their resistance to using these programs.

Questions About Social Security Disability

1. *If someone is under age sixty-five and unable to work due to medical problems, what is the process of establishing eligibility for Social Security disability?*

Social Security rules state that payments for disability may be made if "an individual is unable to engage in substantial gainful activity, because of a physical or mental impairment which can be expected to result in death or which has lasted, or is expected to last, for twelve months or longer." The applicant files a disability claim with the Social Security office, and forms are sent to the providers of medical service for substantiation of the claim.

2. *How long does it take for a decision on a disability claim and what can be done in the meantime for financial assistance?*

In all instances, applicants must wait at least five months from the date of onset of their disability in order to receive a payment. For medical conditions in which the extent of disability takes longer to determine, the waiting period can extend beyond five months. For example, the degree of permanent impairment from a stroke often cannot be assessed until after several months of rehabilitation therapy. If Social Security makes a favorable decision, retroactive payment is made from the date the claim was filed. In the meantime, a person left without income should inquire with their state's health and human services department regarding financial support until the claim is decided. The amount of the monthly payments received from the state are later deducted from the large retroactive Social Security payment so that the Social Security administration can reimburse the state for its coverage during the waiting period.

3. *What can a person do if her original claim is turned down by Social Security and she believes she meets the criteria for eligibility?*

A request for reconsideration must be filed with the local office within sixty days of the written decision denying the claim. It is advisable to file an appeal in most instances, since a substantial percentage of denied claims are reversed through the appeal process. A common reason for denied claims is insufficient detail in the supporting documents, particularly regarding the specific physical and mental impairments that interfere with employability. Appeals cases are heard by administrative law judges retained by Social Security for this purpose. Their judgments are independent of the original decisions and permit the presentation of additional evidence to support the claim.

4. *Should a person hire an attorney to assist them with their appeal?*

The burden of proof is on the claimant to show that the Social Security Administration mistakenly denied the disability claim. The assistance of someone familiar with the statutes and the appeal process can be crucial in some instances. Many communities have legal aid organizations or senior advocacy associations willing to assist with Social Security appeals at little or no charge. Private attorneys are often willing to take cases in exchange for a percentage of the cash award from Social Security, if the chance of a favorable appeal is good. Nonlawyer representation at Social Security hearings is also permitted.

5. *Why can't the Social Security office give a person an estimate of their monthly payment before their disability claim is approved?*

Disability benefits are determined according to the number of quarters that a person contributed earnings to Social Security, as well as the total contributions credited over a person's work life. Workers in local offices do not have this information available. A booklet entitled *How to Calculate Your Benefits,* with formulas for estimating Social Security disability benefits, can be requested.

6. *What if it is too difficult for a person to get to the Social Security office to file a claim?*

Field representatives can come to the home, if medical problems interfere with visiting the office. Although claims can also be filed by telephone, a face-to-face contact gives the Social Security worker a firsthand view of the person's functional problems, which may add credibility to the disability claim.

7. *If a person is almost sixty-two and disabled, should he wait until age sixty-two to file for Social Security retirement benefits or file a claim for Social Security disability?*

If the person has worked five out of the ten years prior to his disability, he is better off filing for Social Security disability than Social Security retirement. A disabled person draws the same amount as he would at age sixty-five and qualifies for Medicare after two years of receiving Social Security disability benefits. In contrast, if the person waited until age sixty-two to apply for regular Social Security benefits, he would receive only 80 percent of full payment and would have to wait until age sixty-five for Medicare.

8. *Can a disabled widow or widower qualify for disability benefits?*

A disabled widow or widower, fifty years or older, may receive disability benefits even without sufficient work credits of their own, as long as their deceased spouse had enough work credits at the time of death. The survivor's disability must have occurred before their spouse's death or within seven years after the death. A divorced person can collect survivors' benefits only if the marriage had lasted at least ten years. For survivors, however, the term disability is defined more strictly than if their spouse had applied for benefits. To receive benefits, a disabled surviving spouse must be unable to perform *any* gainful activity rather than no *substantial* gainful activity before benefits will be paid.

Since financial assistance programs have strict and constantly changing eligibility requirements, families and their older relatives should address specific questions directly to their local Social Security hotline. When in doubt about qualifications for SSI or Social Security disability, an inquiry is generally worthwhile, if only for the peace of mind of having pursued all financial options.

The Management of an Older Person's Financial Affairs

Older people with memory problems, declining vision, and loss of dexterity in their hands frequently need assistance with managing their financial affairs. Most people prefer assistance which allows them to retain as much control as possible over how their money is spent and who has access to private information about their financial circumstances. Giving financial help while preserving the older person's control or privacy becomes more difficult for family members when higher levels of assistance are rendered. For instance, balancing a person's checkbook differs widely from overseeing investment decisions.

The answers to the following questions cover an array of options for assisting with the management of an older relative's financial affairs.[1] Family members can review these with their relative in order to encourage consideration of this crucial topic and to ensure a common base of information during discussions.

1. *What is the difference between putting someone's name on an account as an "additional authorized signature" and "joint ownership with a right of survivorship?"*

Listing someone's name as an additional authorized signature enables that person to sign checks in the event that the owner of the account is unable to do so, or for the sake of convenience to help with bill-paying. By retaining the checkbook, the older person still controls withdrawals from the account. Putting someone's name on the account as a joint owner with a right of survivorship means that this person will own the account upon the older person's death. Many people do not realize that this designation on an account supercedes what is written in a will. Others confuse joint ownership with the option of an additional authorized signature.

2. *What does it mean to grant someone Power of Attorney?*

Power of Attorney can be limited to specific transactions and responsibilities, such as the payment of bills. It can also be general and far-reaching, such as empowering someone to enter into contracts on the grantor's behalf. In granting Power of Attorney, a person does not lose the right to manage his own affairs, but rather extends this right to someone in addition to himself. The person granting Power of Attorney must be mentally competent and must fully understand the written agreement.

3. *Are a lawyer's services necessary for granting Power of Attorney?*

Forms are available in banks and stationery stores that can be completed without a lawyer's assistance. The form must be signed in a notary's presence and filed at the County Auditor's office. When specific limitations need to be written in, however, a lawyer should be consulted for the precise wording in order to ensure maximum protection.

4. *What is a "durable" Power of Attorney?*

The heading "durable" refers to a clause which specifies that the agreement continues after the grantor becomes mentally incompetent. A Power of Attorney can also be granted which begins only in the event of the grantor becoming incompetent.

5. *What can an older person do to make things easier for her family in the event that she suddenly becomes incapacitated?*

Compiling a list of relevant information, putting it in an envelope, and informing adult children and other relatives of its location is the best strategy. The list should include: sources of income, insurance policies, bank accounts, location of titles pertaining to property, location of a will, rent or mortgage payment information, safety deposit boxes, Social Security number, and the names of accountants, brokers and lawyers.

6. *What does the term "representative payee" mean?*

Social Security benefits can be paid to someone else on the older person's behalf. A representative payee application can be obtained at the local Social Security office; a "physician's statement" form is mailed directly to the physician after the application is submitted. The physician must assess the older person's capability to manage benefit payments in her own interest.

7. *What is legal guardianship and under what circumstances is it obtained?*

While granting Power of Attorney is a voluntary means of relinquishing financial control by a competent person, guardianship is usually sought when an older person is unaware of or unwilling to acknowledge the loss of competence. Limited guardianship removes only the rights and responsibilities specifically delegated to the guardian. Full guardianship removes all the person's legal rights as an adult, such as the right to vote, marry, enter into contracts, write checks, buy or sell property, provide consent for medical treatment, or operate a motor vehicle. In both forms of guardianship, an attorney prepares the papers and files for a hearing, and a physician submits a report to the court, including a medical assessment and a recommendation about the person's ability to manage his affairs. Legal expenses and the time involved in the process of going to court often make this option unattractive.

8. What is a revocable living trust?

A living trust is operative during a person's lifetime, in contrast to a testamentary trust, or trust under will, which is not in effect until a person dies. A living trust can be changed or terminated during the person's lifetime, and can pass on to heirs without going through probate. Trust arrangements supersede those in a will and may be less vulnerable to legal contest than a will. In addition, an "incapacity" clause can be included which allows the trust to continue if the older person becomes mentally incapacitated. This advantage eliminates the cost and stress of guardianship proceedings.

9. When does it make sense to set up a living trust?

In many instances, older people requiring assistance with financial management prefer to assign this responsibility to an uninvolved third party rather than to a family member. This allows them to retain privacy and control while avoiding accusations of favoritism that often arise when a particular relative is designated as a money manager.

A spouse who has managed the finances throughout a long-term marriage frequently seeks to spare his partner financial confusion upon his death by establishing a living trust. Another useful aspect of a living trust is that a third-party manager can help mediate competing requests from adult children for loans and gifts from the trust, for example, "I've got to consult my trust officer before I can give you a loan." For older people who want to give gifts but are worried about their long-term financial solvency, consulting a professional financial planner can provide significant relief.

Older people cashing out the equity of a long-term home may suddenly find themselves with a large amount of money to manage, especially if this cash is added to sizable life savings. Those lacking sophistication in money management may gain more income from their assets by establishing a living trust than they could by managing the new wealth on their own. The income they earn may more than cover the fees incurred for services acquired.

10. *What services do trustees generally offer in addition to overseeing investments?*

A list of services included in the basic fees along with estimated charges for additional services should be obtained when the trust is established. Services may include tax return preparation, bill payment, record-keeping, assistance with arrangements for extra help in the home, and other more personalized benefits.

11. *What are the average fees for trust accounts?*

Fees vary widely, depending on included services and who manages the account. For instance, most banks levy an annual charge of between 1 and 1 ½ percent of the value of the assets to be managed. Their minimum charges make it feasible to open a trust only if assets exceed $100,000.

12. *Is it less expensive to have a lawyer or friend be the trustee rather than a trust officer in a bank?*

The fees charged by a lawyer may be less than a bank's. A friend or private financial consultant may charge still less for the same services. The advantage of the bank's trust department is long-term institutional continuity. For some older people, this lends an additional sense of security to the prospect of third-party management of their finances. Increasingly, private financial managers are offering more personalized services than banks and at lower costs.

Many older people view dependence on someone else to manage their money as an admission of their increasing vulnerability. Others may have a life-long mistrust of financial institutions. Family members need to be sensitive to such sources of resistance when discussing with older relatives the advantages of accepting assistance in the management of their financial affairs.

Tax Credits for Family Caregivers

Only a few federal tax relief programs specifically assist family members who provide care for their relatives. Caregivers who need to pay a housekeeper or home health aide to care for a disabled parent or spouse in their own home so that they can earn income outside the home may be eligible for a tax credit of up to 30 percent of the amount paid for these services. A maximum of $2400 of the cost of purchasing help can be counted in determining the credit for one dependent, and up to $4,000 for two or more dependents who are household members. To qualify for the credit, caregivers must have income from work during the year. The work requirement, however, can be met by part-time jobs, self-employment, or by actively seeking work. The person receiving care must have a physical disability that prevents dressing, bathing or eating without assistance, or a mental defect requiring constant supervision.

If a caregiver's adjusted gross income is $10,000 or less, the tax credit is 30 percent of the expenses for hired help. The percentage is reduced as gross income increases, as shown in the following table:

ADJUSTED GROSS INCOME		APPLICABLE %
Over	But not over	
$ 0	$10,000	30%
10,000	12,000	29%
12,000	14,000	28%
14,000	16,000	27%
16,000	18,000	26%
18,000	20,000	25%
20,000	22,000	24%
22,000	24,000	23%
24,000	26,000	22%
26,000	28,000	21%
28,000		20%

The dependent care credit is not refundable, but can be used to limit tax liability. The cost of care provided outside the home, such as fees paid to an adult day care center, also qualifies the caregiver for the credit, provided the dependent person spends at least eight hours a day in the caregiver's household. In addition, the adult day care center must serve more than six individuals.

The examples that follow are provided by the Internal Revenue Service to illustrate how the tax credit is computed.

Example: Dependent Care in the Home

A single daughter works and keeps up a home for her dependent father and herself. Her adjusted gross earned income is $25,000. Her father is disabled and incapable of self-care for six months. To keep working, she pays a housekeeper $500 a month to care for her father, prepare lunch and dinner, and do housework. She would figure her credit as follows:

Total work-related expenses (6 × $500)... $3,000
Maximum allowable expense... 2,400
Amount of credit (22% of $2,400).. 528

Example: Spouse Care in the Home

A married man works and maintains a home for his wife and himself. They file a joint return and have an adjusted gross earned income of $29,000. Because of an accident, his spouse is incapable of self-care for the entire tax year. To keep working, he pays a housekeeper $6,000 yearly to care for his spouse, prepare lunch and dinner, and do housework. His credit is calculated on the smallest of the following amounts:

Total work-related expenses ($6,000 but limited to $2,400
for one qualifying person)... $ 2,400
His earned income... 29,000
Income considered earned by his disabled spouse (12 × $200).............. 2,400
Allowable credit (20% of $2,400).. 480

Families should request the latest edition of Publication 503, *Child and Dependent Care Credit,* to determine further restrictions regarding the caregiving tax credit.[2]

Care costs included as part of a deduction for medical expenses cannot be applied toward this dependent care credit. Medical and dental expenditures that exceed 3 percent of a taxpayer's adjusted gross income may be deducted, provided these expenses are incurred on a dependent's behalf. Under this provision, a dependent must live in the taxpayer's household and derive at least 50 percent support from the taxpayer. In order to be able to claim a personal exemption of $1,000 for each dependent, the taxpayer must have furnished at least one-half of the support during the calendar year for a dependent whose gross income is less than $1,000. Because of the dependency test's restrictiveness, these provisions give only limited assistance to taxpayers. Since a few states have additional tax expenditure programs to relieve the financial burdens incurred by families who provide care, families should inquire with their state internal revenue department as well.

Psychological Effects of Long-Term Care Costs

These tax benefits, although helpful, do not begin to compensate families for the expense of long-term care. Whether incurred at home or in a nursing home, the costs create tremendous financial pressures on most families. Even when an older person does have substantial resources, worry about the depletion of such assets can produce stress among family members, which adds to the other emotional burdens of providing care.

The uncertainty of how long a care service will be needed (and hence, its total cost) can be a primary obstacle to care planning. This unpredictability may be intensified by newspaper stories or friends' accounts of older people left penniless by the expenses of long-term care. Unaware of all the service options and their costs, families and their older relatives can find the unknown overwhelming. The following comparison of the private costs of various long-term care options can be used to reduce some of this uncertainty and to support long-range planning. The figures used in this chart reflect the national range of costs at the time of this writing.

Comparison of Long-Term Care Costs

| | | ESTIMATED CHARGES | |
TYPE OF CARE	DESCRIPTION	Daily	Monthly
Home health aide services	*Hired through agency:* 3-hour minimum, $8–$9/hour for help with bathing, dressing, medications, and meal preparation	$24 $27	$720 $810
	Private Hire: $7–8/hour	$56–$64	$224–$256
Overnight Aide	*Agency:* Nurse's aide provides personal care as well as ensures safety. To hire only for the night on an hourly basis surpasses the cost of the 24-hour rate.	$90–$105	$2700–$3015
	Private Hire: Hourly rate, such as $6/hour from 9 P.M. to 7 A.M.; rate increases if there are hands-on care needs rather than companionship needs.	$60	$1800
Live-In Helper (assuming five days a week)	*Agency:* Lump sum $24-hour fee	$74–$83	$2200–$2506
	Private hire: The two days off per week must be covered by family members or other options above	$20	$600 (plus food)
Full-Service Retirement Homes	Including 3 meals a day, call button, housekeep-	$20–$40	$600–$1500

Comparison of Long-Term Care Costs   (*Continued*)

		ESTIMATED CHARGES	
TYPE OF CARE	DESCRIPTION	Daily	Monthly
(excluding those with large down payments, founder's fees where monthly payments are lower)	ing services, recreational programs (not including help with personal care) (Price varies with size of room, nature of facilities)		
Adult Foster Care (care homes)	Person lives in the home of a paid caregiver; fee depends on care needs.	$20–$30	$600–$900
Nursing Home	Levels of care determine the private-pay rate.	$60–$80	$1800–$2400

Specific information about care costs can also intensify worries about the depletion of savings. Most of the current generation of older people vividly remember the Depression, which fuels their fears about dipping too deeply into their savings and then facing either poverty or reliance on government support. Anxiety about money may also be increased by news reports of inflation, service cutbacks, and legislative demands to limit outlays on Social Security and Medicare. Some older people benefit from having a third party, such as a lawyer or banker, objectively review their financial picture and present some management options.

People who have lived frugally and saved carefully over the years tend to be uncomfortable with spending large amounts of money on their care needs in later life. They are likely to want to try to "get by" or "make do" with the least expensive alternatives. This reluctance to spend money may be deeply habituated and may lead to angry reactions when family members ask "what are you saving it for?". When such a long-standing personal style is challenged, defensive reactions are inevitable. Family members should instead emphasize their own need for "peace of mind" when asking their relative to purchase services.

A particularly painful situation is when family members wish for the death of a relative who is living unhappily in a nursing home. They may perceive that the assets spent to maintain an unsatisfying existence could fund a grandchild's education or something equally productive. Their relative may feel the same way as she hangs on month after month, aware that thousands of dollars are disappearing to pay for time she experiences as tedious and unrewarding. When a private-pay nursing home resident says, "I wish I would die already," her eagerness for death may be largely motivated by this discrepancy between the financial expenditures and the value she places on her present life. Family members tend to reply to such feelings with statements such as "Don't say things like that, Mom," while privately agreeing and consequently feeling guilty, especially after their relative dies.

Openly admitting disappointment over the depletion of savings by costly services is a preferable approach for family members, for example, "Sure, there's lots of things we could do with the money, but as long as you're alive, we're going to pay to make you as comfortable as possible." Some families find that being able to laugh at the absurdity of the exorbitant expenses can remove guilt-laden taboos surrounding this topic. A remark such as, "Gee, at this rate, you could be staying at a top class hotel in Bermuda" can relieve the older person through the very honesty contained within it.

Siblings frequently disagree over how extensively to drain their parents' assets to pay for hired help. For instance, a son living next door to his mother may exhaust himself in order to avoid spending money on a home health aide to provide care every morning and evening. According to the $8 hourly fee and the three-hour minimum required by private agencies, he calculates that he saves his family $48 a day by going over before and after work. His frugality may be motivated by his desire to preserve the inheritance and to be justly compensated later for his caregiving efforts. His out-of-town sister may plead with him to use their mother's funds to pay for aide services rather than complain to her by phone about his fatigue from caregiving, for example, "It's Mom's money, so let's spare no expense for her comfort." One solution in these instances is to pay a fair hourly wage to the adult child who is providing care in lieu of hired services.

The expense of nursing home care may create particularly intense conflicts in this regard. With yearly private rates of $24,000 or more, only assets over $240,000 are likely to generate sufficient income to pay for such care without eroding an inheritance. Disagreements may arise between family members who prefer to utilize the less expensive home care options and those who would rather "get it all settled at once" in a nursing home, despite the depletion of their inheritance. Conflicts about the inheritance may remain unverbalized during heated discussions about what is best for the parent.

Spouses usually have the most reason to worry about depleting their savings for long-term care. For example, a woman who has been a homemaker most of her life may have a small Social Security income from her limited work history, while her husband may have both his Social Security income and a private pension. If her husband has not elected survivor's benefits under his private pension, her income will be reduced upon his death to the amount of his Social Security check. If they were to spend a large portion of their savings on hiring help to care for him at home, she would be unable to maintain her standard of living after his death. In states where the couple must spend down in order to qualify for Medicaid-funded institutional care, the woman may be left feeling guilty and also penniless from placing her husband in a nursing home.

Some states, under Medicaid waivers through the Health Care Financing Administration, have set up demonstration programs which provide a monthly stipend to family members willing to forgo employment to meet an older person's need for home care. While such stipends tend to be too small to replace a full-time salary, they sometimes cover a family member's expenses sufficiently to make a leave of absence financially feasible. These stipends are approved only when the older person's income and assets fall below the state's limit for Medicaid eligibility. Despite these limitations, families should be encouraged to inquire through the department of health and social services in their state about the status of such programs.

More than any other factor, income determines the number of care options available to older people and their families. Those with the private means to purchase services face primarily psychological barriers to their use. Medicare was intended to assure health care to all older people, but covers only about two-thirds of health care bills. The percentage of health care costs born by older people will grow even more with the cost containment restrictions being placed on Medicare coverage.[3]

For low- and moderate-income older people, Social Security, SSI and Medicaid were intended to provide a minimal level of protection. A growing public perception, fueled by the fact that these programs account for the most rapidly expanding part of the federal budget, is that the elderly are better off than younger generations and are responsible for escalating service costs. Despite the number of benefits available, approximately 15 percent of older people live near or below the poverty line. Of these, only about one-third are covered by Medicaid, since many states do not include all aged recipients of SSI under Medicaid.[4] Increased state limitations in defining "medical indigency" are producing even larger gaps in health care coverage for "just poor" older people. Inflationary medical costs and cutbacks in federal contributions to states have led to a decrease in services covered by Medicaid, more stringent eligibility requirements, and fewer providers willing to serve Medicaid clients.

Public scapegoating of older people as responsible for expanding federal spending also overlooks structural causes underlying long-term care costs. These include high unemployment which reduces the number of people paying into Social Security and a privately controlled medical market that profits from Medicare costs.[5] Another structural limitation of the long-term care system is that institutional care is better funded than home care. Because reimbursement for home health care is generally limited to skilled medical care, many older people are forced to enter a nursing home to obtain ongoing reimbursable care. Older people's care needs thus become subordinate to programatic reimbursement regulations.

Most policymakers and gerontologists agree on the need to change the long-term care system. The disagreement lies in whether and to what degree cost considerations should supersede care needs. Older people and their families, as the primary consumers of long-term care and the central constituency of policymakers who are concerned with escalating costs, need to become politically active to ensure that care needs are not forgotten in a cost-containment era.

Notes

1. Parts of this section were derived from an interview with Ms. Wendy Weaver, Trust Officer, Seattle First National Bank.
2. Department of Treasury, *Publication 503. Child and Dependent Care Credit, and Employment Taxes for Household Employers* (Washington, D.C.: Internal Revenue Service, 1984).
3. Laura Katz Olson, "Aging Policy: Who Benefits?" *Generations* IX, 2 (Fall 1984): 10–14.
4. U.S. Congress, 1982, *Every Ninth American, An Analysis for the Chairman of the Select Committee on Aging* (Washington, D.C.: 97th Congress, 2nd Session, U.S. Government Printing Office, 1982); Laura Katz Olson, *The Political Economy of Aging* (New York: Columbia University Press, 1982): 148–150.
5. James R. Storey, *Older Americans in the Reagan Era: Impacts of Federal Policy Changes* (Washington, D.C.: The Urban Institute Press, 1983).

Suggested Resources

BOSSHARDT, JOHN, DORTHY GIBSON, and MARILYN SNYDER. *Family Survival Handbook: A Guide to the Financial, Legal and Social Problems of Brain-Damaged Adults* (San Francisco, Calif.: Family Survival Project, 1981).

A general introduction and guide to the kinds of problems that may arise for brain-damaged adults and their families, and the alternatives available for coping with these problems. Developed by a self-help project.

BROWN, ROBERT N., CLIFFORD B. ALLO, ALAN D. FREEMAN, and GORDON W. NETZORG. *The Rights of Older Persons: The Basic ACLU Guide to an Older Person's Rights* (New York: Avon, 1979).

CLIFFORD, DENNIS. *Plan Your Estate: Wills, Probate Avoidance, Trusts and Taxes,* 1983. NOLO Press, 950 Parker Street, Berkeley, Calif. 94170.
>This work is detailed and accurate. The major limitation is that much of the information pertains specifically to Californians.

MATTHEWS, JOSEPH. *Sourcebook for Older Americans: Income, Rights and Benefits.* NOLO Press, 950 Parker Street, Berkeley, Calif. 1983.
>Comprehensive and practical review of Social Security, Medicare, Medicaid, SSI, and private pensions. Publishes an *Update Service* to review recent changes.

Special Issue on Social Policy, *Generations* IX, 2 (Fall 1984).
>Readable collection of articles on some of the major issues surrounding Medicare, Medicaid, Social Security, and housing in the 1980s.

Your Medicare Handbook (Washington, D.C.: U.S. Government Printing Office, 1984).

Your Pension Rights at Divorce. Women's Pension Project, 932 DuPont Circle Bldg., Washington, DC 20036.
>A useful guide for divorced women.

CHAPTER 9

Bringing Services into the Older Person's Home

Most families try to care for older relatives on their own, until they reach some crisis or breaking point when they resort to institutionalization. For a variety of reasons, most families do not fully use the community services that could support them in their care tasks. They may be unaware of services, or not know how to maneuver within what appears to be a complex system. Both older people and their families may be confused by eligibility requirements, provisions for insurance coverage, and paperwork. Many feel uncomfortable accepting goverment-funded services. Another important factor may be resistance by either the caregiver or the older person to a worker's entering the older person's home, an issue discussed in depth in the pages which follow. This chapter also presents specific community resources and techniques for using them to extend older people's abilities to remain in their own homes. The chapter concludes with strategies for making the older person's home a safe and supportive environment.

Locating Community Resources

A professional can best encourage families to use support services by first helping them clarify their attitudes toward such services. Some may believe that they are not entitled to services, approaching agencies timidly or apologetically. Others may see acceptance of services as a sign of weakness or failure. Still others may have heard second-hand information from friends or relatives that is misleading or negative, thus deterring them from seeking assistance. In many instances, families may be at a loss about where and how to begin to contact community agencies, feeling intimidated by complex listings in the phone book or curt responses to their phone inquiries.

Finding the time to make multiple phone calls when feeling pressured by caregiving can be difficult for families; as a result, days can go by, filled with excuses of being too busy to call. Obtaining support services is so essential, however, that caregivers should be urged to set aside a block of uninterrupted time to make exploratory phone calls. Other family members or neighbors can be enlisted to make time for the primary caregiver to locate resources.

A useful starting point for families is to contact the senior information and referral hotline in the older person's local community. If the number is not prominently displayed in the service listings at the front of the phone book, an operator can easily obtain it. The person answering this hotline will know how the family can obtain a directory of services tailored for older people in that community. Questions about specific services can also be aired during this initial call and the name of someone to contact with further questions can be obtained. If such a hotline does not exist, families can contact the local area agency on aging or the state department of social and health services.

Before phoning agencies directly, families may find it helpful to review the following guide to searching for community resources by phone:

Community Resources Phone Search Guide

1. State your name, relationship to the person needing services, and the nature of the problem or desired service.
2. If no one is available to answer questions, clarify when to call back or how you can be reached.
3. If the agency representative is unhelpful, ask for referral to another person or organization.
4. Write down notes from each phone call, especially the name of the person providing information. The phone contact sheet on page 202 of this chapter could be xeroxed so families can complete it after each phone contact. This is a way to keep track of information, and it makes comparisons among agency options easier after all the calls are completed.

Dealing with rigid agency boundaries or inflexible rules and policies can often frustrate families. Rather than expressing irritation about the

Phone Contact Sheet

Name of Agency _____ Phone _____

Date of call _____ Person spoken to _____

    Services they can provide

_____

_____

_____

_____

_____

_____

    Cost of services/eligibility requirements

_____

_____

_____

_____

Waiting period for services (How much lead time is needed?) _____

_____

Method of payment _____

_____

Will they be mailing program brochures or applications?

           _____ Yes   _____ No

_____

Person to contact if services are desired? _____

_____

General impression/other notes _____

_____

_____

_____

limited knowledge of staff who may answer the phone, families should firmly and clearly ask to speak to the person's supervisor; for example, they could say "I appreciate your help, but I'd like to ask your supervisor some additional questions." The supervisor may have information about comparable programs in the community or may be able to explain agency limitations in a more comprehensive fashion. If the supervisor is not available, family members should ask for the best time to call back and whether a direct phone number can be provided for reaching this person. Persistence in making these contacts can pay off in terms of effective referrals and a sense of satisfaction.

The remainder of this section briefly describes services to support the older person at home:

- In-home chore and personal care services
- Home health care services
- Home delivered meals
- Home safety and repair programs
- Electronic in-home alert aids

In-Home Chore and Personal Care Services

In some instances, hiring hourly help with chores and personal care solves an older person's care needs. Families can consult employment listings at senior centers, newspaper ads, or synagogue and church bulletins to hire workers directly. An advantage of hiring through agencies is that workers can be obtained on short notice, in contrast to families' time-consuming efforts to review listings, conduct interviews, and check references on workers they hire directly. The chief disadvantage of hiring through agencies is the higher cost and structured gradations of the services they provide.

Gradations of Services from Private-Pay Agencies

Companion services—social contact, accompaniment on walks or errands (not including housekeeping, meal preparation, or personal care)

Chore services—housekeeping tasks, grocery shopping, laundry (sometimes including meal preparation but not personal care)

Homemaker—all of the above chore services, with the addition of meal preparation and help with some personal needs, such as getting dressed (usually not including help with bathing)

Home health aide—all of the above chore and homemaker services as well as help with personal care needs, such as the management

203

of incontinence (not including skilled services which a licensed nurse must perform)

The hourly rate for help hired through agencies tends to increase one dollar for each gradation from companionship through home health aide services. Requirements for a minimum number of hours at a time can make the use of such services awkward, since an older person's need for help may occur once in the morning and once at night. In the instance of an older person simply needing assistance getting in and out of the tub, an agency which offers a flat rate for bath assistance would be preferable to one with a minimum requirement of three hours for a home health aide.

If the older person's income and assets fall within eligibility guidelines, state-funded chore services may be available through the local health and human services office. In most states, services are authorized on an individual basis through an assessment interview.

Medicare-Covered Home Health Care Services

Specially licensed home health care agencies can provide services that are fully covered by Medicare. To qualify for such services, the following requirements must be met:

- A physician must approve each type of service received.
- The older person must be homebound, that is, have a medical condition which makes it difficult for her to obtain services outside her home.
- The older person must be in need of skilled nursing or rehabilitation services, rather than only help with personal care or assistance tending to a chronic, unchanging condition.

Phone calls to agencies listed in the yellow pages under "home health care" enable families to determine which are licensed by Medicare. In most instances, the agency will ask screening questions over the phone. Therefore, family members should have handy a list of the person's medications, the name and phone number of her physician, and a list of her current medical problems. The agency will then contact the older person's physician for approval of the services and send out a nurse to conduct an initial assessment. Family members can request that the nurse contact them after completing the assessment to inform them of how long services can be expected to last, which additional services will be provided, and how frequently visits to the home will be made.

The services which home health professionals can offer are described below. Family members should review the role of each professional with their relative, perhaps asking the nurse to write the name of each person next to the services to be provided.

- *Nurse*—supervises the care provided by the home health aide; evaluates and reviews the older person's use of medications; teaches caregivers to do dressing changes and other skilled tasks; maintains contact with the physician as the older person's condition changes
- *Home health aide*—assists with bathing, personal care, housekeeping tasks, and meal preparation
- *Occupational therapist*—evaluates the home for needed adaptive devices; works with the older person on skills of daily living, such as getting dressed independently, and teaches family members to help effectively
- *Physical therapist*—establishes a home exercise program to increase the older person's mobility and independence; teaches caregivers transfer techniques and safe methods for assisting with exercises
- *Social worker*—offers referrals to other supportive services; works with the older person and family members toward removing obstacles to effective care, such as financial stresses, disunity among caregivers, and lack of respite
- *Speech therapist*—facilitates recovery from speech and swallowing problems; works with the older person and family members on adaptive devices and techniques for communication

Family members wishing to meet personally with their relative's nurse or other home care professional during a visit to the home should contact the professional by phone at least several days prior to the anticipated visit. Because of unavoidable scheduling complexities in home care, exact choices for visiting times may be impossible. Family members who can allow a morning or afternoon during which to expect the professional's visit are less likely to be frustrated than those who designate a specific hour. For family members who work full-time, phone conferences can be arranged if the professional is given enough notice to set aside a block of time.

Home-Delivered Meals

Meals on Wheels, one of the most frequently used community resources for homebound older people, can prevent unhealthy eating habits. Difficulties with cooking, the loneliness of eating alone, or forgetfulness about the timing or content of meals can cause older people to snack rather than eat nutritiously. Generally delivered on a weekly basis, government-subsidized frozen meals are also less expensive than frozen dinners of equivalent nutritional value available in grocery stores. In addition, they are suitable for low salt diets. Some programs may offer delivery of liquid dietary supplements by the case and of packaged grocery items.

Home-delivered meals may also provide the older person with a regular and predictable social contact. In areas where prepared meals can be delivered more often than once a week, the delivery person may be not only a social stimulus, but also a means to check whether the older person is out of bed, dressed, warm enough, and so on. By placing the meals in the freezer, the delivery person can monitor how frequently the older person is eating. In localities where government-subsidized meals are unavailable, churches can often organize the delivery of meals to homebound parishioners and neighbors.

Obstacles to the use of frozen meals include insufficient freezer space, freezers which are not cold enough, and inoperable or nonexistent ovens. In such instances, neighbors may be willing to store meals in their extra freezer space and then deliver individual meals daily. Countertop ovens can be purchased to accommodate the meals, offering the advantage of accessible heat controls for low-vision or wheelchair-bound people who cannot manage conventional ovens. Especially useful are countertop ovens with loud buzzers which can alert the person to remove the meal.

Memory loss is a more complex obstacle. An older person may have difficulty remembering to phone in her order or to set the timer on her oven. Unless reminded, she may forget to use the meals in her freezer. In some home-delivery programs, the phone staff keep a list of those who need reminders to place orders or who need assistance in choosing meals compatible with their diets. The older person who burns food may need to have a family member provide phone cues for putting food into the oven and removing the food.

The most common obstacles to home-delivered frozen meals—boredom or outright dislike for the meals' taste—are more difficult to address. In such instances, people can be encouraged to store the meals in their freezer as a backup, in the event that access to other sources of food is unexpectedly cut off. Another strategy is to urge the older person to replace the cardboard covers with foil when heating the meals, since the taste of cardboard is otherwise often a legitimate complaint. The addition of seasoning, such as mild herbs, sauces or garnishes can also make the food more appetizing, without interfering with dietary restrictions. If, despite these modifications, the commercially produced meals still fail to stimulate the older person's appetite, neighbors or family members can freeze individual portions of their own meals, and deliver these to the older person's freezer.

Home Safety and Repair Programs

Doing routine repairs, such as replacing windows or painting a forty- or fifty-year-old home, may seem insurmountable for older persons on fixed incomes. Weatherization can make a major difference in daily comfort, especially in areas with severe winters or extremely hot summers. Many communities have home repair and energy assistance programs, with fees varying according to income. For older persons whose income is too high for subsidized assistance, small repair companies which specialize in home maintenance to older persons exist in many communities; these are generally advertised through senior centers and community newspapers. In using such services, however, it is essential to obtain more than one bid and to read the written contracts carefully.

In-Home Alert Programs

A number of electronic aids can be combined with human assistance to ensure the older person's safety in the home. In some localities, Lifeline Telephone Emergency Response Service has been made available to frail older people living alone. Lifeline service combines electronic and human assistance around the clock to bring help, if needed. An emergency response center, generally in a hospital, receives the signals transmitted by phone from the home. The older person wears a wristwatchlike, pushbutton controlled "Lifeline" monitoring device that can be activated by radio signal to alert the hospital if emergency medical help is needed. If the person is unable to press the button, an electronic clock timer responds to his unusual activity and automatically sends an alerting signal. At the center, the operator retrieves a file of information on the older person and calls back. Depending on the need, the operator may then phone "emergency responders,"—neighbors, relatives or friends who were prearranged with the older person.

Similarly, the Life Safety System consists of a digital communicator that functions through standard telephone lines transmitting signals from a smoke detector or a hand-held medical alert device. When the communicator is activated, it can send three types of alarms: fire, medical emergency, or "no activity" by the user—all of which go directly to a fire department computer. This system, developed by the International Association of Fire Fighters and the Muscular Dystrophy Association, is maintained by local fire departments. While electronic services are currently limited, they will undoubtedly become more available with advances in computer technology.[1]

When In-Home Services by Hired Workers Are Resisted

Although in-home workers are a critical resource for maintaining older people in their homes, families frequently encounter resistance from their relatives to receiving such assistance. This resistance can be an outright statement of refusal or can be expressed indirectly, such as through sabotaging arrangements made by family members. Family caregivers who need time off from helping may react with anger, viewing their relative's resistance as a lack of consideration for the pressures they experience as caregivers. Common sources of such resistance are explored in the discussion which follows.

Sources of Resistance to In-Home Workers

- The need to maintain the illusion of independence
- Worry about depleting savings to pay for services
- Lack of supervisory skills
- Fear of victimization
- Racist feelings toward particular workers
- Reluctance to accept reduced contact with family members

Maintaining the Illusion of Independence

Needing to maintain the illusion of independence, older people often insist that they are managing on their own when family members are in fact providing numerous services. A daughter may drop over at lunchtime with several bags of groceries for her mother, which she puts away while catching her up on family news. She may throw in a load of wash before preparing lunch, knowing that the clothes will be ready for the dryer by the time she finishes washing the lunch dishes. As the drying cycle finishes, she may vacuum the living room and scrub the bathroom. Later, her mother may describe the visit to a friend with the remark, "My daughter came by and we had a nice lunch together," omitting any reference to the tasks her daughter performed for her.

A chore worker arriving at the door to perform these same services represents an entirely different experience for an older person. Service by a hired person makes the fact of receiving help too prominent to be denied and thereby removes the pretext of social contact as the basis for such a visit. What may have been seen as favors done by caring family members to make life more convenient become tasks for which help is necessary due to the incapacities of aging. For those whose acceptance of help from family members evolved so gradually as to be virtually unnoticed, the prospect of a hired worker providing services for even a few hours each week may require an acknowledgement of diminished independence that has been long delayed.

In dealing with this need for maintaining a sense of independence, it is important to give the older person as many choices as possible, within the limits set by the hiring of outside help. If the family has funds to hire a private-pay worker, the older person can be involved in writing the newspaper ad, interviewing applicants, and making the decision of whom to hire. Even when the older person is restricted to government-funded workers, she can maintain some control over the situation by practicing some of the supervisory skills described later in this chapter.

Worry About the Depletion of Savings

Paying for such services not only makes their necessity more prominent, but can also evoke worry about the eventual depletion of savings. The fact that the state will pay for chore services when an older person's savings balance drops to a certain level does not usually comfort someone accustomed to financial self-reliance. Those who have accumulated substantial amounts of money "for a rainy day" may resist spending money on in-home services, to their families' frustration and bewilderment. Beginning to spend even a plentiful savings account can be experienced as both opening up financial vulnerability and acknowledging that the last stage of life has arrived. Family members may feel less angered by the older person's refusal to spend money on needed services if they recognize that the dread of poverty or fear of death may lie behind the refusal.

Since inflexibility in the desire to hold onto money usually stems from nonrational sources, family members' pleas for respite or teasing comments such as, "You can't take it with you" may only serve to increase the older person's stress without affecting his inflexibility. One possible strategy for dealing with financial fears is to multiply out the cost of services for a defined number of weekly hours over a year's time to demonstrate exactly how much of the person's savings would be spent. Occasionally, comparing the size of this sum to the whole of the person's assets can help facilitate the realization that ample funds will remain for "the future," despite this opening of the financial spigot. It is also important for family members to listen to the meaning or emotion behind these fears. Expressions of financial worry may be an indirect request for a chance to talk about dying with family members.

An older person's wish to leave savings intact in order to ensure a substantial inheritance for family members is often a prime source of financial reluctance. The person may insist, "I worked hard all of my life, and I want to know when I leave this world that my family is secure." In effect, some older people transfer their own need to defend against financial vulnerability to their family. They may prefer maintaining a disheveled household or performing unsafe tasks rather than reducing their estate, since they see the size of the inheritance as a measure of their success as a parent. Occasionally, family members can convince a relative with such concerns that this stockpile of cash exceeds the family's needs and that the surplus should be used to give them peace of mind now rather than luxuries in the future.

Lack of Supervisory Skills

A common frustration to both family caregivers and older people is hired workers' poor work performance. Older people often need to learn how to provide clear instructions and appropriate supervision. When they become confident in their ability to supervise workers' performance of assigned tasks, they tend to use these services more willingly. For example, an older person may stand by silently while a chore worker vacuums the open spaces of her living room without moving a coffee table to clean underneath. The incompleteness of the task may infuriate the older person as much as her failure to correct it embarrasses her. Those who have had little experience with other people working for them can find giving instructions awkward until they practice it. Family members can help by modeling the giving of instructions in the first few sessions and working with the older person to devise a written checklist which specifies how tasks should be completed.

Copies of a checklist which can be handed to the worker at the beginning of each session can have a substantial impact on the development of supervisory confidence. Relieved of the need to remember what to ask of the worker, the older person can use the list as a step-by-step supervisory tool. For example, after a worker has cleaned the kitchen, the older person can dispense praise or correction while checking off the parts of the task specified on the list: "I see that you wiped the counters with cleanser, but it looks like you forgot to sweep under the table." Instead of feeling infuriated and embarrassed by such omissions, the older person can become skilled at making it possible for in-home workers to produce satisfaction.

Older people may need specific instruction in how to give praise without being patronizing and how to offer correction without being insulting. Some older people cause their own unhappiness with successive workers by their dictatorial, nagging, or otherwise offensive style of supervision. As with any human interaction, decency and respect in a supervisory relationship go two ways. If older people create a comfortable work environment, they are more likely to elicit good work. As a teaching tool for professionals or family members, the following list of supervisory techniques can be used with older people who need to improve their skills in this area.

Instructions for Supervising In-Home Workers

1. *Make a list of the steps for each task,* including preferences for cleansers and implements to be used, the location of these items, and reminders of parts of the task which could be overlooked, for example, "please separate out the white wash" or "please sweep under the table."
2. *Avoid following the worker around the home.* Instead, ask to be notified after each task is completed. Then, check off each step on the list that has been finished correctly and simply remind the worker if any step has been left out.
3. *Be sure to acknowledge any extra effort or thoughtfulness,* even if what has been done does not fit exactly with your specifications. It is important to focus on the person's good will rather than insignificant errors.
4. *Correct major errors by giving information rather than criticism.* Unless an error occurs repeatedly, assume that the person has been lacking information about how something should be handled within the home.

Fear of Victimization

Another source of resistance to in-home services is the fear of being victimized by the in-home worker. The thought of receiving services from a stranger while alone in the home can be frightening to older people who perceive that they could be hurt or exploited in some way. Not only are there no witnesses to what occurs between the worker and the older person, but the worker also gains access to household items which may have high monetary or sentimental value. Older people with poor vision, hearing, or memory may feel particularly vulnerable to the extent that their supervisory abilities are impaired by these deficits. Even when family members assure them that the person's references have been checked or that the state provides on-going supervision and training to chore workers, older people may still feel highly vulnerable.

On the other hand, the positive experiences of friends and neighbors can strongly influence an older person's level of receptivity to in-home services. If an older person's trusted friend vouches for the integrity of her own privately hired worker, family members can often prevent anxiety by arranging for that particular worker to serve the older person. Similarly, if an older person has a chance to observe firsthand a neighbor's warm and successful relationship with a chore worker, she may be more willing to give such services a try. Unfortunately, even a single story of someone being robbed or abused by an in-home worker can increase an older person's fears to the point that receptivity is blocked.

To begin addressing these fears, family members can offer to take time off from work or other responsibilities in order to be present during a worker's first few sessions in the older person's home. In addition to allowing time for the older person to develop enough trust to accept the service unaccompanied, this tactic permits family members to form their own impressions of the worker's reliability and competence. Often the greatest benefit from family members' presence is conveying to the worker that they will monitor the quality of the services and will be concerned about the older person's satisfaction. Later, family members may make unplanned appearances to reinforce their role as observers.

To protect the older person further, family members need to become familiar with common types of abuse by in-home workers. The most prevalent variety is the misuse of time, a problem which can often be overcome through the use of the supervisory methods described previously. Some workers will attempt to use up the available time on easy tasks in order to avoid doing the more demanding tasks. By using a checklist, the older person can structure the work sequences to leave the easiest tasks for last. Other workers may try to waste time by taking frequent breaks, making social phone calls, or attending more to the television screen than to their work. As an antidote to these delay strategies, the checklist can be emphasized as a written record of what is accomplished, subject to the scrutiny of the older person's family.

The type of abuse which is hardest for family members to monitor occurs when a worker wins, and then takes advantage of, an older person's sympathy. An older person may deprive herself of needed services by doing "favors" for her state-funded chore worker, such as signing for hours that the worker never provided, or repeatedly allowing the worker to arrive late, leave early, or bring her children to the older person's home. By sharing her personal problems, the worker plays upon the older person's loneliness and desire to be a confidant. Initially perceiving herself as a friend rather than a victim, the older person may feel she is helping out with the financial or family problems which the chore worker has described in vivid detail. The worker may even solicit "loans" of cash, which the older person provides out of this same concern. Stress from the realization that she is being abused may eventually manifest itself through the older person's sleeplessness and loss of appetite.

Older people who are abused by in-home workers may choose not to talk about the situation to family members for a variety of reasons. As in the previous example, the older person may feel protective of the worker and worry about the worker getting fired if family members complain to the agency responsible for her employment. An older person who is lonely may not want to relinquish this opportunity to be a "friend." Additionally, the older person may blame herself for the abuse in the way that a rape victim can feel guilty about not resisting strenuously enough or somehow bringing the victimization on herself. Fear of reprisal if the abuse is reported can be one of the strongest reasons for silence, especially if the older person has felt intimidated by the worker's friends or relatives who may also have entered the home, for example, "If she gets fired because I tell on her, they'll break into my house." Periodic checkups by family members are the best way to guard against such abuse and to remain aware of the nature of the relationship between the chore worker and the older person. Neighbors can be particularly helpful in their ability to scrutinize the comings and goings of in-home workers and in their capacity to drop in for a visit during the worker's hours.

Racist Feelings Toward Particular Workers

Racist feelings against particular workers may also underlie resistance to in-home services. Families and professionals may be unaware of these feelings, finding it hard to understand the older person's obstinancy. If they are aware, they may not know how to broach the issue with the older person. How racist feelings manifest themselves and how to deal with them are complex, often unspoken issues that may need to be addressed in order to assure the older person's care, family members' relief, and decent treatment of in-home workers.

While some individuals consciously implement racist attitudes in how they relate to other people and conduct their lives, others remain only minimally aware of these feelings until a life experience brings them into view. Many older people discover such feelings during hospitalization, when a member of a different ethnic or racial group assists with their bathing and dressing. Having this person make the bed or deliver a food tray may be acceptable, but being touched by this person may evoke uncomfortable reactions. Those who had previously prided themselves on their tolerance may find it painful and embarrassing to acknowledge these feelings as racism.

In contrast, those who feel entitled to their racist feelings usually have no difficulty making their feelings known to others. Family members and professionals may be faced with an older person who demands that another worker be assigned. As with any morally complex problem, family members and professionals tend to vary in their opinions about how racist attitudes should be handled in personal care situations. One view can be summarized as "You can't change lifelong beliefs, so why upset an ill person who has little time left?" Another is, "By going along with a racist reaction, you affirm it." Some take a middle ground, believing that racist statements should be corrected verbally, but that forcing an unwilling older person to adapt is not productive for either the worker or the older person.

In many instances, the older person does have to adapt, or do without the service. The head nurse in a hospital or the supervisor in a chore service agency may simply refuse to accommodate racial preferences when they are expressed. For family members who find racism offensive, the most difficult situations may be those in which they have some control over who will serve the older person, such as when they seek to hire an in-home worker privately. They may be faced with the choice of forcing adaptation or accommodating in a way that is both morally reprehensible to them and infeasible in terms of service. If family members differ in the ways they believe an older person's racism should be handled, further stress can result. For example, one family member may express sympathy with the older person's feelings while another tries to stop the disparagements, or one prefers accommodation and another believes in forced adaptation.

A particularly frustrating situation for family members is when an older person repeatedly sabotages in-home workers due to her racist feelings, but does not express them directly. The older person may pick at insignificant errors or criticize the worker's cooking, making personal remarks which are actually fueled by underlying racist feelings. When confronted, such an older person is likely to deny that anything but the worker's job performance has formed her opinion of the worker's competence. Despite family members' attempts to teach improved supervisory methods, the older person may enact a self-fulfilling prophecy by oppressing the worker so intensely with condescending comments and hovering suspiciousness that the worker responds with poor service. The older person may then use the evidence of poor service to justify her point of view.

Recognizing the futility of arguing against nonrational feelings, family members and professionals who are offended by racist terms nevertheless have the right to ask that the older person not use particular words in their presence. When an older person makes blatantly racist remarks, it may be useful to practice a less confronting style of response which does not tacitly reinforce the attitudes behind the allegations. The following dialogue illustrates this type of response:

OLDER PERSON: Did you see how the chore worker left grease on the dishes? Her kind doesn't know the meaning of cleanliness.

214

FAMILY MEMBER: Lots of people leave grease on dishes. Next time she comes, let's tell her that she needs to use hotter water and more suds.

OLDER PERSON: But they never learn, so what's the use? And if they learn anything, they're too lazy to do it right, anyway.

FAMILY MEMBER: She seems willing to learn and to work hard if we give her a chance, so let's try.

The essence of this approach is to bring generalized statements back to the immediate situation. Talking about an individual's specific actions is more helpful than arguing about perceptions of an entire race's behavior.

Some older people manage to put aside racist feelings after repeated contacts with an in-home worker. While still retaining generalized beliefs, they may rationalize that a particular worker is a lucky exception to the rule. The older person resolves the dissonance between her racist beliefs and the reality of an appreciated worker by adding a subgrouping: those who belong to a certain racial group but who manage to avoid absorbing the group's characteristics. After an older person experiences a succession of forced adaptations with a variety of workers who contradict her beliefs, she may begin to hold the idea that positive human traits have no connection to race.

Fear of Reduced Contact with Family Members

As in-home workers are hired to replace the help of tired family caregivers, some older people fear that contact with family members will decrease. By providing help with household chores, family members may have established routines of contact that will, in fact, become unnecessary when in-home workers fill these needs. Whether consciously or not, older people in this situation may seize upon the other sources of resistance to explain their not wanting hired workers to provide services. These reasons may be so eloquently articulated that family members do not realize that reduced family contact is dreaded more than the stated reasons, such as fear of financial depletion or victimization.

In such situations, family members should listen carefully to the feelings behind their relative's protests, not just the content. Offering frequent phone calls at prearranged times and setting dates for social outings are ways to reassure the older person that contact with the family will continue. Family members who are convinced that the older person will benefit from their becoming rested can best address this most basic source of resistance. By stating clearly and directly that their intention in hiring help is to prolong their ability to provide care, family members can sometimes show the older person that this action is the very opposite of abandonment.

Medical Equipment and Adaptations to the Home

The purpose of modifying the home environment is twofold: to support the older person's competence and independence, and to reduce the family's burden. A fine line exists, however, between simplifying the environment to support the older individual's capabilities and making the environment too unchallenging. For example, concerned family members might insist that a stroke victim use a wheelchair, when the person could manage with a walker. The goal of any adaptations in the home should be to develop an environment that is both supportive and challenging and has the overall effect of preventing accidents and injuries.

Lacking the skills and money required for extensive adaptations, families may feel overwhelmed when they confront obstacles to modifying their older relative's home. Every situation, however, does not require major structural changes in the home or the purchase of costly equipment. This section explores a range of practical problems that vary in the effort and resources required to solve them. Professionals can help families be creative in devising innovative strategies consistent with their own capacities. (See Chapter 6 for adaptations tailored to changes in vision, hearing, memory, and mobility.)

Medicare provides for the rental or purchase of home care equipment, so long as a physician certifies its medical necessity. The purchase prices of items such as hospital beds and wheelchairs are almost always far above the amount Medicare reimburses; as a result, equipment purchased from providers not accepting Medicare assignment may leave the older person responsible for a considerable portion of the cost. Specially adapted wheelchairs, for example, can leave the purchaser with as much as 60 percent of the cost after Medicare makes its payment, depending on how large the gap is between the allowable charge and the provider's charge. For equipment without special adaptations, providers can usually cite the amount of reimbursement that can be expected from Medicare, but may have to be pressed to do so.

Despite their expectation of using certain equipment for years, older people on limited incomes will often choose to rent rather than incur a sizable debt for the purchase of the more expensive pieces of equipment. The monthly payment of the portion of the rental fee left over by Medicare is usually easier to meet than those asked by providers on the balance of purchased equipment. Additionally, if equipment is rented during the course of receiving services from Medicare-certified home health agencies, the rental fee is covered by Medicare 100 percent for the duration of home health services, making purchase an even less attractive option for those in this position. Medicaid can be used for the purchase of equipment from providers who accept assignment, but requires prior approval from the state's health and welfare system.

Purchasing or borrowing used home health care equipment is an option which can save money, often without sacrificing safety. Nonprofit home health care agencies, senior centers, and Easter Seal, MS and Cancer Societies are examples of agencies which may maintain loan closets of medical equipment or sell reconditioned equipment. Even if such loans are only short-term, families and older people can then gauge the utility of various equipment prior to its purchase. Loans can also extend the time for families to shop around for the best prices on new equipment, or perhaps to advertise for buying used equipment from private parties. For example, posting signs in the lobbies of senior apartment buildings or senior centers may yield wheelchairs, walkers, and bath benches which people are willing to trade, sell, or give away. For the sake of safety, used equipment should be examined for loose attachments and other defects, and scrubbed thoroughly with antiseptic cleansers.

One way for families to become familiar with the range of available equipment is to request catalogs from major suppliers, such as Abbey Medical, Sears, Care Medical Equipment, and others, as listed in the Yellow Pages under "Home Health Care" or "Hospital Equipment." Obtaining these catalogs also enables families to compare cost and quality without the pressures of salespeople and the inconvenience of visiting each supplier. In making phone calls to local suppliers, the phone contact sheet on page 202 may be useful for conveniently organizing the information obtained. Some of the most important questions relate to how the supplier handles Medicare billing, for example, "Do you bill Medicare directly? Do we have to lay out the full cash payment while we wait for Medicare reimbursement? How gradually do you permit payment for the uncovered portions of purchase prices?"

The following survey of practical problems encountered in home care explains the uses of the most common types of medical equipment and home adaptations.

Home Care Problems and Solutions

1. *The older person is unable to get out of a chair, couch, or toilet without assistance.*

Wooden blocks placed under the feet of a chair or couch can often raise it high enough for an older person to stand independently. Even a younger person may have difficulty standing up from a couch in which his knees are tilted higher than his waist. The blocks can be made on home shop equipment or obtained through the rehabilitation departments of hospitals and home care agencies. Professionals in these organizations can advise how high to raise a particular piece of furniture, how to score the blocks' surfaces to prevent skidding, and how to position the body for optimum leverage. For instance, a person who moves himself forward to the seat's edge and then places his feet close in to the bottom of the chair, under his center of gravity, will be able to stand more easily than if he extends his feet away from where his body most needs support. Family members can help by reminding their relative to practice until this technique becomes habitual.

A *raised toilet seat*, attached over the existing seat, can significantly ease an older person's getting down and up on his own. Such seats are among the least expensive and most widely available pieces of home care equipment. When used in combination with a grab bar installed beside the toilet and the positioning technique described above, independent use of the toilet can often be restored.

2. *The older person is unable to get in and out of the tub without assistance.*

A *bath bench* is a small waterproof chair, placed inside the bathtub, onto which the person slides from the tub's rim. When the bench is the same height as the tub's rim and wide enough for a smooth slide, getting in and out of the tub can be dramatically simplified. The limitation is that the older person may not be able to have the pleasure of being immersed in a hot tub of water, instead being restricted to showering while seated on the bench or using a hand-held spray device. Once on the bench, some older people are able to lower themselves to the bottom of the tub, putting the bench back in the tub when they are ready to get out. Instruction from a physical or occupational therapist and experimentation with benches of different heights and sizes often yield the most successful approach. Grab bars attached to the wall beside the tub are advisable for maximum safety.

3. *The older person is unable to get out of bed without assistance.*

A *triangle*, hanging from a bar attached to the bed's headboard, can be used by the older person to pull himself to a sitting position and to exercise stomach and arm muscles. If the older person's bed lacks a headboard or if the device cannot be securely attached, a hospital bed may have to be obtained. The manual or electric means of raising the head of a hospital bed can aid with sitting up, making the task virtually effortless. As indicated earlier, adaptations which leave room for effort while increasing independence should be chosen whenever possible. For instance, a grab bar attached to the wall beside an older person's bed, along with a course

218

of exercises for strengthening his stomach muscles, might enable him to sit up on his own without removing the need for exercising.

A *transfer board* is a polished wooden or plastic slab onto which an older person can slide when moving from his bed into a wheelchair with collapsible arms. The chair wheels need to be securely locked and the board's surface may require powder to ease the slide, but an older person with sufficient muscle strength can usually learn to accomplish this transfer method independently. Often, the bed's height has to be adjusted to match that of the wheelchair, and a mattress with firm edges has to be obtained. Training in transfer techniques by rehabilitation therapists can be requested from hospital or home health care rehabilitation departments. The older person may also be able to use similar techniques for transferring himself onto a commode, toilet seat, or kitchen chair.

4. *The caregiver is unable to lift the older person out of bed, in and out of chairs, or off the floor in the event of falls.*

A *Hoyer lift* is a hydraulic device with a cloth sling. The caregiver positions the sling under the older person's body by having him roll to one side and then the other. The sling's ends are then attached to the device and a hydraulic arm is pumped until the older person is suspended in the sling. Becoming accustomed to the sensation of being suspended in this way generally requires a few practice sessions, but the advantages of being moved in and out of bed frequently are usually sufficient motivation. Families can receive rental information and instruction in the use of this device from most home health care agencies.

5. *Steps separate crucial areas of the older person's home.*

The transformation of a living room into a bedroom can make life easier for caregivers, especially spouses who may be coping with their own physical impairments which interfere with climbing steps to a second-floor sickroom. Similarly, a daughter with small children will find care less tiring if she has to maneuver fewer levels. Placing the older person's bedroom on the same floor as the kitchen eliminates going up and down steps with meals or to tend to intermittent needs. Moving the bed near a large picture window or the family meal table may have the secondary benefit of improving the sick person's mood. By being more centrally located, the bedbound person can feel less secluded and less confined by bedroom walls. A standing screen or a curtain run along tracks installed in the ceiling can create visual privacy. For an older couple residing in a large house, fuel costs saved by heating only one level could pay for respite caregivers and other benefits to ease care demands.

When the house's only bathroom is on the second floor, the technique of moving the older person's bed near a first-floor kitchen becomes complicated. A *commode,* or a portable toilet, can be used, but carrying the catchbasin upstairs to empty in the toilet can be an onerous strain on caregivers. An older person living alone may have to live with unpleasant odors until a family member or hired helper arrives to empty the commode. Nevertheless, commodes are an effective method of coping with toilet needs when accessibility is a problem. They are available from health equipment suppliers at a wide range of prices and styles.

Installing a bathroom on the level needed is often worth the cost, especially if nursing home placement is likely to result otherwise. Contractors are often willing to give estimates and recommendations regarding the feasibility of preferred locations. For example, a laundry room adjacent to the kitchen may contain the necessary plumbing, if the homeowner is willing to forfeit a washing machine hookup. Some localities have loan programs for older people needing to make such adaptations and will send out housing rehabilitation advisors. Families can contact the senior information hotline or the housing authority in the older person's community to determine a program's availability and qualifying requirements.

6. *Outdoor steps prevent the older person from getting outside without assistance.*

Installing sturdy railings alongside an older person's front steps can often prevent her becoming homebound. The psychological security of having something to hold onto may induce her to go out, as well as make her safer when she does. If steps are particularly steep or uneven, rebuilding them or constructing a wooden ramp over them is often worth the cost. The greatest disadvantage of ramps is that space proportional to the height to be surmounted is required in order to construct a safe, gentle slope. Some older people have backyards large enough for a long ramp, but dislike making their disability prominent to neighbors or resist having plywood intrude upon their beloved garden. Cost is an obstacle for others, who do not realize that retired carpenters in their area may donate their labor, or that organizations associated with churches and synagogues may supply volunteer help. In some communities, home repair programs for seniors provide free labor for such projects, if the older person pays for materials.

Another option is for a home health care physical therapist to teach the older person to maneuver on stairs. In many instances, older people with walkers and canes do not know how to properly use these ambulation aids on steps. Some may also need muscle strengthening exercises to increase their safety on steps. Combining these modifications with railings of the proper height and shape can enable some homebound people to regain independent access to the outside world.

Safety Adaptations

The rest of this section details adaptations to the home which significantly enhance safety. Among the dangers older people face in their homes, fire is one of the most threatening. Sensory impairments can impede the early detection of fires, and slower physical responses can interfere with efforts to put out small flames, to phone for help, or to exit the residence. For example, it is estimated that of all the people killed in the United States when mattresses catch fire, 42 percent are over the age of fifty-five.[2] The "Fire Safety Checklist" on page 222 can be used to survey an older person's home for the removal of fire hazards.

Falls within the home are another major danger to older people for which preventive measures can be taken. Bathrooms and kitchens are accident-prone areas because of wet surfaces and should therefore be subject to scrutiny with this in mind. The list on page 223, "Precautions for Preventing Falls," reviews precautions for the whole household.

This chapter has reviewed home care, the weakest aspect of the current long-term care system. This component has become even weaker with recent cost-saving program cuts. Some religious organizations and social service agencies have set up volunteer programs to try to meet the growing demand for in-home personal care. Yet recruiting and maintaining volunteers to perform burdensome personal care tasks is difficult. Volunteers, with diverse motivations and expectations for their altruism, are generally better suited to provide light housekeeping help and companionship rather than perform heavy household or intimate personal care tasks for an older person.

Publicly funded home health care must be expanded. Even minor changes within the existing long-term care system could make home care options more available, especially for low-income older persons. One change would be a voucher system, based on a test of the older person's functional disability, that would allow the person to purchase in-home services. Vouchers have been implemented on a demonstration basis in several states. In California, a supplemental payment through Supplementary Security Income has been allowed for attendant care. Another proposal is that every person over age seventy-five—the age when the incidence of chronic diseases and therefore functional limitations increases—should automatically receive an additional Social Security payment to allow them to purchase in-home services.[3] Currently, the

Fire Safety Checklist

_____ Light bulbs should be the proper voltage to avoid blowing fuses and causing fires.

_____ Exits to the residence should not be blocked.

_____ Ashtrays should not contain paper items and should be kept far away from the bed.

_____ The insulation around wires should be kept intact.

_____ Space heaters should be placed far away from bedspreads, drapes, and other flammable materials; they should be located out of areas where the older person walks.

_____ Rugs should not cover electric wires.

_____ Newspapers should not be stacked near the stove or near baseboard heaters.

_____ Fireplaces should be cleaned regularly.

_____ Smoke alarms should be installed in the bedroom and kitchen.

_____ The older person should establish the habit of using an egg timer when placing food on the stove.

_____ Heat controls on the stove should be easy to read.

_____ Clothing with loose sleeves (bathrobes, for instance) should not be worn while cooking.

_____ Emergency phone numbers should be displayed on the phone itself.

From Nancy R. Hooyman and Wendy Lustbader, Taking Care: Supporting Older People and Their Families *(New York: The Free Press, 1986). Copyright © 1986 by The Free Press.*

Precautions For Preventing Falls

_____ Nonskid mats or abrasive strips should line the bathtub and the floor beside the tub.

_____ The shower or bath should have at least one grab bar within easy reach.

_____ Sturdy rails should be available by all steps.

_____ Adequate lighting should illuminate steps and hallways. Light switches should be located both at the top and bottom of the stairs.

_____ Light switches should be located by the doorway of each room.

_____ A light switch or lamp should be reachable from the bed.

_____ Electric cords should be out of pathways.

_____ Rugs should be smooth, with folds and wrinkles regularly removed.

_____ Throw rugs should be eliminated unless they are secure around the edges and have slip-resistant rubber backing.

_____ Carpeting on steps should be in good condition and smoothly tacked down; steps should be sturdy and of equal height and width.

_____ A long-handled sponge mop should be available in the kitchen for mopping up spills.

_____ Areas of clutter should be cleared.

From Nancy R. Hooyman and Wendy Lustbader, Taking Care: Supporting Older People and Their Families *(New York: The Free Press, 1986). Copyright © 1986 by The Free Press.*

political and economic climate will not support such entitlements to older people. In the meantime, older people and their families should become advocates for legislative changes that can benefit future generations.

Notes

1. *Life Safety Program for the Disabled*, International Association of Fire Fighters, 1750 New York Ave, N.W., Washington, DC, 20006; Andrew S. Dibner, Louis Lowy, and John N. Morris, "Usage and Acceptance of an Emergency Alarm System by the Frail Elderly," *The Gerontologist*, 22, 6 (December 1982): 538–540.
2. Lisa Balkin, "Making Homes Safe for the Elderly," *The New York Times* (August 2, 1984): 15.
3. Judith Meltzer, Frank Farrow, and Harold Richman, *Policy Options in Long-Term Care* (Chicago: University of Chicago Press, 1981).

Suggested Resources

ARCHBOLD, PATRICIA. "Impact of Parent-Caring on Women," *Family Relations* 32 (1983): 39.
>Identifies two main types of parent-caring: care-provider who performs needed services herself and care-manager who manages service provision by others. Care-providers suffer more negative consequences and fewer positive ones than care-managers. Advocates companion and homemaker services, day care, respite care, and collective parent-sitting.

"Family Home Care: Critical Issues for Services and Policies," *Home Health Care Services Quarterly*, 3/4, (1983): 3.
>Special issue on home care for dependent family members. Discusses the demands placed on families as well as policy options.

Handle Yourself with Care: An Instructor's Guide for an Accident Prevention Course for Older Americans (Washington, D.C.: U.S. Government Printing Office, 1984).

MORONEY, ROBERT. *The Family and the State: Considerations for Social Policy* (London: Longmans Ltd., 1976). Also *Families, Social Services and Social Policy: The Issue of Shared Responsibility* (Washington, D.C.: U.S. Government Printing Office, 1980).
>Both present a model for analyzing the relationship between the family and the state in caring for dependent persons.

"Safety of the Elderly Kit," National Retired Teachers Association, American Association of Retired Persons, 1909 K Street N.W., Washington, DC 20049.
>Includes pamphlets, worksheets and checklists for community safety education programs.

SHEEHAN, SUSAN. "Kate Quinton's Days," *The New Yorker* (Nov. 21 and Nov. 28, 1983).

A moving account of the difficulties of setting up and maintaining home care and some of the abuses that can occur.

SILVERSTONE, BARBARA, and ANN BURACK-WEISS. *Social Work Practice with the Frail Elderly and Their Families. The Auxiliary Function Model* (Springfield, Ill.: Charles C. Thomas, 1983).

Views both professionals and family members as part of a supportive environment, that is, auxiliaries. Oriented primarily to geriatric social workers. Focuses on the worker–client relationship and environmental interventions, including natural helping networks and social services. Includes one chapter specifically on working with the family.

STOLLER, ELEANOR PALO, and LORNA L. EARL. "Help with Activities of Everyday Life: Sources of Support for the Noninstitutionalized Elderly," *The Gerontologist* 23, 1 (1983): 64.

A major finding was the absence of reported reliance on formal service providers. The older respondents did indicate a willingness to hire help with difficult tasks if they could afford it.

CHAPTER 10

Using Services Outside the Home

As family members and professionals often discover, the existence of specialized services outside the home does not guarantee their use by older people. Families may become especially frustrated by their older relatives' unwillingness to try services which could be beneficial. Likewise, well-intentioned professionals may be perplexed when their recruitment efforts fail to attract older people with apparent needs. The most frequent barriers to using services outside the home involve transportation difficulties and psychological reticence. At the same time that health problems force older people to relinquish car keys, other transportation options may be unavailable, inaccessible, or too expensive. This chapter focuses first on the issue of transportation, particularly the meaning of curtailed driving ability to older people and the array of alternatives to private automobiles. Senior centers, adult day care centers, and support groups are then surveyed as three out-of-home services which can be of primary benefit for reducing social isolation, once practical and psychological barriers to utilization are overcome.

Giving Up the Car Keys

For many older people, the ability to drive signifies an active, independent lifestyle. Driving is particularly important in rural areas, where distances between communities are greater and public transportation options scarcer than in cities. Depending on family members for rides may not be practical, especially if they have only one car, are employed full-time, or live at a distance. In addition, the perception that asking family members for rides intrudes on their busy lives may be accurate. Even if family members are available and willing to provide rides, the freedom to leave the home at will, without needing to ask or wait for anyone, is a privilege few people willingly relinquish.

Driving ability is particularly vulnerable to the aging process. Vision, hearing, reaction time, manual dexterity and memory are components of driving skills which typically diminish as people grow older. Even among people with adequate daytime vision, night blindness is common. Driving also entails the expense of owning, insuring and maintaining a car, costs

---

Problems Experienced by Older Drivers

Vision problems: Loss of night vision, depth perception, peripheral vision, and the ability to read signs

Memory loss: Forgetting destinations, directions, where the car is parked, and the meaning of traffic signs

Slowed reaction time: Produced by the combination of sensory deficits with slower reflexes, muscular weakness, and tremors in hands and feet

Heart problems: Physicians may advise against the episodic stress of driving and the danger of an incapacitating episode while driving.

Deficits from strokes: Visual field cut, in which a section of the visual field cannot be seen; one-sided weakness that interferes with handling the wheel and pedals; reading or communication problems

Fainting episodes, seizures, bouts of dizziness, or drowsiness: Result from neurological, respiratory, inner ear and heart conditions as well as from medications and insomnia

High blood pressure: Physicians may advise against the stress of driving.

Back problems: Spinal fractures and disk deterioration can be aggravated by driving.

Arthritic changes: Problems with manual dexterity; shoulder pain increased by the position of driving; reduced range of motion in the arms and neck

Diabetic problems: Loss of sensation in hands and feet; episodes of low blood sugar during which mental acuity may be decreased.

---

which can be burdensome for those on fixed incomes. Despite these vulnerabilities and burdens, many older people cling to their car and driver's license, symbols of their personal power and independence, with a tenacity both perplexing and frustrating to family members. Medical conditions which can impede a driver's safety are listed above, along with their implications on the road. This chart can be used for identifying an older driver's skill deficits.

Attempting to compensate for any one of these problems, older drivers may adopt a rigid driving posture. They may sit forward in the seat, grasp the wheel tightly, and keep their gaze focused directly ahead in a kind of exaggerated concentration. This posture often contributes to a reduced ability to attend to events on the periphery, such as a pedestrian starting to enter a crosswalk or a car approaching from behind during merging. A woman who tenses her neck to compensate for poor vision and hand tremors may be unable to glance back to check her blindspot. Unaware of the near-accidents she causes by merging without checking to her left, she may continue to drive for months, leaving a host of frightened drivers and pedestrians in her path.

Denial of driving errors is common to drivers of all ages. Those threatened by the physical changes of aging, however, are even more likely to blame close calls on other drivers, poor brakes, or road conditions. As indicated in the above example, older people can be oblivious to deficits which have come on gradually and almost imperceptibly, especially decreases in vision, hearing, and muscle flexibility. Denial often continues, even when passengers or other witnesses complain about blatant driving errors. A wife may repeatedly warn her husband about his near-misses, only to be told that she is too critical or "a backseat driver." Caught in a bind, she may be terrified by his driving but also fearful of his wrath if she were to enlist her daughter's support in getting him off the road. To avoid being in the car with him, she may feign illness, but then be left worrying that he will injure himself or others. When driving problems are suspected as the cause of a spouse's changed behavior, family members should try to accompany the older driver to observe firsthand the suspected deficits. After this experience, they may feel compelled to stop his driving, while finding that they are at a loss for effective strategies to do so.

Family members' initial attempts to persuade older relatives to give up the car keys usually meet with strong resistance. Many older men attach their remaining sense of personal power to their driving ability and can feel especially demeaned and emasculated by such a request. In a traditional marriage, for example, the man may have consistently assumed the driver's role, never accepting passenger status with his wife behind the wheel. Although his wife may be a competent driver, this role differentiation may be so deeply incorporated into his self-image as a protective, directive male that he resists becoming a permanent passenger long beyond the point deemed safe by his wife and family. Resistance may also stem from maintenance of an attractive car as one remaining focus of identity, time, and money, especially for those who have experienced numerous other losses. Older men often derive considerable satisfaction from polishing and tinkering with cars. The void left by removing these activities is not easily filled with other sources of comparable pride.

Sensitivity to the symbolic significance assumed by driving, in addition to its practical advantages, can help families channel their worries about an impaired older driver into constructive responses. Often, the problem can be narrowed to particular situations, such as loss of ability to merge safely onto freeways or to maneuver in congested city streets. Instead of asking their relative to surrender the car keys entirely, families can sometimes negotiate an agreement that driving be restricted to situations of optimal safety and practical necessity. They could ask their relative not to drive at twilight, or to park the car and take a bus in the crowded downtown areas. Families can also help their relative find alternative routes to necessary destinations. A parallel service road alongside the freeway might triple travel time but eliminate the problems of merging and lane-changing on the freeway. Similarly, an older person could follow a series of side roads, rather than the busy main arterial, avoiding the need to make risky left turns through traffic. In areas with handicapped parking, obtaining a disabled parking sticker permits the older person to park in specially reserved spots near a store's entrance, thereby eliminating the distracting search for parking spaces, the long walk to the entrance, and the need to remember where the car was parked.

Another strategy to increase their older relative's safety on the road is for families to offer to pay for a series of private driving lessons. To overcome resistance to this idea, families can present driver retraining in the positive light of learning to compensate for normal changes of aging as well as to brush up on driving skills and recent rule changes. Facing driving deficits under a trained, impartial observer can be easier for an older person than receiving similar information from close family members. Outside the power struggles and emotionality of his family, the older person may be able to approach his deficits less defensively and learn some skills that actually prolong his tenure as a driver. If the instructor determines that no amount of training can surmount the older person's problems on the road, facing this in impartial company may make it easier for the older person to withdraw voluntarily from driving.

Once defensiveness about deficits is overcome, adaptations to the older person's car may be a further option. Hand controls, special steering wheel grips, additional mirrors, glare-reducing glass, extra warning signals,

229

and adapted brake and gas pedals are examples of such modifications. Many older people and their families are unaware of the availability of these devices, or associate them only with severely disabled people. Families can contact their state's motor vehicle department or the occupational therapy department at their local hospital for referrals to agencies or car shops which specialize in such adaptations. Although these modifications may not solve all the older person's driving problems, they may add a margin of safety which extends the person's driving ability for months or years. In addition, during the process of testing for devices and learning their use, an older person who has resisted recognizing the extent of his impairments may become more receptive to examining them.

Rather than secretly removing one of the car's spark plugs or hiding car keys, families can help an older person relinquish this cherished instrument of freedom by exploring other transportation alternatives with him. Older people tend to want options which do not require their calling upon family members, preferring continued privacy and the feeling of control over their own comings and goings. For instance, a psychological obstacle to using public transportation can be a lack of experience with bus routes and timetables. When family members accompany their relative on exploratory trips, they help transform buses from alien conveyances to familiar and welcome options. Practice mounting the steep bus steps with a family member standing by or becoming comfortable with asking younger people to give up seats on crowded buses can gradually induce an older person to substitute public transportation for a private vehicle.

To soften the impact of the loss of driving, family members can identify in advance the aspects of the person's life which will be most affected by this change. In rural areas and suburbs where public transportation tends to be limited, it is especially crucial to plan for alternate ways to meet practical and social needs. The following questions may be useful for analyzing the older person's situation and for advance planning.

1. *What basic needs has the older person met by driving?* (food shopping, picking up medications at the pharmacy, going to the bank to deposit checks, visits to the doctor)
2. *What social activities will probably be forfeited once the older person can no longer drive?*
3. *What psychological needs may be left unmet once he can no longer drive?* (The ability to render assistance to others, time alone or away from a spouse, the stimulation of a change of scene, the release of aggression on anonymous people in other cars, the satisfaction of controlling an inanimate moving object, the role of the protector, the sense of success in owning an attractive or late-model car)

Despite a family's careful efforts, an older person may become depressed in reaction to the psychological losses just depicted. Often dictatorial passengers during the adjustment period, frustrated ex-drivers may alienate friends, family and neighbors who are trying to be supportive by offering rides. Reminders that it usually takes time for former drivers to find other ways to exert control may give substitute drivers extra patience. Families can also help by emphasizing the benefits of the change, such as increased exercise through walking or time to socialize with others while sharing rides. Gradually, as personal habits disrupted by the change fade from prominence, and as new routines fall into place, the older person's mood is likely to improve.

Expanding their relative's use of transactions by mail and phone can also help return a sense of control and independence. Many older people are accustomed to handling their banking, bill payments, and purchases in person. Unaware of other options, they do not benefit from the increasing range of business or domestic activities that can be taken care of at home, such as mobile markets for home delivery of groceries, shopping via catalogs or banking by mail. Families can support their relatives' transitions to these options by showing them how to write out an order prior to a phone call, assuring them of the safety of mailed business transactions, and assisting with the paper work entailed by catalog shopping. Despite the absence of driving, many older people derive satisfaction from continuing to conduct transactions privately and independently.

Technology holds promise for vehicular innovations, some of which may prolong the driving ability of older people with sensory deficits and other health problems. For example, video screens on dashboards are being developed which can link car computers with satellites for navigational purposes. Dashboard controls may be centralized onto the screen, taking the place of various switches and buttons which older people have difficulty manipulating. Conceivably, cameras focused on blind spots will one day project warning images onto the screen, or sensors attached to stoplights and stop signs will set off signals within cars to compensate for vision and reaction-time deficits.[1]

In the meantime, families of impaired older drivers will have to go on mediating between their safety worries and their respect for the need for independent transport. Their relatives' relinquishment of driving may be triggered by the final malfunction of a beloved old car, a minor collision, or traffic violation from running an unseen stop sign. Others may wait until they fail the vision test for license renewal or a neighbor with small children leaves an angry note in their mailbox, claiming they are a hazard on the road. For many, only a physician using medical authority to prohibit their driving convinces them that they have to stop. The negotiation of limited driving agreements, described earlier, is an effective interim strategy family members can employ while they await these triggering events. The section which follows can be used to guide an older person toward other alternatives.

Other Transportation Options

Once older people are unable to drive, alternative modes of transportation become pivotal in preventing them from becoming homebound and isolated. In areas where public transportation is minimal or nonexistent, special options designed for older people may be available. Often, these are restricted by eligibility requirements or in the number and types of trips provided. The following chart summarizes the typical options along with the problems and solutions associated with them. It can be helpful for families to become familiar with these as they attempt to identify what is offered in their relative's local community.

Transportation Options

	PROBLEM	SOLUTION
Buses	Steep steps to get up or down	Practice handling the steps along with a companion for safety; obtain special training from occupational or physical therapist.
	Bus begins moving before the older person is seated; danger of falling	Ask the driver to wait until you are seated when seats near the front are full.
	Bus stop does not have a bench	
	Bus is often crowded, with no seats available	Contact the bus headquarters; have others who use the stop sign a group letter asking for a bench.
	Bus driver discourteous; does not announce stops so older person can hear them	Practice asking younger people to give up their seats, and asking drivers to announce stops.
Cabs	Too expensive	Contact the senior information and referral line to see if programs for reduced cab fares exist in the community.
	May be slow in responding to call for service	
		Plan ahead to share a cab for shopping or doctor visits with a group of others.

Transportation Options   (*Continued*)

	PROBLEM	SOLUTION
Volunteer Escort Programs	May be limited to vital needs, such as food shopping and medical appointments Other needs, such as personal shopping or attendance at a religious service, remain unmet	Identify other participants at religious services, club meetings, and recreational activities who could offer rides. Ask one of the organizers to solicit members for a driver who lives nearby, either directly or through a newsletter.
Van Service	May be limited to certain catchment areas and in the number and types of trips they provide Driver may not have time to provide door-to-door assistance	Older neighbors who also live outside these catchment areas may be willing to form a car pool in which family members' help is rotated. Take a bus to a van's catchment area to gain personalized service for the latter half of an errand.
Trains/ Subways	Older stations may have steps instead of escalators Fear of crime, especially purse-snatching	Petition with others in the community for renovations of inaccessible public facilities. Travel without a purse; keep wallets inside clothing or attached to special belts. Travel with a companion.

Options for Reducing Social Isolation

Senior Centers

Psychological obstacles can keep older people from using services outside the home, even when low-cost transportation is convenient and accessible. Stereotypes of senior centers prevent many from attending, for example, "I don't knit or play bingo, so why should I go?" Others may reject all social events, recreational activities and volunteer opportunities specifically targetted for seniors because they dislike contact with their age peers or feel they have not yet crossed the line to join the population known as "old people." Those who value work more than leisure may stay home to devote themselves to solitary projects rather than gain contact with others through dances, trips, and dinners. For still others, the loss of lifelong friends may have created a fundamental weariness toward the idea of making new friends, blocking their interest in social activity.

Family members can induce their relative to take a second look at senior centers by obtaining detailed descriptions of the activities at the center nearest the older person's home. Some centers provide exercise and relaxation classes, writing groups, lecture series, action-oriented issue groups, and other educational programs, a far cry from knitting and bingo. Others have active volunteer task forces in which members bring meals to the homebound, help others with transportation needs, craft specialized items for disabled people, lobby for additional services, and assist with running the center. The opportunity for inexpensive, nutritious meals with others, and weekly blood pressure checks and foot care by community health nurses can be other motivations for attending. Families may place their relative's name on the center's mailing list as a way of highlighting these options and perhaps kindling interest. Accompanying their relative on an initial visit to the center is another way to overcome resistance. In such instances, families may want to phone ahead to ensure that center staff or volunteers are available to greet them. Staff can also help identify a neighbor to invite the older person to senior center events.

Older people who dislike spending time with their age peers may further support their stance by making derogatory comments regarding "what old people talk about." They may complain that conversations about the weather, aches and pains, and the price of meat bore and alienate them. Most likely, such people have been repelled by small talk all their lives. Reminding them that "old people" are simply people who have become older, family members can perhaps point out that the full range of human possibility continues throughout the life span, even among any group of "old people." By participating in activities likely to be attended by other older persons alienated by "chitchat," they may meet those who are also eager to talk at a more substantive level and who share common interests. Examples of such activities are book discussion clubs and lectures sponsored by public libraries, continuing education classes and Elderhostel at local colleges, and legislative and issue-oriented organizations, such as the Gray Panthers, the American Association of Retired People, or the Older Women's League.

For deeper and more complex reasons, many older people remain determined to avoid programs with "senior" in their titles, even if the word is attached to employment programs and meaningful volunteer involvements. For such people, the idea of living in a subsidized senior apartment complex can seem an abomination, no matter how low the rent. Similarly, the prospect of accepting discounts and other age-related benefits may offend their need not to feel segregated by an arbitrary chronological status. Living and feeling "young at heart" may be an integral part of their self-esteem, expressed in this avoidance of "senior" activities and benefits. Adult children may become impatient with their older relative's unwillingness to take advantage of age-based services, not realizing that such avoidance fills a deep need.

Family members may find it helpful to examine whether they are inadvertently limiting their relative's options. In subtle ways, families often promote traditionally "senior" pursuits and steer older relatives away from activities they perceive as youthful and therefore inappropriate. Adult children frequently feel resentful at a parent's refusal to "act his age," reacting to an inner need to maintain separate identities and to keep the parent a parent and not a peer. Some may hold youthfulness as an advantage over the parent, having looked forward to a time of life when they would be stronger or freer than the parent. Others may be unaware that their relative has interests beyond those normally assumed for older people. A man in his seventies who would have enjoyed attending a campus lecture on nuclear disarmament with his twenty-three-year-old grandson may strenuously decline the grandson's offer to drive him to a talk on "foot care" at his local senior center. The grandson may erroneously conclude, "Grandpa doesn't want to do anything anymore," never thinking to invite his grandfather along to campus with him.

Another cause of social isolation and inactivity in an older relative may be a lifelong lack of practice with leisure time. For many older people, a traditional work ethic led to mistrust of nonproductive uses of time and a strong value on hard work. Having failed to develop leisure interests earlier in life, such people can feel especially lost within the open time of retirement. In contrast, those who have enjoyed a weekly bridge game most of their adult lives are likely to continue to play the game as long as they can see, handle, and remember the cards. Some older people need encouragement to learn pleasurable uses of leisure time and to try out activities they previously scorned.

For those more comfortable working than relaxing, social opportunities that are encased in work projects may be the best options. Shrewd organizers usually manage to spot such people at club meetings and put them to work, but families may need to suggest the possibility of working while socializing to get relatives to the first meetings. Becoming a food server, helping with a club's clerical tasks, and answering phones are examples of such jobs. Families can also identify volunteer opportunities that utilize their relatives' past work skills, since such projects are ideal for forming social bonds while simultaneously satisfying an inner work ethic. The Retired Senior Volunteer Program (RSVP) is a helpful resource in this regard. When an older person feels reluctant to try out new activities, family members can help by accompanying their relative to orientation sessions or first meetings of clubs and volunteer organizations.

A relative's daily routine of doing housework, watching television, and talking with friends on the phone may appear boring and empty to busy family members. Yet such activities may reflect their relative's realistic adjustment to their life circumstances. Younger family members need to recognize that being inactive and alone does not necessarily signify boredom and loneliness. Many older people learn to derive satisfaction from contemplative activities, often watching people out their window, studying old papers and photographs, or immersing themselves in a review of memories. Some become deeply involved in the lives of soap opera characters, obtaining vicarious emotional experiences that substitute for actual occurrences. Derogatory judgments on the uses of such time can be conveyed subtly in jests and questions, for example "What did you do all day?," which can be embarrassing for older people who are trying to make the best of their circumstances.

Despite the pleasures they may be able to derive from such solitary pursuits, the loss of lifelong friends to death, incapacity, or geographic relocation can leave older people feeling profoundly isolated. Family members may parade social options before them which are stimulating in their content and intergenerational focus, but evoke only disinterested responses. Concerned family members may worry, "Don't you want to meet new people?," believing that filling the gaps left by these painful losses is essential. Paradoxically, older people who have had friendships of the most depth and devotion may feel the least motivated to try again, fully appreciating the number of conversations and shared experiences needed to build friendships of this magnitude.

The types of experiences where people cross the boundaries from themselves to others often become physically impossible in older age. Long treks in the woods, fishing trips, all-night conversations, or other activities dependent on physical capacity may no longer be options. Practical constraints, such as the need to catch a bus before dark, can also curtail conversations long before their natural endings. Even before decreased stamina and transportation logistics diminish an older person's willingness, many become weary of making friends as a result of frequent moves during their working years and perhaps a final move during retirement. Those who had long marriages may have concentrated their friendship and conversational needs in spouses, finding in widowhood that they have forgotten how to converse with others at a deeper level than polite chitchat. One of the most exasperating dilemmas of later-life friendships can be mutual short-term memory problems; for example, each tells the other detailed stories from her past, but neither remembers the other's stories.

Learning how to eat alone in restaurants is a skill which requires practice to master, but which is useful for people feeling too weary to initiate new friendships. Just being in the midst of other people can lessen an older person's loneliness. The sound of human voices, watching others come and go, and overhearing neighboring conversations can make a solitary dinner a satisfying entertainment. Bringing a book or magazine to read can also make eating alone enjoyable. After the restaurant's staff becomes familiar with a "regular," their greetings at the older person's arrival may provide a welcome sense of continuity and warmth.

Adult Day Care Centers

For some older people, the severity of their impairments makes attendance at senior centers or enjoyment of active leisure pursuits difficult. For these people, adult day care centers can provide meaningful activities as well as respite for their families. These centers offer a structured environment for social contact, mental stimulation, exercise, supervision with medications, and nutritious meals. Unlike the less structured programs of senior centers, adult day care center programs are designed to accommodate the needs of people with severe memory loss or extensive physical disability. In addition, people who would be uncomfortable at senior centers due to hearing problems, visual deficits, or speech impairments tend to be at ease in day care centers, because of the presence of others with similar limitations on social interaction.

The staff–client ratio in most adult day care centers is small enough to permit staff assistance with eating, bathroom transfers, and other personal care needs. Recreational and social activities are led by trained staff. Depending on funds, licensure requirements, or space constraints, other possible services include round-trip van transportation and nursing service for blood pressure checks, foot care, and other health needs. Quiet areas with beds are available for participants who need frequent rest. Social work staff often provide counseling and community resource referral.

Fees for adult day care depend on the range of services offered and the extent to which costs are subsidized by public and private funds. Some centers utilize a sliding fee scale, which can reduce fees to a nominal amount for low-income people. The demand is increasing for adult day facilities to become licensed as day health centers, thereby making Medicaid reimbursement possible in some states. Day health centers provide more extensive medical supervision and rehabilitation services.

In addition to cost, other obstacles may interfere with participation in adult day care. A major barrier may be the older person's resistance to attending. A trial visit to the facility with a family member can provide an older person with a firsthand acquaintance with the benefits of participation and thus remove some of her fears of the unknown. Staff are usually willing to allow family to accompany the older person to sessions until she feels comfortable with the setting. As the older person develops familiarity with the other participants, staff, and program routines, family accompaniment can be gradually tapered off.

Lack of transportation is another common obstacle. The day center may not own a van, or the older person may live outside the van's catchment area. Family members may work during the center's operational hours or live at a distance from their relative's home. At times, families can carpool with others who are transporting relatives to the center, or can organize a system of neighbors, friends and other relatives to rotate the driving.

A more difficult obstacle is when an older person who lives alone is unable to get dressed or perform other personal care tasks independently. Van or car pool arrangements may be available, but they are not of much value if no one is able to help the older person prepare to be picked up. Although van drivers will often assist center participants with the finishing touches, such as buttoning coats and getting down steps, they cannot be expected to supervise more extensive care needs regularly. In such cases, neighbors may be willing to assist with the morning preparation, especially if the older person's attendance at day care relieves them of the need to provide other forms of assistance during the remainder of the day.

Support Groups for Older People

Local chapters of organizations, such as the Lung Association, American Cancer Society, and the Arthritis Foundation, sponsor monthly educational meetings in which various speakers address a fairly stable core of participants. The core members develop bonds through their casual mingling after presentations as well as through their responses to lectures. When such programs are skillfully led, the audience volunteers anecdotes and opinions without feeling pressured to do so. Shy people control the timing of their responses, and private people choose the content of their contributions. The larger educational and social format makes acceptable the "therapy" implicit in interacting with others who are coping with similar health problems.

A framework for more focused support groups can result from such educational programs. Building on the participants' comfort and safety with each other, professionals can invite them to form smaller groups around selected themes. The group's support and self-help functions can be openly acknowledged and individuals asked to actively participate. The group leader's role is to draw out the helping abilities brought to the group by members' life experiences rather than to serve formally as a teacher or therapist. After modeling leadership skills, professionals may be able to withdraw from the group leader role, allowing participants to rotate this responsibility among themselves.

The fear of being called upon to "say something" is one of the most commonly cited obstacles to older people's attendance at such support groups. Members of the generations which reached adulthood prior to the therapeutic explosion of the 1960s generally prefer to take in information without revealing their personal concerns. Lectures allow such passive anonymity, while support groups carry an expectation that individuals will personally contribute. Older people are especially likely to reject groups led by mental health professionals, often believing that only individuals with severe psychiatric problems utilize mental health services. Free of this psychiatric stigma, educational programs possess the advantage that participants do not have to define themselves as needing help in order to attend.

Those likely to benefit the most from educational meetings and support groups often are the least motivated to attend. A persuasive response to people immobilized by an illness or bereavement is the idea that life experience is the best teacher: "Nobody can help you more than someone who's been through this." Few dispute the argument that those who have experienced a particular situation know best how to cope with it, or that gleaning practical hints from others might speed their own recovery process. Some groups are willing to send members on home visits, providing people with a sample of the potential benefits from attendance without the exertion of mobilizing themselves. This personal contact with a member combined with supportive phone calls and offers of introductions to other members then serve to motivate attendance.

Embarrassment about physical changes resulting from illness often deters people from all out-of-home ventures. A man recently confined to a wheelchair may feel keenly self-conscious, preferring to remain home rather than risk others' stares at his partially paralyzed body. A woman who needs to carry a portable oxygen tank and wear tubing in her nose may dread the curious looks of others on the street or in stores. Group meetings of stroke and respiratory clubs are ideal settings for breaking through such reticence, since everyone in attendance has firsthand knowledge of the needs bringing them together. Others' accounts of how they moved past social embarrassment often free those still encumbered by such fears. Observing people who go about their lives despite wheelchairs or oxygen tanks can have an inspirational effect that far surpasses the verbal encouragement of family members and professionals.

Hearing impairments deter many older people from attending lectures and groups. Planning to arrive early at a lecture to obtain a front row seat allows for both lip reading and maximum volume from the speaker's voice. Group leaders can encourage members to clearly enunciate their words and request that chairs be arranged to allow a close range for the sound of voices. Someone can be seated beside the hearing-impaired person to summarize the content of inaudible portions of the group discussion. Professionals in these situations need to convey a welcoming attitude toward adaptations for hearing-impaired people rather than displaying signs of annoyance or implying that the adaptations are a nuisance. In contrast, this welcoming spirit and willingness to adapt demonstrates to people who do not have hearing impairments alternatives to the common impulse to exclude hard-of-hearing people from their activities.

Driving a relative to and from group meetings can seem to be one more burdensome task to family members, who perceive it as less vital than tasks directly related to the older person's physical health. However, professionals can portray such group involvement as an investment in the eventual reduction of their care responsibilities, since improvements in their relative's motivation and mood may result in increased self-care efforts. In addition, as family members talk informally with each other before and after meetings, supportive relationships among them tend to evolve. Car pool arrangements may develop as well as exchanges of health care equipment and supplies, tips about specialized community services, and joint ventures beyond the meetings, such as recreational outings and shared care arrangements.

Transportation, especially in rural and suburban areas, is often the greatest obstacle for older people who want to take advantage of services outside the home, such as support groups. The older person who has to give up driving faces more transportation barriers than alternatives. Subsidized escort services tend to focus on transporting older people to essential appointments and not for visiting or recreation. Even when adequate public transportation exists, older people may be deterred from using it by their fear of crime and their unfamiliarity with the system. To some older people, automated bus and subway systems are not welcoming, but rather a confusing maze of computer screens and escalators. Passenger cars are generally not suitably equipped for a physically impaired person. Clearly, transportation is a critical area for program development and the advocacy efforts of older people and their families.

Transportation difficulties may also underlie the fact that a high percentage of day care centers are not operating at full capacity.[2] This underutilization also reflects the fact that many centers do not reach the most impaired older people, where the caregivers' need for respite is greatest. Because of budgetary limitations, most adult day care centers are unable to accept severely demented people who wander, are incontinent, are combative, and require close staff supervision. Adult day care centers with a staff–client ratio that permits the care of severely impaired older persons are sorely needed. Without heavily staffed centers, the families who most need the relief and the older persons most in need of supervision remain at risk.

Notes

1. *New York Times* (December 13, 1984): 34.
2. Nancy Mace and Peter Rabins, *The 36-Hour Day: A Family Guide to Caring for Persons with Alzheimer's Disease, Related Dementing Illness, and Memory Loss in Later Life* (Baltimore: Johns Hopkins University Press, 1981).

Suggested Resources

MELTZER, JUDITH, FRANK FARROW, and HAROLD RICHMAN. *Policy Options in Long-Term Care* (Chicago: University of Chicago Press, 1981).
> An excellent collection of essays on long-term care policy that consider future options, cost constraints, and underlying dilemmas of who should be served in a time of scarce resources. Provides a policy framework for services discussed in this chapter.

The OWL Observer: National Newspaper of the Older Women's League, 3800 Harrison Street, Oakland, CA 94611.
> OWL is a national organization with chapters throughout the country. The major issues of concern are access to health care and health insurance for older women, Social Security, pension rights, and caregiving. They are a major resource for advocates wanting to increase services and their accessibility outside the home.

SILVERMAN, PHYLLIS. *Mutual Help Groups: Organization and Development* (Beverly Hills: Sage Human Services Press, 1980).
> A how-to book about building mutual help and support groups. Guidelines are applicable to the elderly.

U.S. DEPARTMENT OF HEALTH AND HUMAN SERVICES. *A Guide to Medical Self-Care and Self-Help Groups for the Elderly* (Washington, D.C.: National Institute on Aging, 1980).
> Reviews findings on self-care and self-help groups; lists major self-help groups.

CHAPTER 11

Alternative Living Situations

Many options exist between living alone in a private residence and going to a nursing home. Yet older people and their families often dread the last resort without learning about the intermediate alternatives. In other instances, families grasp at the idea, "If we could only find someone to live with Mom, she'd have help whenever she needed it." The possibility of paying someone through the provision of room and board seems attractive when compared to the cost of hiring hourly help. When they attempt to find live-in helpers, however, families discover that few people are willing to accept such positions. The first part of this chapter discusses realistic expectations and terms of employment for live-ins, as well as specific hiring strategies. Home sharing arrangements are then depicted, followed by a question and answer section differentiating the other care alternatives: retirement homes, subsidized apartments, adult foster homes, and congregate care settings. The kinds of resistance felt by older people as they face leaving long-term homes for these alternative situations are described. The chapter concludes with ways to help with the wrenching task of packing up a lifetime's accumulation of possessions and with adjusting to a new residence.

Hiring a Live-In

Prior to attempting to hire a live-in helper, it is important for families to distinguish between applicants intending to share a home with an older person and those wanting to provide a primary service. Homesharers expect to reduce their personal expenses by living with an older person, usually planning to attend school or work at the same time. The other type of applicant views caregiving as employment, expecting a salary in addition to room and board. While the distinction can become blurred in practice, starting out with this framework helps families weigh their relatives' care needs and finances against the likely realities of the live-in applicant pool.

As this distinction implies, home-sharing applicants seek a living situation different from that of salaried helpers. For example, an older woman needing only companionship at dinner and someone's presence in the house at night might be able to rent a room to a student at a discounted rate. If she later wanted the student to take over her household chores, she could offer free rent and a small cash payment. In contrast, a woman needing someone to prepare and serve her three meals a day, along with helping her to and from the bathroom at unpredictable times, would not be able to attract someone with school or job commitments. She needs to seek a person who regards caregiving as a primary occupation, and offer a salary reflective of both the tasks involved and the short supply of such helpers.

The degree of restriction on personal freedom is one of the key aspects considered by home-sharing applicants as they choose a living situation. If an older person's personal care needs can be managed during the early morning and late evening, for example, these duties would not interfere with out-of-home daytime commitments. Similarly, the chores and errands that can be performed on an impromptu basis, in and around other involvements, may be acceptable in exchange for free rent. As a general rule of thumb, tasks requiring daytime availability, such as assistance with midday medications, eating, wheelchair transfers, and cleaning up after incontinence episodes, rule out unsalaried live-in arrangements.

When family members realize that paying a salary is unavoidable, they next face the reality that financial compensation is only one of the factors considered by applicants choosing a live-in position. Since the demand for live-in helpers tends to far exceed the supply, families usually need to work to make their relative's situation as attractive as possible. The following chart can help family members identify the advantages and disadvantages of the situation they are offering and enable them to promote the former while they try to correct the latter.

*Factors Which Prospective Live-ins Consider
in Choosing Employment*

- *Privacy of the living accommodations*—Is a private room available? How separate is it from the older person's living area? Is there a

243

private bathroom? Use of kitchen facilities? Space for having own guests?

- *Nature of the care needs*—Does the older person need assistance or wander during the night? Is incontinence a frequent problem? How much lifting is required? Are the care needs constant and anxiety-producing?
- *Household cleanliness and order*—Is the home pleasant to spend time in? Are there odors or areas of clutter? Is the helper expected to make up for pre-existing deficiencies?
- *The older person's personality*—Is the person dictatorial, demanding, or manipulative? Is there a feeling of respect toward the helper or will the older person try to undermine the helper's efforts?
- *Availability of transportation*—Are family members able to drive the helper to and from the home? Is public transportation nearby? Will the helper be expected to provide transportation for the older person?
- *Degree of support from family members and friends*—Will the helper be left in a lurch if the care needs suddenly become more difficult? Are people available to be called upon in emergencies or for respite care?

Of these factors, family members and friends' support is frequently most important to live-in applicants. They want to be able to rely on substitute help to come promptly on their days off, as well as on someone to relieve them when they have a personal emergency. Experienced live-ins prefer situations in which families espouse a spirit of partnership in the care, rather than an attitude of dumping all responsibilities on the live-in. Applicants find that the availability of next-door neighbors who will step in for an hour or two while they run their own errands, exercise, or tend to incidental needs is especially appealing. Family members can demonstrate their sensitivity to this need for ongoing support by providing a list of nearby friends and relatives willing to assist the live-in helper.

Days off are another key issue for prospective live-ins. Most insist on two twenty-four-hour periods per week when they can leave the residence and forgo all responsibility for the older person's needs. Some will request weekends off, while others will ask only for consecutive days off or single days at a time. Families who present applicants with an organized plan for substitute help will tend to have more hiring success than those less prepared to deal with this problem. Experienced candidates may have been previously burned by families who did not plan for substitutes and then forced them to give up their days off.

Live-in applicants often have unspoken concerns about whether the older person is likely to die soon after they move in. While some prefer short-term commitments, others desire a situation in which they can settle in for a long stay. Applicants may ask family members detailed questions about the older person's health status, without divulging this concern as the motive underlying their question. It is helpful for family members to be prepared to address this issue, perhaps by asking applicants to state during the initial interview their ideal length of employment. Family members may want to offer final candidates a chance to discuss these concerns privately with the health professional who is involved in the care situation.

Prior to placing ads and setting up interviews, a final step is to determine whether the older person has strong racist feelings that will complicate the hiring process. Some older people are explicit with family members about their racial attitudes, while others express their feelings by covertly sabotaging the hiring of particular individuals. In some localities, for example, a large proportion of the applicants will be newly arrived immigrants with minimal English-speaking ability. However uncomfortable the issue may be for family members, advance awareness of the older person's feelings can prevent awkward or hurtful moments for applicants. A professional's skills can also be enlisted here to help the older person become more realistic about the paucity of choices and to begin facing the need to adapt (see Chapter 9).

The Mechanics of the Hiring Process

Senior citizens' hotlines, senior centers or home health agencies often maintain listings of those seeking salaried live-in positions. Occasionally, job programs at community colleges or state unemployment offices will accept such listings. Posting notices in neighborhood laundromats and supermarkets may reach applicants attracted to living in particular neighborhoods. Another effective means is placing ads in community newspapers, church or synagogue bulletins, and advertising supplements with local neighborhood distribution.

Becoming adept at screening applicants over the phone and eliminating inappropriate callers is a time-saving skill. The following questions can help families separate out people they want to interview from those placed on a backup list.

Questions for Screening Live-In Applicants over the Phone

1. Why are you interested in living with an older person? Have you done this before?
2. What employer and landlord references do you have in the local area? Can you give me their phone numbers?

3. Do you drive? Do you own a car? Is access to public transportation necessary?
4. What are your usual bedtime and waking hours?
5. Are you a smoker? Do you use alcohol?
6. Do you expect to be able to entertain friends in the home?
7. (Read off a specific list of tasks and expectations.) How do these sound to you?

The following sample ad may be useful to family members as a basis for devising their own. Generally, ads for salaried live-ins should stress the family's support, days off, and the nature of the care responsibilities. Since waiting at home for calls can be a nuisance, the family member who volunteers to screen calls should select a narrow time period for receiving calls, for example "between 7:00 and 9:00 P.M. weekdays." Telephone answering machines ease the intrusiveness of this process, but discourage applicants uncomfortable with leaving messages. Those who are currently in live-in positions, for instance, usually do not have a private phone number to which a call can be returned. Additional statements in the ad to help applicants screen themselves include "nonsmokers only," "experience necessary," and "must have local references."

SAMPLE AD

Older woman recovering from a stroke
needs a LIVE-IN HELPER

• Salary offered and free room
  and board

• Two days off per week

• Private living area

• Family nearby and involved

• Meal preparation, personal care,
  and household chores, but no lifting
  or strenous tasks

CALL: 683-9162, 7–9 PM, Mon–Thurs

Some older people fear that prospective live-ins who tour their homes are "casing" the house for a break-in. In these instances, setting up initial interviews at other locations is advisable, such as meeting for coffee at a restaurant. Once applicants are narrowed down to a few choices, second interviews can be held at the home to include both a detailed tour and a chance to converse with the older person. Conducting initial interviews in this way has the further advantage of allowing applicants to ask questions they would withhold in the older person's presence, thereby giving family members a glimpse of their attitudes toward older people.

It is helpful for families to have a list of questions for the interviews. Possible topics include the applicant's family background, past job experiences, places lived and traveled, food and music preferences, favorite television programs, uses of leisure time, and other nonintrusive yet personal areas of discussion. Having the older person ask these questions establishes an immediate involvement in the hiring process and conveys to the candidate that the family respects their relative's judgment and supervisory role. Watching how applicants respond to the older person often reveals more about their competence and compatibility than the content of their answers. For example, someone who persists in directing her responses to family members, as if their relative was incompetent or insignificant, shows inherent disrespect for older people. Likewise, candidates who fail to ask the older person questions about her life history or personal preferences demonstrate their disinterest in these areas. A serious red flag is an applicant who supplies names of references who cannot be reached by phone, or references whose prior relationships with the applicant are only vaguely linked to employment. Even in circumstances with no other available live-ins, it is preferable for families to extend their search efforts rather than risk hiring a skilled con artist.

Another issue which may arise during the interview process is whether Social Security contributions are to be deducted from salary payments. Some salaried live-ins prefer that payments not be filed with the government, while others insist upon Social Security contributions and proper recording. These stipulations may conflict with family members' preferences, such as those who want to maintain careful records for tax purposes or those who view the paperwork needed for legal filing as a nuisance. To determine legal requirements, families can phone the local Social Security office listed in the phone book and inquire about the salary level at which payments to household employees must be declared through quarterly filing. The form for obtaining an employer's identification number can be obtained by calling the Internal Revenue Service. After the first filing, forms are mailed quarterly by the IRS and are relatively easy to complete.

The following is a sample agreement in which the terms of employment can be specified. While many families are inclined to believe the relationship will work on "good faith," putting these terms in writing avoids misunderstanding, prevents future problems, and lends an organized formality to the hiring process.

SAMPLE
Salaried Live-In Helper Agreement

1. *Room and Board:*
   We will provide three meals a day and a private room.

2. *Salary:*
   We will pay $_____ gross weekly. $_____ will be deducted for Social Security, leaving a net pay of $_____.

3. *Time Off:*
   We will provide two twenty-four hour periods off per week, on _____ and _____. At least one week's notice should be given if these days need to be changed.

4. *Extra Work Days:*
   If substitutes for days off fail to arrive, the rate of pay for extra work days is $_____ in cash.

5. *Duties of the Live-In Helper:*

   _____

   _____

   _____

   _____

   _____

   _____

6. *Termination of the Agreement:*
   Either party can terminate this agreement with two week's notice. If a hospitalization occurs, full pay will continue for _____ days. $_____ per day will then be accrued if the helper does not seek other employment, payable in a lump sum once the hospitalization ends.

Employer _____ _____
                    (Signature)   (Date)

Live-In Helper _____ _____
                        (Signature)   (Date)

When the Older Person Resists Live-In Help

Some older people express indignation when they learn that a live-in helper is to be paid a salary as well as room and board. Those who do not perceive the extent of their care needs, or the disadvantages of their living situation from an applicant's perspective, may believe that family members are foolishly throwing away money by offering a salary, for example, "We have to pay her to live in such a nice home?" If the salary is to be paid from the older person's funds, these perceptions can become a substantial obstacle during the hiring process. In some instances, a professional's experience in this area can convince an older person that the salary level is indeed realistic and that the outlay is well worth the services to be rendered. In addition, family members can use the checklist below to enumerate the advantages that will accrue if the arrangement is successful.

Advantages of Successful Live-In Arrangements

- *Sense of security at night*—Having someone in the home during the night is comforting.
- *Improved nutrition*—Having company at meals increases both appetite and motivation to prepare interesting foods.
- *Increased visitors to the home*—Friends of the live-in helper can expand social contacts, making the home more lively and stimulating.
- *Economically practical*—The cost of hiring a similar amount of help on a per day basis is much more expensive.
- *Prolonging the family's ability to help*—Having someone to help in the home spares family members driving back and forth for incidental needs, and reduces their overall stress by enabling them to focus on social rather than practical needs.

An older person who has never lived with anyone but a spouse, parents, or siblings may feel frightened or intruded upon by the image of a stranger residing in the home. Worries about what this unknown person will do can multiply to the point where the older person tries to disrupt the hiring process or bargains with family members to drop the whole idea, for example, "If I promise not to ask you to come over so often, can we do without this?" Some interpret the family's desire to hire a live-in as punishment for their requests for help, while others regard it as an indication that family members are tired of them and want to have less contact. As family members attempt to prevail over such resistance, the potential for hurt and misunderstanding can be extensive.

When initiating the idea of live-in help, families can be most persuasive and least hurtful if they explain the advantages from their perspective rather than telling their relatives "You'd have someone right here to talk to." A more forthright and honest statement is "We would not feel so worried about your loneliness if you had someone here with you." Likewise, a statement such as "You wouldn't have to wait to get things done" is not as direct nor convincing as "We wouldn't feel so pressured to come over each time you need help." When family members admit their own worry and exhaustion as legitimate motives for hiring a live-in, they take responsibility for initiating the hiring process and for the benefits they will gain. The rest of their assurances then become more believeable.

An older person's fear of abandonment by family if a live-in takes over care responsibilities should also be discussed directly, for example, "It's not that we'll stop coming over, but that we'll be able to spend time with you in other ways." Some of the intensity of this fear can be alleviated by planning an evening each week for a family outing. Another option is for family members to arrange to fill in on the helper's days off, instead of hiring substitute help. While not always possible, such joint arrangements convey the sense that the live-in will supplement the family's help rather than replace it.

Other worries possibly harbored by an older person at the prospect of a live-in helper are portrayed in the following vignette:

> Will I ever get to have solitude? What if she hovers around me all the time? I might not like her cooking. What if she eats me out of house and home? She might want to have a man stay overnight in her room. What if she brings in guests I don't want in my house? How about a stereo blasting when I'm trying to get some sleep? She might watch television programs I don't like. What if she hogs the telephone or runs up long distance bills? What if she isn't tidy enough to suit me?

When people share a residence, a certain amount of friction is inevitable, usually arising in the areas suggested by this vignette. One strategy is to air some of the predictable concerns during the interview process, allowing the applicants to react to them specifically, for example, "How would you handle the need for privacy and solitude? Do you expect to have overnight guests?" Another way to relieve worry about potential disagreements is to enact a two-week trial period after the live-in is hired. A trial period gives both parties a chance to evaluate the situation and to attempt to resolve conflicts through negotiation and compromise. In addition, family members can enlist the services of a professional for a mediation session midway through this period to ensure that grievances are addressed rather than held in as resentments. Family members possessing mediation skills can adapt the negotiation techniques described for family meetings in Chapter 3.

Home-Sharing Arrangements

As depicted earlier, the attitudes and expectations of people interested in sharing a home differ widely from those of individuals applying for employment as live-in helpers. A guideline for older people wanting to attract homesharers is to view themselves as landlords rather than employers. They must offer a situation based on the fair exchange of benefits, recognizing that they will retain people only as long as the living situation's advantages outweigh the practical restrictions. The challenge

250

is to determine which benefits to offer and how much to expect in return, since an advantage for one person may be regarded as a restriction by another. For instance, an older housemate might perceive companionship as a mutual advantage, while a younger housemate might have competing social interests that make such expectations a chore rather than an advantage.

Agencies to match homeseekers with those hoping to share their homes exist in many communities. After a match is made, home-sharing staff may assist with negotiating conflicts that develop from living together. Home-sharing agencies can also help older people assess the terms they are offering against the pool of homeseekers in that particular community. College towns usually have students seeking housing every fall, which increases the likelihood that older people in these areas can charge rent for rooms in their houses. In other communities, the housing market may be such that better terms need to be offered to draw applicants. Whether they use a matching service or not, people offering their homes should narrow their expectations to specific guidelines and realistic terms. The following list portrays the most common reasons that older people give for wanting to share their homes and the ways these reasons can be translated into concrete expectations.

Expectations in Home-Sharing Situations

"Someone in the house with me at night"	Every night? Could the person go away on weekends? At what time in the evening would you want the person at home?
"Someone to eat meals with me"	Which meals? How often? Who prepares the meals and who cleans up afterwards?
"Someone to help with the chores"	Which chores? How often? Laundry? Food shopping? Who scrubs the bathroom?
"Companionship; someone to talk to"	Do you expect the person to be home with you every evening? Saturday and Sunday? Is companionship at the evening meal enough?
"Shared expenses"	Are utilities to be divided? How is the food budget to be determined? What items are personal expenses?
"Someone to run errands and give me rides when I need them"	How available does the person have to be? Is the use of your car involved?

Homeseekers also need to be prodded during the interview process to delineate exactly what they hope to gain from the living situation. For instance, a woman with a young child may identify "help with child care" as one of her goals in seeking a shared home. Does this mean that she expects the older person to be home when the child returns from school each day? How many evenings per week does she hope to leave the child in the older person's care? Some home-sharing agencies have staff to help with such interviews to ensure that key questions are asked and that both parties clarify their expectations. In lieu of this service, family members can offer to be present during the interview to lend support and to help later in deciding between applicants.

Some older people refuse to consider housemates considerably younger than themselves. Citing lifestyle differences, they believe that the generations are too different to share living situations. Since people generally prefer to remain in long-term homes, a greater number of older people want to share homes than seek homes. Those who prefer someone close to their own age thus face a limited pool of possibilities, unless they decide to give up their home in order to move in with others. It can be helpful to ask an older person to identify the generational differences that seem most divisive and to venture solutions to the hypothetical conflicts. For instance, the fear that "stereos will be blasting at all hours" can be countered with the suggestion of establishing quiet hours when both parties agree to minimize music and other noises.

Conflict around the practice of sexual freedom is a key problem dreaded by many people in this position: "I couldn't stand it if my housemate had a man stay overnight in her room." Some dislike the idea of a man visiting a housemate in her room at any time, insisting that guests remain in the common areas of the house. For others, worry about guests centers on privacy issues more than on sexuality, for example, "I don't want to step out of the shower and find a strange man in the hallway." These are issues which should be aired during the interview process. One way is for the older person to state her preferences clearly, allowing applicants with contrary intentions to rule themselves out. Another solution is for the housemate to stay overnight on weekends at her friend's house rather than violate the older person's sense of propriety or privacy.

When the services of home-sharing agencies are unavailable, family members can assist by placing ads as described earlier. The following is a sample ad that can be adapted to individual circumstances. Home-sharing ads should emphasize the freedom to pursue outside commitments and any features of the residence that enhance personal privacy.

Similar to landlords checking applicants' references and finances, older people should verify information given by home-sharing candidates. It is also advisable to obtain a sample rental agreement, comparable to that

252

used by apartment managers. This agreement can be used to devise a written statement of rent to be paid, amount of notice to be given upon termination, and other pertinent issues. Services that are to be rendered in exchange for free rent should be itemized on the written agreement to prevent future misunderstandings.

An older person with organizational skills and sufficient motivation could join with one or two friends to purchase or rent a large house, and rent out the remaining rooms to people obtained through such ads. Intergenerational group homes are becoming popular among healthy older people who enjoy collective living. Sharing expenses, housekeeping tasks, meals, and companionship offer obvious financial and social advantages. Such living arrangements also contain an inherent caregiving potential, due to the number of household members. If one of the members becomes ill, many hands are available to give assistance and to fill in for missed chores and other tasks for the duration of the illness.

Although home-sharing options are increasing in number and popularity, professionals and families need to be sensitive to the fact that some older people are uncomfortable with shared living arrangements. Those accustomed to arranging their possessions in the same way for years or who jealously guard their privacy may prefer to endure loneliness or high housing costs rather than accept intrusions on their personal habits.

Retirement Homes, Subsidized Apartments, Foster Homes, and Congregate Care

Many older people and their families are unaware of housing alternatives. They may confuse the term "congregate care" with nursing home care, or assume that retirement homes are rest homes. This next section explains these housing options and ways to choose among them.

1. *What is a simple way to distinguish between retirement homes and nursing homes?*

A definition which removes confusion is: "A retirement home is an apartment complex with extra services included in the rent." Frequently, family members and professionals praise a particular retirement facility without realizing that the older person pictures a "home" where people lie in bed and receive nursing care. The requirement that residents manage their personal needs independently should be emphasized as well as the fact that individual units are locked as in any apartment situation. Extra services that are usually part of the rental fee are meals, light housekeeping, and recreational programming. The following checklist can be used for comparing the services of different retirement homes. It also can help serve as an overview of the advantages of such facilities for skeptical older people.

2. *What is meant by "senior housing" or "subsidized senior apartments"?*

In various localities, federal and state funds have subsidized the construction of apartment complexes for older people. These buildings are usually designed to be accessible for the disabled and are often located near shopping and other services. The rent is adjusted to a percentage of the older person's income, but most types of subsidized housing disqualify applicants whose assets exceed certain limits. Information can be obtained from the city or county housing authority in the older person's community. Most of these buildings offer few services beyond an on-site manager and vans to take residents shopping once a week. Meals are normally prepared by residents in their own apartments.

3. *What are the "founder's fees" and "buy-in plans" offered by retirement homes?*

Some facilities require a large initial payment, called a founder's fee or buy-in plan, which guarantees the residents access to a nursing home within the retirement complex or other care services. Although this guarantee may seem attractive, such large initial fees are a gamble that the older person's care needs will eventually justify the investment. In some cases, these initial fees do not cover the full cost of nursing home care, such that the older person who later requires skilled nursing care may face unanticipated additional costs. If the fee is entirely nonrefundable, signing a contract with the facility also removes the older person's freedom to change her mind. In all cases, the older person and a family member should read the contract carefully, and be encouraged to ask questions about parts of the contract they do not understand.

254

Checklist for Comparing Retirement Homes

_____ *How close is the facility to the nearest family member's home?* Is there easy access to public transportation? Are vans available for transportation to shopping or medical appointments?

_____ *What are the duties of the on-site manager?* Are call buttons in the apartment answered by staff 24 hours a day?

_____ *How often is a nurse on duty?* Is assistance with medications provided? Are the services of an infirmary available?

_____ *What kind of recreational programming is provided?* Is there a comfortable and accessible activity room or lounge area? Where do people congregate?

_____ *Are laundry facilities conveniently located in the building?* Is linen service included? Is help with laundry obtainable? Are housekeeping services provided as part of the rent?

_____ *How often is meal service in the dining room?* Is the number of meals negotiable? Are they served at the table or cafeteria style?

_____ *Are there safety rails in the bathrooms?* Does each apartment have individual heat controls? Do the windows open?

_____ *How large are storage areas in the apartments?* Is additional storage available elsewhere in the building?

_____ *Is the kitchen fully equipped in each apartment?* Is private telephone service available in each? How soundproof are the apartments?

_____ *Are guests allowed on a per meal basis in the dining room?* Is there a room or apartment available on a per day basis for out-of-town visitors?

_____ *What is the nature of the surrounding neighborhood?* Are there safe places to walk and interesting destinations nearby? How close is the nearest bank, pharmacy, or grocery store?

_____ *Does the waiting list require a fee?* How long is the average waiting period?

_____ *Can rent be paid on a month-by-month basis,* or is there a founder's fee, buy-in plan, or other initial payment? Is this fee refundable on a prorated basis if the person leaves the facility?

4. *What level of independence is required for admission to most retirement homes, and what happens if the older person's health condition deteriorates while she resides there?*

As part of the selection process, family members should ask admissions directors the circumstances under which residents are requested to leave the facility or not permitted to return after a hospitalization. While most retirement homes are explicit about admission requirements, some are vague about their termination policies. An admission criterion for almost every retirement home is that residents transport themselves independently to the dining room. Individual residents who become more frail may be permitted to use wheelchairs for long distances; some homes, however, do not allow wheelchairs under any circumstances. Another admission criterion for most retirement homes is the ability to dress and bathe independently. If the older person's condition deteriorates, some homes permit personal care aides to be privately hired, whereas others insist that a resident needing such help be moved to another facility.

5. *What are the chief benefits of moving to a retirement home?*

Having neighbors in such close proximity and organized activities on the premises can dramatically reduce social isolation and boredom. When the evening meal, and perhaps other meals, are served in a common dining room, cooking tasks are eliminated and the stimulation of eating with others is added. Retirement home living for a couple ensures that when one spouse dies, the other can rely on established and available social networks during the bereavement and adjustment process.

6. *Why do monthly rates of retirement homes vary so widely?*

Retirement homes affiliated with religious organizations and those sponsored by other nonprofit organizations are generally less expensive than for-profit, privately owned facilities. Rental rates are also affected by a facility's age, its location, and the range of services included in the monthly fee. Rates sometimes vary widely within a single facility due to differences in apartment size and in the meal and care plans selected. When older people and their families decide in advance what they most want from a retirement home, they can more easily compare costs and services as they visit different facilities. For some, choosing the facility closest to a family member's residence is paramount, while cost is the deciding factor for others.

7. *Does Medicare or Medicaid help pay the cost of retirement homes?*

Medicare only pays for certain types of skilled care in nursing homes. Medicaid, or state-administered programs of medical assistance, pays for custodial or "intermediate" care beds maintained by some retirement homes on a limited basis.

8. *What are "adult foster homes" or "care homes?"*

These are private homes in which up to four older people receive care from a person licensed by the state. Regulations vary regarding the residences' physical layout and accessibility, the type of meals served, and the training levels of the people who deliver the care. Families can obtain a list of licensed residences from the division of the state's health and human services responsible for long-term care. Older people who meet the state's requirements for Medicaid nursing home funding are usually also eligible for payments to adult foster homes. As with nursing homes, the monthly fee paid by states to these homes tends to be less than private-pay rates. As a result, the better homes tend to avoid accepting Medicaid residents, preferring the few hundred dollars more per month possible from private payees. At this writing, private charges range from $600 to $800 per month, depending on the level of care required. Adult foster homes are thus significantly less expensive than private rates in nursing homes.

Before selecting one of these homes, family members should carefully interview the people who deliver the care. They should also follow up with frequent visits to ensure the quality of services. At their best, care in these homes is personalized and the atmosphere more homelike than in institutions. At their worst, an older resident is vulnerable to neglect and abuse due to the infrequent inspections and minimal licensing requirements.

9. *What is meant by "congregate care?"*

This term is used to designate a wide variety of settings. The smaller facilities in remodeled houses differ from the "care homes" described previously, in their having from five to ten people in residence. Others with individual cooking facilities in the rooms and recreational services resemble retirement homes. Distinctions become blurred in the upper range of such facilities. Whether a setting is licensed for Medicaid reimbursement as an "intermediate care facility" (ICF) is crucial for Medicaid recipients. Intermediate care signifies basic custodial services and minimal nursing supervision, suitable only for those who are semi-independent and not in need of skilled nursing care.

Resistance to Alternatives

While searching for suitable alternatives to home care, family members often find that they are more enthusiastic and motivated than their relative. The older person may acknowledge her need for increased safety, services and social contacts, yet sustain a reluctance that outweighs her rational agreement with family members' suggestions. A fundamental inertia against a change of this magnitude, deep attachment to a lifelong home, love for a pet who cannot be brought along, dislike of high-rise apartment buildings, and worry about living among a "bunch of old people" are common sources of resistance to such moves.

In both emotional and practical payoffs, family members almost always stand to gain more initially than does their relative. They may look forward particularly to relief from the responsibility of maintaining their relative's house. Their honest statement to this effect provides the older person with an external motivation for moving: "We're now taking care of your house and ours. If you move to a retirement home, we could take care of just one house and use the leftover time and energy to spend enjoyable time with you." The move then becomes a means for the older person to give something to her family: "I'll move so that my daughter won't have to do all that extra work."

No matter how they present the reasons for a move, family members may need to wait for a precipitating event that overcomes their relative's resistance. Family members may be less frustrated if they anticipate the human tendency to make changes in response to painful experiences rather than a desire for future benefits. An older person who struggles daily with steep steps is not likely to find this sufficient reason to leave a lifelong home until she has a frightening stumble. Although family members may dread her breaking her hip in a fall, a close call may be necessary before her fear is strong enough to make a move appealing. Fortunately, a less dangerous event such as the breakdown of a water heater or major repairs to a roof often serves as the "last straw," causing an older person to conclude that remaining in her house has become too difficult.

In addition to emotional inertia as a source of resistance, home ownership may be integral to the person's identity. A house and yard often function as an extension of the self. Those who have tended gardens for years may continue to derive considerable satisfaction from this form of self-expression. For others, the house itself may be something to show for years of hard work and mortgage payments. Frequently, a house provides older people with their only remaining ways of spending time meaning-fully: "If I move to an apartment, I'll have nothing to work on." When a garden or a workshop is unavailable in the proposed residence, older people's fear of idleness may outweigh the advantages of moving.

One of the most formidable forms of reluctance arises from relation-ships with pets. Although many people maintain deep attachments to pets throughout life, pets can assume the heightened importance of sole companions for isolated older people. Ever-available, affectionate, and noncritical, pets afford older people who live alone the opportunities to talk out loud and express emotion. Some actively chitchat with their pets and satisfy their need to nurture by spoiling their pets. For such older people, parting with a pet in order to move into a retirement home may constitute an insurmountable obstacle. An occasionally successful stra-tegy is for family members to find someone to care for the pet and to allow periodic contact so that the separation is not total. Unfortunately, some older people will not agree to move until a beloved pet's death, which serves as a powerful precipitant of action.

As another reason for putting off a move, some older people refuse to accept an apartment more than a few floors above ground level. Although seemingly a stubborn pretext, people who have always lived in a house commonly react uncomfortably to the thought of living "up high" away from green grass or shrubs. Those who have difficulty managing steps may dread depending on an elevator in the event of a fire or elevator mal-function. Discussing this special need with the manager of the prospec-tive facility is usually better than trying to argue away such feelings. The waiting period for a ground floor apartment may be lengthened, but a strong psychological obstacle to the move may be eliminated.

During first visits to retirement homes, the older person may dislike a certain facility because she sees someone using a cane or a group of people who appear to be "old." While the older individual herself may be in her eighties, she may be opposed to any identification with disability or aging. If a facility which has been rejected on this basis seems otherwise well suited to the older person's needs, family members can ask the manage-ment for the name of a particularly active resident who would give a per-sonalized tour. Meeting someone who has maintained a lively spirit within the facility can often relieve these concerns about proximity to inactive people.

Disposing of Possessions

The thought of sorting through years of accumulated possessions can be a major obstacle to an older person's moving. For some, packing up and giv-ing away household items is symbolic of dying. The disposal process feels

259

synonymous with throwing away the future as well as the past, as if the disappearance of the accumulation is equivalent to the person's disappearance. Parting from possessions that have been tied through memories to previous roles, such as wife and mother, is especially painful. By disposing of the tangible signs of such roles, the older person may react as if she is losing confirmation of her sense of worth.

In many instances, an older person who asks a family member to "help" with the sorting needs a listener more than an assistant. The older person may be unable to allow items to vanish into a box before explaining how they were acquired, their purposes over the years, or the memories attached to them. By permitting an older person to complete experiences through the telling of them, such stories serve to make sense of life. Transmitting these memories to family members is a means of passing on the past instead of seeming to lose it. By viewing the sorting process in this light, family members can transform what is otherwise a chore into a meaningful life event.

Because storytelling is central to the sorting process, however, it can slow progress to a pace that exasperates those giving assistance. No matter how much interest and respect a family member may feel for the process, time constraints are a reality which can produce legitimate impatience. A family member who flies out to use a two-week vacation period to help a parent with the disposal of possessions may need to hurry the stories in order to make the most of limited time. To be both practical and respectful, family members can ask the older person to anticipate the importance of the longer stories and make tapes prior to the actual packing time. A friend or neighbor can listen as the older person records the stories in advance of the family's assistance. Such recordings have the additional value of preserving stories for family members who are unable to help sort the household.

Further problems can arise when the older person agrees to a garage sale, but insists on prices that are too high. Aware of the items' original value, the older person may feel infuriated by the idea of selling them for a fraction of the cost. To deal with this, families sometimes accept the items as gifts, while privately planning to dispose of them. Instead of resorting to deception, family members can avoid future hurt by storing some items until after the older person is settled. Once the move's emotionality has subsided and an acceptable future is assured in the new setting, the stored possessions may seem less important and the older person may be less upset by disposing of them at a low cost.

An older person's gifts of emotionally sacred items present even more complex dilemmas. Such gifts often function as trial balloons for the older person to observe how respectfully various family members will treat the memory of her life. Implicitly, she may be wondering "If they don't take care of these things, how will they handle what I leave when I'm gone?" A woman who gives a childhood painting to a son and then discovers it under several crates in his basement may feel that by dishonoring her memento, her son dishonored her. It may be helpful for family members to realize the loaded nature of such gifts and to ask the older person to explain their significance prior to accepting them. Citing limited space and a desire to give her mementos a place of honor, family members can then ask the older person to choose only the most precious items for this purpose.

Overwhelmed by a mountain of small decisions, some older people are unable to find a beginning point in disposing of possessions. The following decision-making categories can help set the thought process in motion:

Categories for Sorting

1. If I had just one box to fill, what would I take with me?
2. What would I enjoy having with me, if I had room for ten more boxes?
3. What things do I want to keep, but I don't mind storing?
4. What am I ready to part with, but would prefer to keep in the family, if possible?
5. What am I prepared to give away, sell or throw out?

The older person should be encouraged to make such categorized lists in advance of the need to start packing. Imagining the items to go in the first box can be particularly helpful in freeing the person to make the rest of the decisions. Having named the "necessary" items, the person may feel the confidence that "If I had to, I could live without everything else."

Widowed people, needing to break up a household previously shared with a spouse, may experience a profound inertia when faced with the task. Items as mundane as a magazine rack may hold significance for the couple's past life together. Disposal of such items may seem disrespectful to the deceased person. Sorting through the spouse's things can evoke unfinished grief, particularly if such items have not been touched since the death. Many bereaved older people leave the spouse's clothing hanging in the closet and dread being pressured to part with it during the moving process. Family members should anticipate the intensity of grief likely to be unleashed in such situations in order to be prepared to extend added sensitivity and patience.

For family members, the most difficult situations are when the older person refuses to participate in the choice process. Unable to feel enthusiasm for the new phase of life ahead, some older people express their feelings of despair through statements such as, "Do what you want with my things. It doesn't matter, anyway." Older people entering a structured living situation directly from a hospital may insist that they are glad to be spared the necessity of sorting through and grieving their life's accumulations. Family members should view this attitude as transitional, which will change as the older person develops friendships and interests in the new setting. By renting a storage area for six months, family members spare themselves the responsibility of making these choices, and allow the older person to make decisions about personal belongings when her spirit for life resumes.

Adjusting to Alternative Settings

People who leave a lifelong home to move into senior apartments or retirement homes tend to adjust more slowly than those parting with a more recently acquired home. Arriving in the new setting, they generally feel as if their connection with the past has been severed. The memories surrounding their furniture and other transportable possessions may not sustain links with the past powerfully enough to prevent a mourning period. As with any grief, separation from a lifelong home requires a healing period before a readiness for the next attachment can develop.

How older people view the move also affects the rate of their adjustment. Those who equate leaving a long-term home with a death knell tend to feel depleted and resigned about entering a retirement home. Others who define the move as a life transition, with inherent benefits and challenges, may be enthusiastic about this new phase. For those who have simultaneously left a known geographic area, the adjustment can be complicated by their struggling with an unfamiliar dependence on relatives for visits. They may have expected more time with their family: "I did this to be near my kids, and I only see them once a week." They may not have envisioned themselves needing to reach out to new friends.

Hoping for a smooth adjustment, family members are often puzzled when a relative holds back from making friends in the new environment. Initial resistance toward becoming part of the community can last for several months, depending on how intensely the person refuses to identify with "all those old people." The person may maintain a separation by rejecting neighbors' friendly overtures or by watching for experiences that confirm her derogatory perceptions of fellow residents. Couples are especially prone to remaining aloof, since they carry a compact social world along with them to the new setting and may feel little impetus to reach beyond this comfortable sphere.

A willingness to establish roots in the new environment often evolves with time. Once they have accepted the change, most newcomers become receptive to forming attachments. Others find that the sheer repetition of daily contact with people breaks through their resistance. Some people hold out until an illness forces them to depend on their neighbors' thoughtfulness, a situation which rapidly forges bonds.

Compared to home ownership, residence in a managed community necessitates an increased degree of passivity. Waiting for a custodian to handle maintenance problems is a relinquishment of control as much as a relief from responsibility. To someone accustomed to modifying his living space at will, a large psychological shift is required in receiving services from others. In a similar way, new residents usually miss their former control over when they had their meals and what they ate, even though the burden of food preparation may have been a reason for the move. Being served in a central dining room entails such passivity that some older people insist upon having a kitchenette where they can occasionally prepare meals.

Loss of control over other people's access to them is another major shift. Unaccustomed to strangers scrutinizing their affairs, those who previously lived in private homes are often unnerved by people in the lobby observing them as they come and go. Being cornered in the elevator by a nonstop talker or a particularly intrusive neighbor may rattle them more than those accustomed to apartment life. For some, needing to be conscious of the volume of their music and voices as well as being subject to the sound levels of adjacent apartments is a new experience. In settings where meals are served in a central dining room, facing the same people three times a day can seem a drastic loss of privacy compared to former patterns of occasional meals with friends.

Within all communities, gossip flourishes when people have little else to occupy their attention. Who was seen leaving a neighbor's apartment at midnight and who leaves a urine odor behind after she occupies a couch are topics which can seem engrossing in the absence of larger concerns. Unless people stay involved in outside interests, petty aspects of their environment come to assume an unwarranted prominence. Friends within such a community can pledge to each other not to indulge in these "easy" topics, but rather to push themselves to talk about political events, stories from the past, or anecdotes from experiences outside the community. Acknowledging the effort involved to focus on topics beyond their immediate circumstances, such friends can prod each other when they slip into gossiping rather than conversing.

To assert an adventurous spirit despite such scrutiny requires a secure sense of individuality and personal confidence. Without this, many residents of retirement homes and senior apartments have a difficult time achieving indifference to what others may say about them. Some residents may so intensely dread walking past observers in the lobby that they

263

leave early for outings or omit them entirely. If the building has a back door, they will sacrifice convenience to avoid intrusive queries such as, "Where are you headed at this hour?" or "Gee, you're all dressed up." Since saying or doing things out of the ordinary attracts attention, many find safety in adopting bland conformity as their response to such over-concern with others' affairs.

The power of gossip to disrupt residents' personal freedom in these settings needs wider professional recognition and intervention. When the majority of residents are homebound, insularity should be countered with planned invasions of information and experience from the outside world. Guest speakers, slide shows, and other regularly occurring programs can serve to relieve internal pressures by providing an external focus. Shared cabs and car pools for residents to go out to concerts and films can compensate for insufficient recreational staff or lack of van services in certain settings.

When older people are grouped together, death looms as a presence more than in communities with a mix of younger and older people. The frequency with which ambulances appear remind residents of their fragility, confronting them with death and illness as the chief methods of exit from the community. These reminders can contribute to residents feeling confined, such as when a woman forgoes her weekly walk to the grocery store in reaction to a neighbor's breaking her hip while shopping. When dining partners die, the surviving occupants of the table may not have the spirit to invest as strongly in the new residents who replace them.

Many people who move into these settings begin enjoying them immediately. The services relieve them from worry about practical details of daily life. They welcome the social contacts and feel protected by others' scrutiny, knowing that neighbors will check on them if they fail to come to the dining room or the mailboxes. The ability to watch out for others and to exchange helping efforts provides a pleasing sense of community. Eating in the company of others increases their enthusiasm for meals and thus improves their general nutrition. Family members enjoy a similar freedom from worry, usually finding that the quality of their time with their relative improves in proportion to the extent to which they are spared assisting with practical details. Family members can focus on the kinds of conversations and activities previously deferred in the effort to maintain their older relative in a private home.

Appropriate housing is a major factor in sustaining an older person's independence. The housing options described have the advantages of providing concrete services and opportunities for contact with other people. Unfortunately, these options are limited in many communities. Most policy debates have focused on institutional versus home care, with insufficient attention given to intermediate living arrangements. Federal incentives to the private sector to experiment with housing is one way to stimulate more alternatives. Another policy direction would be to expand the use of SSI supplementary payments for group housing arrangements. With the development of more visible and affordable housing options, older people's resistance to such moves might also be reduced.

Suggested Resources

"Call for Decent Housing," Gray Panthers National Task Force on Housing, Quarterly Newsmagazine, 4534 47th Street N.W., Washington, DC 20016.
　　Presents a legislative action agenda to improve the housing conditions of older people.

Center News, National Policy Center on Housing and Living Arrangements for Older Americans, University of Michigan, 200 Bonisteel Blvd, Ann Arbor, MI 48109.

Crone's Nest, 207 Coastal Highway, St. Augustine, Florida 32084.
　　Intergenerational group of women that aims to provide a living environment as an alternative between isolated independence and institutionalized care.

Planning and Developing a Shared Living Project: A Guide for Community Groups (Boston, Mass.: Community Development Inc., 1979).
　　Useful reference on group living for older people.

Shared Housing Resource Center, Inc., 6344 Green Street, Philadelphia, PA 19144.
　　National nonprofit organization that promotes shared housing alternatives for older people. Provides an educational clearinghouse, technical assistance, research and advocacy, and a *Shared Housing Quarterly.*

CHAPTER 12

Living Together
in the Caregiver's Home

Older people commonly stay in family members' homes following discharge from the hospital or the death of a spouse. Responding to the immediate need, family members often do not have time to plan or discuss this arrangement with their relative. Since periods of recuperation and bereavement are assumed to be short-term, family members generally approach them with stamina and a spirit of accommodation, working toward their relative's resumed independence. When the expected improvement does not occur or happens more slowly than anticipated, stress may develop from the adaptations which were acceptable only because they were temporary. Never having intended a long-term arrangement but reluctant to consider nursing home placement, families often feel trapped and helpless.

In other instances, families make decisions about living together when their relatives are fairly independent. They make a long-term commitment to a certain level of care, not conceiving of medical problems that could substantially alter the nature of their care tasks. For example, a stroke or broken hip can result in round-the-clock care which dominates their lives. Ruling out nursing home placement as an avenue of relief, they find themselves providing more care than they anticipated.

This chapter identifies the advantages and disadvantages of giving care in a family member's home, addressing factors to be weighed when

*Factors to Consider Prior to an Older Person's
Move into a Family Caregiver's Home*

Expense: Does a family member have to give up employment or reduce working hours in order to provide care?

Confinement: Will caregivers have to forgo many out-of-home involvements? How available are other family members to stay with the older person to enable primary caregivers to get out of the home?

Accessibility: Does the family's home have features, such as steps and narrow doorways, that will require modification?

Space: Is an extra room available to ensure privacy? Will family members be displaced in order to create adequate space? Is a bathroom located near the room that is designated for the older person?

Privacy: Are both the older person and the family willing to sacrifice personal privacy? Will too much access to each other harm their relationship?

Emotional pressures: What emotional strains pre-exist within the household? How will the older person's presence complicate or relieve these pressures?

Noise level: Is the house structured in a way to segregate noise?

Retirement plans: Will long-awaited retirement plans have to be disrupted? To what extent can plans be modified?

In-law Relationships: Does the son- or daughter-in-law concur with the choice of the older person's moving in? What is the nature of their relationship?

Grandchildren: What changes will be required of the grandchildren? Have grandchildren been involved in the decision?

Lifestyle compatibility: What aspects of either generation's lifestyle would engender conflict or discomfort?

Cultural and personal expectations: Does the older person or family view in-home caregiving as a duty? Is it highly valued?

Future plans: How long can the family envision themselves providing care? Do they have long-range plans that may conflict with having their older relative in their home?

advance planning is possible. Suggestions for solving the most common dilemmas of such an arrangement, along with architectural modifications and options to make living together feasible, follow this exploration. Shared households can be satisfying to family caregivers and their older relatives when needs for privacy, respite, and support are adequately met.

Deciding to Live Together

Advantages of Shared Households

Many families invite older relatives into their homes out of a desire to make caregiving more convenient. Weary of driving back and forth to help with incidental tasks and problems, they perceive that caregiving would be easier in their own surroundings. A daughter with young children may be attracted to the idea of being able to spend time with her own family while helping her mother. Maintaining one household rather than two may also seem appealing, especially if a relative's health status has left the family responsible for household tasks and yardwork. Preparing one set of meals, doing laundry all at once, and mowing one lawn can seem a vast improvement over the split arrangement.

Saving money is another prime reason for living together. After investigating the costs of hiring a live-in worker, paying hourly helpers, or subsidizing a move to a retirement home equipped with the necessary services, families may realize that the older person's living with them is less expensive than other options. Without sufficient funds to pay for live-in or hourly help, sharing a household may be the only viable alternative to nursing home placement for a person whose care needs become extensive. If a family is experiencing financial difficulties, they may perceive living together and merging the older person's income with theirs as a way to gain financial relief. Additionally, an older person who is able to cash in the equity on a home owned for many years may receive a sizeable interest income; this money could be contributed to the family to compensate for employment forfeited to provide care or perhaps to pay for respite helpers.

In some cultures or families, especially in rural areas and among ethnic minorities, taking an older relative into the family's home is regarded as fulfilling a basic responsibility rather than an extraordinary sacrifice. This expectation may have been shaped by childhood experiences of a grandparent living with the family as an integral part of the household life. To the extent that this experience was positive, family members may want to give their children similar daily proximity to an older person's guidance, nurturance and storytelling. If the older person is particularly beloved due to the help and support she rendered earlier in life, or if the present relationship is one of great affection, her living with them may also serve as an expression of gratitude and a fulfillment of the desire to enjoy the relationship more readily.

With increasing numbers of women in the work force, another advantage of moving the older person into a daughter's or granddaughter's home may be the potential for child care. Especially for low-income or single parent families unable to afford day care costs, the ability to leave young children at home can be an important motivation for sharing a household with an older person. The extent of assistance which an older relative can provide varies with the degree of the person's mental or physical disability. Even those who cannot provide extensive help with housekeeping can contribute their presence when children arrive home from school, an advantage that is reassuring to working parents and their children. A physically disabled older person may still be able to play a game or read to a child, thereby relieving the mother to prepare meals or run errands.

An immediate gain for the older person in making such a move is increased contact with relatives and their social networks. The daily mental and emotional stimulation from these interactions gives the older person more to talk about and more reason to be alert and animated. The phone rings more often and people come through more frequently in the family's household than in the person's solitary home. Everyday experiences, such as watching children with their friends, are more stimulating than sitting alone watching television. Friends and neighbors of family members may develop bonds with the older person and be willing to spend time in the home, freeing the family for out-of-home involvements.

For an older person in good health, the opportunity to contribute to the family may be another benefit of sharing a household. In addition to assisting with child care and chores, the older person may be able to answer the phone and take messages, do mending or work on time-consuming projects, such as furniture refinishing, which family members have put off. In some instances, a satisfying emotional role in the family's life may evolve, allowing the older relative to feel a greater sense of purpose and value. Some grandparents are able to serve as buffers between parents and teenagers, giving the advantage of their more detached perspective to both parties during times of conflict.

In contrast to her life alone, the older person living with family may acquire a more comfortable lifestyle. Her family's home may have features which she enjoys, such as a yard or garden, closer access to bus routes and safe places to walk, more spacious or attractively furnished common areas, and more labor-saving appliances than her home. Sharing expenses may free a portion of her income. If she is able to get out, she may thereby be able to afford more recreational activities, such as shows or concerts. Special personal purchases may become possible such as a new dress or having her hair done. The ability to afford such "extras" may raise her spirits and lead to the formation of new friendships. For an older person subsisting on a minimal Social Security check, sharing a home with relatives may provide her such basics as adequate food and a well-heated home.

For some older people, the safety accorded by others' presence in the home, especially at night, may be the chief attraction of sharing a household. Those who have had frightening experiences with being unable to get out of a bathtub or up from the floor after a fall may regard others' presence in the home as a primary asset. For those who dread dying alone, shared living arrangements might seem especially vital. For example, someone on oxygen for advanced respiratory disease may view having others nearby as an advantage in the event of a respiratory emergency, which more than compensates for the loss of privacy and autonomy in a shared household.

Disadvantages of Shared Households

In deciding whether to offer their home to an older relative, family members often fear their becoming homebound above all other consequences. This fear may be justified in instances where the older person's care requires someone's continuous presence in the home. The older person's move into the home can also postpone adult children's long-awaited plans for travel upon retirement, unless respite caregivers are found. Those in the midst of active careers may worry about burning themselves out coming home every evening and weekend to caregiving demands. Middle-aged women eager to pursue their own interests after years of child-rearing may especially resent alterations of their immediate plans as well as the inability to make long-range plans.

In many family relationships, the emotional balance achieved at a distance is likely to be disrupted by close proximity. Lifestyle differences in child-rearing practices, choice of friends, or even food preferences can become areas of contention when living space is shared. Seemingly insignificant details of daily life, such as vegetarian cooking, omitting prayer before meals, or hurriedly setting the dinner table, can become areas of conflict that would not otherwise have emerged.

Another common dread is that the older person will meddle in matters that family members prefer to handle without interference. Family members may be reluctant to establish a situation in which their relative's participation in their affairs cannot be controlled. Parent–child control issues long ago laid to rest may be revived. Despite the span of years, for instance, a forty-year-old career woman may find herself acting like a rebellious twelve-year-old around her mother. After extended time in the same house, she may discover that her boundaries as an autonomous adult have become vulnerable through her mother's access to information about her personal life. A natural reaction is to use verbal sparring to defend against a parent's attempts to give advice or make judgments. Unless

270

such reactions are channeled into more productive responses, relationships between a parent and adult children can be injured when they share a household.

In making the decision to invite the older person into the household, the adult child and her spouse may differ regarding the necessity or desirability of doing so. The spouse who already resents the adult child's time spent on caring for a parent may view a move into the household as a final violation of both time and privacy. In addition, the spouse may be concerned that his own parents will feel slighted by "the other side" moving in with him or that his parents will eventually need care while his energies are diverted for an undetermined length of time. Whatever the disagreement's source, marital conflict over this decision can be a major obstacle to its accomplishment and eventual success.

Grandchildren may also have doubts about their grandparents' moving into the home. If grandchildren must give up the privilege of having their own room to make space for their grandparent, the feeling of being intruded upon can outweigh the most intense bonds of affection. The prospect of sharing a room with a younger sibling, or using a pull-out bed in a den without a door to close off family noise and traffic is reprehensible to most teenagers. Their private spheres can also be invaded in other ways. They may resent their grandparent's expressed displeasure at their music, hair style or clothes, generational differences to which their parents may have adapted. Some may remain silent about their sense of intrusion, but simmer internally, unless their parents include them in the decision-making process and make it acceptable for them to express their negative feelings about the move.

A common fear, difficult for family members to verbalize, is that the decision to live together cannot be altered once their relative moves in with them. Some families worry that they will want to change their minds once the reality of the older person's presence in the home makes unforeseen problems more evident. Other families fear unexpected changes within the family unit. A middle-aged daughter's husband may have a heart attack while her father is living with them. Unable to care for both of them, she may feel guiltier about institutionalizing her father in order to care for her husband than if he had earlier established his own life in a congregate care facility or nursing home. Such worries suggest the importance of including the relative in the preliminary dicussions where family members can honestly assess their own capabilities and openly share their concerns about key issues that could result in the use of other care options.

Older people also perceive numerous disadvantages to shared households. In exchange for anticipated benefits, they first must contend with leaving their own homes. An emotional attachment to the dwelling itself may be compounded by attachments to furniture and other belongings which cannot be moved to a family member's residence. Trees outside the home's windows, familiar walks and views, a garden or yard, and neighbors of many years' duration are among the emotional losses experienced during such a move. Sorting through and packing possessions, and distributing items among family members can be heart-wrenching (see Chapter 11).

The loss of space necessitated by leaving a house or apartment for a bedroom in a family member's home can also be a difficult psychological adjustment. After years of controlling extensive personal space, an older person can feel claustrophobic in a single room. Common areas of the family household may be maintained less fastidiously than the older person would like, or used for entertaining guests whom the older person would rather avoid. Some family members may also indicate, either directly or through embarrassed glances, their preference that the older relative remain in another area of the home while family guests are present. As a result, the older person may spend most of her time in her room, the one household area over which she can exert control. These reclusive tendencies may frustrate those family members who do attempt to make their older relative feel welcome in the rest of the home. The reality is that for many older people, their son or daughter's house will never feel like "home."

An older person's seclusion in such situations may be partially due to disruptions of her daily routines. Accustomed to eating and sleeping at certain times or watching particular television programs, the older person may be forced by majority rule to concede to the family's patterns of eating, sleeping, and watching television. Noise level during evening hours may be especially disruptive to an older person needing quiet at that time. The sense of abandoning her previous daily patterns for the family's preferences can make an older person's need for the private domain of her room more intense. It may also account for unexplained and atypical grumpiness.

The older person's newly obtained knowledge of family conflicts may be another unfortunate consequence of a shared household. Marital conflicts, discipline problems with grandchildren, and other stresses become unavoidably visible. Adult children who are preoccupied with their parent's care needs may not be aware of the extent to which their own problems become a burden to the parent. Witnessing family disagreements firsthand, the older person may find that the potential of being drawn in as a participant contrasts with the safety of being a distant observer. The urge to give advice or take a stand may be too difficult to restrain, despite an older person's wish to remain exempt from the upheaval: "I'm just too old for this kind of thing." Avoiding such frays is yet another reason older people living with family may choose to confine themselves to their rooms.

Occasionally, the family's expectations of their relative's contribution to the household clash with the person's perferences and physical abilities. A daughter may count on saving day care costs for her children once her mother moves in, without realizing that her mother is apprehensive and unenthusiastic about coping with two active children. Despite her wish to be of use to the family, her mother may feel she lacks the physical stamina required by young children. Alternatively, the older person's desire to help may exceed her cognitive capabilities. A grandmother in the early stages of Alzheimer's disease may insist that she can babysit. Her daughter is placed in the bind of not wanting to hurt her mother's pride while worrying about her children's safety. The daughter may have to enlist a friend or neighbor to check on the well-being of both her mother and children.

No matter how welcome family members attempt to make an older person feel, the perception of being useless and in the family's way may develop. Efforts to arrange schedules to ensure that someone is home all the time are likely to be detected by the older person, especially if she overhears conflicts regarding such arrangements. No matter how graciously a grandson gives up a private bedroom for her, she is likely to remain conscious of his displacement. The idea of money spent to adapt the home, such as installing an additional bathroom or renovating a portion of the house, may weigh on the older person if she is unable to contribute financially. She may also attribute the family's missed out-of-home involvements as evidence of her being a burden, irrespective of her family's repeated assurances that they are pleased to have her in the home.

Problem-Solving Strategies for Shared Households

In intergenerational households, a major problem is maintaining each member's separateness. Norms of interaction are initially unclear, with both younger and older generations uncertain if they are intruding on the other's privacy. An older woman in a basement apartment may wonder how often to accept her daughter's invitations to come upstairs to join family dinners. She may be unable to tell whether she is invited out of obligation or a desire for her presence at the dinner table. When she declines the invitations to give the family privacy, she may worry that her daughter's family misinterprets this as disinterest or rejection. In such situations, families and their older relatives often spend more time together than either finds comfortable or desirable. Both sides may be unable to think of a way to broach the topic without hurting the other's feelings.

Gray areas about interaction also occur when the older person's room is within the main part of the family home. An older man may be ever watchful for cues after dinner about when to go upstairs to his bedroom. Instead of relaxing with the family, he may silently debate how long to linger in their midst. He may watch television programs in which he has no interest in order to be near family members. In turn, his family may tolerate the same programs in order to include him in a comfortable after-dinner activity. A normal family pattern of separating after dinner to enjoy private activities may be disrupted, with all members feigning comfort.

One way to resolve such awkwardness is to create a structure in which periods of private time automatically occur. Instead of continuously negotiating boundaries, the older person and family can establish routines of contact and separateness, thereby omitting the need for psychological guesswork. For instance, the parent in the downstairs apartment can plan to join the family for dinner every Tuesday and Thursday evening on an ongoing basis. Similarly, the parent living within the home can agree to spend the first hour after dinner with the family and the rest of the evening "on his own," similar to everyone else. With preset arrangements, the family can stop feeling guilty about their private time, and the older person need not worry about intruding.

Establishing such structures prior to the older person moving in with the family is usually easiest. The mutual benefits of separateness, however, can be negotiated at any point in shared living situations. A daughter can say "Mom, I've been thinking that we'll all be more comfortable if we organize our time together and apart. Then, no one has to worry about hurting anyone's feelings." Several different ways of dividing evenings and weekends can then be discussed, with all household members included in choosing the most convenient plan. A grandson may insist "I need to have quiet to do my homework after dinner," with the result that a 9 P.M. snack time is selected for after-dinner contact. Even if arrangements are readjusted, the right to private, autonomous time for each household member becomes openly accepted.

The need for privacy and autonomy has more ramifications than the organization of time. Family members may want their phone conversations out of the older person's earshot, but feel awkward in moving to a more private area of the home to talk. Instead, they hold stilted conversations with veiled meanings while the older person tries to appear not to be listening. A more relaxed arrangement is to establish the practice that each family member will seek privacy while on the phone, irrespective of who is nearby. The same expectation can be developed for visitors, with household members allowing each other the private use of common areas, when needed.

Inevitably, an older relative will witness family conflicts which challenge the desire to permit familial privacy and autonomy. An older woman may fall into an uninvited mediator role between her son and his teenage children. Her tolerance for the volume and intensity of their conflicts may be limited. In addition, she may have her own ideas about how a parent should handle adolescent defiance. Her son may feel his role usurped when she injects her opinion into the fray, leaving him in the bind of feeling angry at her yet not wanting to upset her.

Third parties "butting in" to arguments generally serve as lightning rods, draining off the anger onto themselves. A strategy to protect the older person from such stress and to reduce the adult child's sense of invasion is to request the older person to reserve her input until after conflicts have abated. The understanding can be reached that the older person will remove herself from the immediate area when a conflict erupts, becoming a silent observer until she later contributes her thoughts. Removal to the physical periphery, such as moving to the living room when the argument is in the kitchen, can enable an older person to remain on the emotional periphery. When spouses fight, it is especially critical for the older person to avoid the mediator role or taking sides. In families with daily eruptions, an adult child may set aside one evening per week to privately solicit his parent's views, in exchange for her restraint and noninterference the rest of the time.

The recognition of an older relative as a legitimate part of the family system is inherent in the strategies described above. Segregating an older person's input differs from degrading it as "meddling." Intergenerational households often have difficulty accepting the ways an older relative's presence alters the balance of relationships, especially without traditional patriarch or matriarch roles. In the absence of norms for how members of extended families should live together, the role of silent observer is a workable compromise. Such agreements respect the nuclear family's autonomy, without stripping the older person of the dignity inherent in an active familial role.

The older person's place in the family can also be affirmed through her inclusion in the formative stages of household decision-making. Without abandoning final control, for instance, a son could explain to his mother the pros and cons of having the house painted versus doing the work himself. The less trivial the decision, the greater the importance of including the older person as a contributing adult. Whether to accept a job in another part of the country or send a child to a private or state college are examples of decisions with geographic and economic implications, which could seem demeaning if announced after the fact to the older person. Family members may need to periodically remind each other to consult their older relative on family matters. As indicated in Chapter 7, restoring an older person's areas of contribution can be a powerful antidote to depression, even when contributions are largely symbolic.

Devising concrete contributions to the household can be still more difficult for families than permitting their relatives a verbal role in household affairs. Traditional older women may have a particular need for concrete household responsibilities to affirm their identities as homemakers. In some instances, adult children may feel uncomfortable at the sight of a frail parent vacuuming the living room or scrubbing the bathtub. Afraid that she may physically harm herself by working beyond her capacities or that others will criticize them for overworking their parent, they may plead with her to rest. Her housekeeping preferences may seem absurdly detailed to her children, who are more concerned with her health than the gleam on porcelain fixtures. Another problem arises when family members are pressed for time and become impatient with an older relative's slow and meticulous cleaning methods. As with other areas of potential tension, the best strategy is to settle these differences before they develop into larger conflicts.

Housekeeping plans promoting peaceful cohabitation should begin with the premise that household members have control of their private rooms. For an older person newly confined to a small room, having absolute control over that personal space is especially crucial. Even a daughter's well-intentioned "straightening up" in her mother's room can be felt as a violation, leaving her mother with only her own body to manage. When the older person is also disabled and cannot manage her body independently, her ability to direct details within her room becomes still more vital. In exchange for the older person's autonomy in this sphere, families can request noninterference in their control over other household areas. Designing specific household tasks for the older person to participate in, such as folding laundry or mending, can often satisfy an older person enough to prevent her from trying to help in areas family members prefer that she avoid.

Money can underlie or add intensity to many of the problems described above. An older person may be unable to rid herself of the feeling of being a burden unless she pays room and board to the household. Some older people will restrict what they eat, unless family members allow them to contribute to the monthly grocery bill. To continue to feel they belong to the realm of adulthood, many older people need to retain an economic function, for example, "I'll pay the heating bill, since I like the house very warm during the winter." Those too disabled to contribute to the household through concrete tasks may especially benefit from a financial role in the family's functioning. Rather than avoid financial discussions due to embarrassment or fear that siblings will accuse them of exploitation, family members should explore their own and the older person's attitudes. A statement such as "sometimes older people living with families like to contribute financially" can be a way to initiate discussion of this topic.

Architectural Options

Many families also find that structural changes in their home ease some of the difficulties inherent in shared households. Architectural choices include basement apartments, "mother-in-law" apartments, mobile homes, duplexes, and additions to existing structures. For instance, families faced with their older relatives' needs for supportive living situations are sometimes attracted to the idea of turning a basement area into a fully-equipped apartment. They perceive the equity from selling an older family home as a means to pay for the installation of kitchen and bathroom fixtures and other adaptations. An immediate problem is that such arrangements can be confining for an older person who has difficulty managing steps. The transfer of sound from active household areas above the basement is another difficulty, especially for an older person who goes to bed earlier than the rest of the family. A further problem is the fact that basement windows are smaller and higher than those on upper levels. The inability to look out at street activity combined with limited daylight can make a basement apartment a depressing place to live, no matter how lovely the furnishings or modern the fixtures.

A more expensive option that solves the obstacles of steps, noise and windows is to build an extension onto the home for a "mother-in-law" apartment. Limited yard space, zoning restrictions and insufficient funds may preclude this alternative. Instead, a small prefabricated home in the backyard or "granny flat" may meet space and financial constraints. Since such structures can be disassembled when no longer needed, an exception to zoning restrictions may be granted. Problems can arise from neighbors complaining that such structures are "too tacky for the neighborhood," or from modular pieces being too large to fit through the narrow pathway leading to the backyard.

House trailers and small mobile homes can be a practical and economical option for housing an older person near family, but also may invoke neighbors' displeasure. At first an older relative may park a house trailer on the side of the driveway for an extended visit and find that proximity to family compensates for the confined living space. Eventually, the "visit" becomes a permanent arrangement, with the family setting the trailer up on blocks and hooking electric power into the house. Such arrangements are most commonplace in rural areas with spacious yards and distant neighbors. Another way to create this option is for an older person to offer his home to younger family members and then move into a backyard trailer, gaining loved ones' support in exchange for unneeded living space.

An increasingly popular option is for newly retired adult children to move from a large family home to a duplex, thereby gaining the ability to rent the other half until one of their relatives requires care. They may also anticipate their own later years when one of their children may move in the other half to care for them. In addition, duplexes provide the possibility of renting to nonfamily members at reduced rates in exchange for assistance with housekeeping, yard work, and other care needs. In this light, a duplex can be an investment in both giving and receiving care.

Architectural adaptations of a lesser scale include adding a bathroom, soundproofing a bedroom, and dividing den space to make another bedroom. Adding a wall and door to a den can sometimes make it habitable for a teenager, who would then be willing to give up his private bedroom for a grandparent's use. Building a separate entrance into a street level room or installing a refrigerator and sink in a laundry area to create a modified kitchen are adaptations that make living arrangements more attractive to live-in helpers. Professionals can assist families and older people with generating creative ideas for home adaptations to solve problems of privacy and noise, and thereby minimize the stresses of increased proximity.

The Need for Respite

Even with such changes, family members generally find that their relative's constant presence in their home heightens their need for periodic relief, or respite. Opportunities to run errands, to go out to dinner, or just to have time alone can be critical to sustaining the family's ability to assist their relative in their home. One of the hardest services to obtain for caregiving families, respite can include ad hoc arrangements provided by other family members, friends, neighbors, and live-in or hourly helpers as well as formally organized services, such as adult day care.

Family members outside the direct care situation can aid primary caregivers in a number of vital ways. The major way is by performing tasks that reduce pressures on the primary caregivers and thereby enhance their ability to continue the shared living arrangement. For example, running errands or providing transportation for caregivers' children are forms of concrete help not directly related to the older person's care, but which could significantly relieve the caregivers' level of stress.

Another useful form of assistance to primary caregivers is for family members to accompany the older person to medical, dental, and other out-of-home appointments. A dual function is served by removing a time-consuming task from the primary caregiver's realm of responsibility and providing her with private time. Since such appointments are usually scheduled in advance, the primary caregivers can plan their own errands and meetings for those time periods, thus making optimal use of such breaks in their care responsibilities.

Providing large blocks of respite is perhaps the most critical way for other family members to assist primary caregivers. Time to be alone in their own home and to pursue out-of-home involvements becomes especially precious to people sharing their home with an older relative. A sibling who works full-time could relieve his sister and her husband one evening a week by taking his mother out to a leisurely dinner. Another option is for the older person to stay at another family member's home one or two weekends a month, thereby allowing primary caregivers to take a weekend trip or use large blocks of time for their personal needs. If the older person cannot be moved, family members could trade homes for the weekend. Out-of-town family members could spend a vacation in the primary caregivers' home, allowing the caregivers an extended period of rest.

Unfortunately, family members may not provide such crucial support to primary caregivers. Outright refusals or passive avoidance of opportunities to be helpful may be accompanied by the defensive assertion that nursing home placement is the better solution to the older person's care needs: "If you're going to keep her in your house instead of putting her in the nursing home where she belongs, that's your business." Other family members may be unwilling even to help purchase respite for the primary caregivers, maintaining that respite care is an expensive luxury. They can sometimes be persuaded to contribute cash monthly to help purchase services, in instances when the home care achieves significant savings over institutional care.

Neighbors can be a valuable resource for relief. When willing to step in for a few hours, neighbors can dramatically affect the caregiver's level of stress. While assistance from other family members or hired helpers usually has to be scheduled in advance, neighbors' proximity could allow them to meet unexpected or spontaneous needs. Professionals can assist family caregivers in identifying neighbors likely to help and suggesting nonmonetary compensation for them. When deciding which family members should take the older person into their home, the presence of helpful neighbors can be a key determinant in the choice.

If space is available in the home, a further respite alternative is to find someone willing to spend blocks of time with the older person in exchange for free room and board. Having to cope with yet another person in the household often discourages such arrangements, although the loss of privacy is often worth the freedom gained. With such arrangements, the specific time expectations of the live-in should be negotiated in advance (see Chapter 11).

Formal respite services include in-home companions, nurse's aides, and homemakers who can be hired through agencies or obtained through special state-funded programs. In some communities, religious and service organizations coordinate volunteers to provide respite free of charge, although recruiting and maintaining volunteer respite workers is difficult. Respite services in the home have the advantages of keeping the older person in familiar surroundings, avoiding transportation difficulties, and providing caregiver relief for short periods of time. Since public funding for in-home respite is limited, cost is the major obstacle.

Because of the expense, many caregivers put off obtaining this time for themselves, regarding the cost as "not worth it." Female caregivers especially may be reluctant to spend money to meet their own needs. To overcome such resistance, professionals could compute the weekly costs of respite, demonstrating that these represent only a fraction of nursing home fees. As another option to reduce the expense, a group of neighborhood caregivers could pool funds to hire a full-time helper whose time they divide between them.

Another obstacle to in-home respite is the caregiver's resistance to leaving their relative with someone else. In addition, if their relative complains or cries about being with a stranger, locating and paying a respite worker may seem too troublesome. Even when caregivers do hire respite help, they may worry during the time away, thus gaining little mental relief. In such instances, professionals need to emphasize that caregivers' failure to take care of themselves will erode their ability to give care. Resistant caregivers can perhaps be encouraged to try out a respite worker on a temporary basis.

Out-of-home respite care includes adult day care (see Chapter 10) and temporary stays in nursing homes, geriatric units of rehabilitation centers and Veterans Administration hospitals. "Respite care beds," if available, can be reserved for up to a two-month period, thus enabling the family to enjoy an extended vacation. Nursing homes without an established respite bed system may still negotiate a short placement, if the cost of the full private-pay rate can be met through a cash advance. Respite in a nursing home has the advantage of providing trained staff within a licensed facility, thereby assuring a high level of care and emergency medical backup. As a result, the caregiver may feel more at ease than when a stranger comes into the home to provide respite.

States vary considerably in the availability of nursing home respite beds. The major obstacles are the lack of coverage by Medicare or private insurance and the resultant excessive cost and the long waiting lists for a limited number of beds. In addition, the older person, especially if cognitively impaired, may be disoriented by the move to a long term-care facility. The transition to out-of-home respite can be eased, however, by including the older person in the decision as much as feasible, describing the facility and emphasizing the predetermined discharge date to the older person, and providing the staff with a detailed report of previous home care. If the transition is conducted smoothly and the nursing home experience a positive one, detrimental preconceptions of nursing homes held by both the family and the older person may be removed.

Proposed Reforms for Respite Care

Even when families have time to plan and implement some of the problem-solving strategies suggested above, they still may find intergenerational living stressful. To address such familys' care needs, gerontologists and policymakers have recommended numerous policy changes. Of these, the primary proposals are financial incentives and expansion of respite programs.

The financial proposals, while initially appealing, have a number of limitations. If a family needs to structurally modify their home, hire outside help, or forgo employment, they undoubtedly experience financial strains from the shared living arrangement. Most studies of family caregivers, however, have consistently found that financial hardships are secondary to emotional and physical burdens of providing care.[1] Families who are already providing care do not need financial incentives as an inducement. Thus, proposed financial benefits do not recognize the nonmonetary motivations underlying caregiving or the caregiver's preferences for supportive services rather than financial aid.[2] In addition, the amounts proposed represent only a fraction of expenditures for care and do not reimburse the caregiver for her time.

Tax reforms have also been proposed to allow tax deductions for long-term care services, such as home health care workers and adult day care, and one-time costs to make the principal residence barrier-free. Such deductions would benefit families with the economic resources to hire private help, but would not relieve low-income caregivers who provide the care themselves and are financially unable to purchase supportive services.

Proposed reforms also deal with liberalizing eligibility for tax credits to include any dependent care services purchased for persons over the ages of seventy or seventy-five. The maximum credit suggested is $500.[3] The proposed tax credit applies only to employed caregivers and thus gives no relief to caregivers who have either chosen to or been forced to forgo employment in order to provide care. Because only a fraction of the care costs would be reimbursed, women in low-paying jobs might find that skilled substitute care costs considerably more than they can earn.

These proposed financial reforms would also not benefit most caregiving spouses, who are usually women assuming full-time care responsibilities rather than employment. Many of these women exhaust all their financial resources by trying to care for their husbands at home. When their husbands die or are institutionalized, they are often destitute.

Thus, proposed financial reforms do not provide relief from the most stressful daily care tasks, especially for low-income caregivers. On the other hand, a monthly stipend, or attendance allowance, similar to that given in most Western industrialized countries, could offset some of the costs of care, legitimate the value of caregiving, and allow the caregiver flexibility in her use of the monthly income. Such an allowance should be available to all caregivers, regardless of their marital or employment status or their relationship to the older person. The allowance could be a direct monthly stipend or in voucher form for purchase of services, such as respite. While a caregiver allowance is unlikely to be funded in the 1980s, caregivers can act to increase public awareness of the needs.

Most professionals and family caregivers agree on the need for more respite services. The greatest barriers to respite care are the limited funding options. In addition to federally funded demonstration respite programs, some funds are available for respite through waivers in the Medicaid program from the Health Care Financing Administration. Middle income families ineligible for Medicaid but unable to afford to hire private pay workers have even fewer respite options. Ideally, respite programs should have a sliding fee scale adjusted for income.

States have been able to request Medicaid waivers on the assumption that respite care reduces the cost of institutional long-term care. Such presumed benefits, either long-term or short-term, have yet to be documented. Others argue that even if respite does not reduce the risk of institutionalization, it is essential for the caregiver's mental and physical well-being. The Older Women's League has assumed a national leadership role in proposing model respite legislation, components of which have been adopted by some states. In this model, respite, including in-home, in-patient and emergency, is integrated as part of a system of family support functions linked to case management and other coordinating mechanisms.[4]

Beyond financial benefits and incremental programs, more fundamental changes are needed in how caregiving responsibilities are distributed in our society. Caregiving needs to be viewed as a collective responsibility, not only that of an individual family or woman. One step toward this perspective is through job modifications to enable both men and women to assume caregiving tasks, without having to forfeit their employment needs and goals. While some companies have taken small steps in this direction, more companies need to institute flextime, part-time jobs with full benefits, and job sharing options. In fact, if the workplace were modified to be more supportive of caregivers for dependent persons, caregivers might not have to choose between employment and providing care, and the need for financial benefits and respite programs might be reduced.

Notes

1. Amy Horowitz and Rose Dobrof, *The Role of Families in Providing Long-Term Care to the Frail and Chronically Ill Elderly Living in the Community,* Final Report to the Health Care Financing Administration (1982); Elaine M. Brody, "Women in the Middle, and Family Help to Older People," *The Gerontologist* 21, 5 (1981): 471–480.
2. Amy Horowitz and Lois Shindelman, "Social and Economic Incentives for Family Caregivers," presented at the 33rd Annual Meeting of the Gerontological Society of America, San Diego, Calif. (1980); Marvin B. Sussman, "Social and Economic Supports and Family Environments for the Elderly," Fiscal Report to the Administration on Aging, AOA Grant 90–A–316 (03) (January 1979).
3. Lucy Steinitz, "Informal Supports in Long Term Care: Implications and Policy Options," presented to the National Conference on Social Welfare (1981).
4. Older Women's League, Respite Services Bill, 1983, available from 1325 G. Street N.W., Lower Level B, Washington, DC 20005.

Suggested Resources

CROWLEY, DAVID. "Friends Welcome," *Social Work Today* 13, 2 (1981).
Describes England's Invalid Care Allowance, a cash benefit payable primarily to unmarried daughters who care for sick parents, recently extended to friends who meet the caregiving criteria. Its extension to married women is widely advocated.

ELLIS, VICKI, and DWIGHT WILSON. "Respite Care in the Nursing Home Unit of a Veterans Hospital," *American Journal of Nursing* (1983): 1433.
Describes a unit with seven respite beds serving 126 families and some of the positive outcomes of its use.

Respite Services Bill. Older Women's League, 1325 G Street N.W., Lower Level B, Washington, DC 20005.
Model respite legislation that includes a broad array of respite services adaptable to particular states.

SOLDO, BETH J., and JOANA MYLLYLUOMA. "Caregivers who Live with Dependent Elderly," *The Gerontologist* 23, 6 (1983): 605.

Found that situations where care is provided to a dependent, unmarried relative appear to be most vulnerable to dissolution because one in four of these households is headed by a woman for whom working is an economic necessity. Concluded that homecare benefits need to be targeted to such households.

LANG, ABIGAIL M., and ELAINE M. BRODY. "Characteristics of Middle-Aged Daughters and Help to their Elderly Mothers," *Journal of Marriage and the Family* 45, (1983): 193.

Daughters who are older and share households feel more caregiving responsibility. Being married and being employed compete with demands of parent care. Emphasizes the need for a family-focused social policy.

CHAPTER 13

Extending Family Caregiving into the Nursing Home

Few older people willingly choose to live in a nursing home, and most families arrive at this decision only after exhausting their home care resources. Placing a relative in a nursing home is one of the most painful decisions of most people's lives. The pain stems partially from the catastrophic images harbored by older people and their families about nursing homes: "Going to a nursing home would be the end of me" or "Any family who puts their relative in a nursing home just wants to get rid of the person." In instances when nursing home placement signifies an extension of the family's care rather than its abrupt termination, these images do not become realities. In this chapter, an approach to nursing home placement is demonstrated that establishes a partnership between the older person and the family, beginning with the decision to seek placement and continuing through the adjustment period and ongoing life in the nursing home.

When Placement Becomes Necessary

The nursing home decision is often made in reaction to a crisis, such as the older person's imminent discharge from the hospital. Discharge planners pressure family members to make their decision after physicians and other hospital staff press them to "get those beds open." The beds may be needed for patients with more acute medical needs, or their relative may be exceeding the limits of insurance coverage. Family members may reason that their relative's home routines have already been disrupted, hoping to use the momentum of hospitalization to enact nursing home plans.

Increasingly, hospitals are unwilling to serve as "holding areas" while a family waits for an opening in a preferred nursing home. Instead, the discharge planner places the older person's name on several waiting lists, and accepts the first available nursing home bed. If the first open placement is unacceptable to them, the family can take their relative home, negotiate for a longer hospital stay, or go along with the placement on the assumption that they will transfer their relative to a preferred facility when a bed becomes available. Although moving the person twice is undesirable, family members are often concerned that even a brief return home would result in their relative's refusing nursing home placement.

When older people vehemently resist going to a nursing home from the hospital, home care professionals can be enlisted for help during a trial period at home. Such periods allow older people to test their capacity to live independently, especially in instances when their functioning has declined dramatically during hospitalization. Unless permitted this trial, some older people retain unrealistic beliefs about their physical capacities. They are likely to accuse family members of prematurely relegating them to nursing home status: "You just don't want to help me anymore." After returning home, resistant older people generally see firsthand how much assistance they need. When feelings of insecurity and physical discomfort accumulate during the trial period, those in need of care often become amenable to the idea of twenty-four-hour assistance in a health care setting. Once the older person is willing to pursue placement, a rehospitalization can sometimes be negotiated for placement purposes.

In other instances, the nursing home decision evolves in response to intractable circumstances that become increasingly exhausting to caregivers. A prime example of this kind of circumstance is incontinence that requires a helper's constant presence to prevent skin deterioration. Spouses in long marriages are most likely to sustain this burdensome level of care over extended time periods. Their physical exhaustion grows with having to lift their spouse to prevent bed sores and with carrying heavy laundry. Hiring home health aides at high hourly wages to perform incontinence care is usually affordable only as a form of respite. Live-ins employed for the burdensome task of incontinence care tend to resign, unless provided with ample family support and a highly competitive salary to keep them from securing an easier position elsewhere.

Other intractable situations are those in which older people disturb others' sleep. Those who need to be assisted to the commode during the night or who call out at all hours for pain medication quickly exhaust their caregivers' physical strength. Older people who wander at night, reversing night and day in their sleep patterns, may wake up family members by their confusion or by the noise they inadvertently make as they pace. Sleep medications can occasionally resolve these problems, but frequently produce undesirable side effects, such as daytime grogginess and detrimental interactions with other medications. In addition, such medications do not solve the problem of the caregiver who loses sleep from getting up to turn his bedbound relative during the night. Solutions, such as paying an aide to stay overnight regularly, can equal or surpass the cost of twenty-four-hour care in a nursing home.

The primary caregiver's illness or injury is a major precipitant of nursing home placement. When the caregiver is suddenly incapacitated, the older person is usually hospitalized. The placement is then handled by hospital discharge planners, unless other family members come forward to provide home care. To prevent this type of crisis placement, professionals should heed more gradual signs of caregiver incapacity. Early on, health care providers should watch for signs of caregiver fatigue, stress, and depression by interviewing the family members who accompany their older patients to appointments. A contributing factor in many nursing home placements is the family's lack of awareness regarding respite options in the community. Such an omission is correctable by professionals being alert to caregivers' needs. When caregiving has become an excessive burden because of exhausting, abusive, or psychologically disruptive conditions, professional interventions are essential to support the family in considering nursing home placement as a care option.

Accepting Placement

As the decision to pursue nursing home placement evolves in their minds, family members frequently try to shield their relative from awareness of this possibility, reasoning, "It would only make her worry." They may attempt to locate affordable help in the home, placing ads for live-in helpers or phoning home care agencies to compare hourly rates. During this process, they may assure their relative that "everything's going to be okay." An unspoken backdrop to their exploration of community services is the question of the older person's move into a family member's home. The older person may wonder whether she will be invited, while the family wrestles privately with their conflicting loyalties to their relative and their other personal commitments. Concealing their emotional agony, family members often hope that something will happen to spare them the dreaded moment of telling their relative, "We have to start looking at nursing homes for you."

The hope that they will not have to resort to placement is only part of what prevents families from being open about their worries. The deeper source is the pain of admitting that they are unwilling or unable to restructure their lives to keep their relative at home. A daughter may feel intense hurt as she imagines saying to her mother, "Mom, I just can't give up my job right now. I love you and I hate the thought of your being in a nursing home, but I've worked so hard to get where I am." The need to retain a job rather than care for a parent can seem shameful to someone who values human needs over personal ambition. Resolving such dilemmas is a highly individual struggle. Professionals can be instrumental in helping family members cross the emotional barriers to include their relative as an equal partner in the resolution process.

Establishing an attitude of partnership on the issue of nursing home placement is easiest when verbal barriers are crossed early in the sequence of decision-making. For instance, a visiting nurse or social worker can meet with an older woman and her daughter to educate them about home care options in their community. During the discussion, the professional can speak the unspeakable: "Sometimes families try out all these options and work as hard as they can to keep a parent at home, but nursing home care turns out to be the only solution." Mentioning the words "nursing home" and "only solution" almost always evokes strong responses. But the relief after they expose their dread tends to be palpable for all participants in such discussions. The older person can then direct her anger at the inadequacy and costliness of home-based services, rather than feeling that family members are her adversaries. Family members can affirm their intention to support their relative's goals as much as possible: "Mom, we're going to do everything we can to keep you at home. For what we can't do, we'll try to use these services." Having confronted medical and practical realities and mentioned the unmentionable, both are empowered to discuss care alternatives openly.

An older person who witnesses firsthand family members' efforts to surmount care problems on his behalf is less likely later to feel he has been "dumped" in a nursing home. A father who joins his daughter in interviewing live-in applicants may realize how difficult it is to find reliable helpers, especially at the salary he is able to offer. A daughter who talks with her mother about the ways job pressures conflict with her desire to provide care will make her mother feel loved, even if she eventually chooses to continue her employment rather than assume full-time caregiving. Similarly, a son who admits that he is afraid that having his mother live with him would injure their relationship frees her to vent related concerns from her standpoint. To facilitate such discussions, families may benefit from reading relevant sections of this book together and exchanging reactions to specific issues.

Despite family members' efforts, this spirit of partnership often becomes vulnerable to differences about what constitutes a "safe" living situation for their relative. An older person who frequently falls may insist, "Look, if I'm willing to lie on the floor until my neighbor gets home to help me up, that's my business." His son may respond, "Dad, I hate the thought of you lying on the floor like that. What if you were injured? In a nursing home, there'd always be someone around to help you." The degree of danger deemed acceptable depends on the motivation for tolerating it. In many instances, older people are willing to withstand threats to their safety because of their intense desire to retain their privacy and independence. Motivated by a desire for peace of mind, their families may regard the same dangers as intolerable.

Unless such a division of perspectives is openly addressed, the older person may begin to conceal medical and practical problems from family members. In the instance of falls, the older person may ask the neighbor who assists him not to tell his son the frequency of his need for help getting up off the floor: "They think it's too dangerous for me to keep living here alone, so you'd better not tell them I fell five times last week." Family members concerned about safety become a "they" with opposing goals. When professionals encounter this adversarial mindset, they can easily be drawn into choosing sides. The more productive approach is to acknowledge that a divergence in how older people and their families see such situations is common and stems from their possessing different priorities and motivations. The following dialogue is a distillation of these differences:

> FAMILY: We love you and want you to be safe.
> OLDER PERSON: Safe for what? I don't care how long I live; I just want to stay here until I'm gone.
> FAMILY: We worry about you all the time. We'd never forgive ourselves if you got hurt here.
> OLDER PERSON: So, I'm supposed to give up my home to make you feel better?
> FAMILY: We would feel better if there were people with you at all hours of the day.
> OLDER PERSON: I hate the thought of people with me all hours of the day.

Families can make progress in such dialogues when they admit that placement is largely for their benefit: "Yes, we'll be relieved, and you'll have to put up with a huge change in your life." Avoiding or covering up this truth with fake reassurances only makes older people feel more frightened. The dread that family members will abandon them once they have made the transition is one of the deeper sources of resistance to placement that can be intensified by initial dishonesty. A son who says "Dad, it's going to be a hard adjustment for you, but we'll stick with you all the way" will produce more comfort than one who says, "Dad, it's not such a bad deal. You'll have all those nurses around and plenty to do." The immediate advantage of nursing home placement is relief for family members. Later on, benefits for the older person will become more apparent.

The argument that "not all nursing homes are alike" requires specific and vivid clarification to impress those who have seen the worst types of homes firsthand, such as an understaffed home where a relative was physically neglected. In order to address anxieties about nursing homes, it is crucial for professionals to determine the images that older people and their families hold from past experiences. The idea that some older people thrive in nursing homes due to intensive rehabilitation programs or increased social contact may be entirely foreign to those unfamiliar with decent nursing homes. The following chart depicts the positive aspects of life in such homes and can be helpful for families and their older relatives to review together.

Potential Benefits of Nursing Home Life

1. Increased social contact
   * Roommate relationships can be close and supportive.
   * Sitting with the same people at meals can produce a small community, characterized by warm interactions; eating with others tends to improve appetite.
   * Nurse's aides often become close to the people for whom they provide personal care.
   * Meeting others with similar interests is possible at special events and activities at home; transportation obstacles do not interfere with seeing new friends frequently.
2. Accessible activities
   * Religious services and clergy may be available at the home.
   * Musical programs, craft activities, discussion groups and outings in the home's van may be regularly offered.
   * Common areas may include recreational equipment (pool tables, chess boards, etc.)
   * Barber and beautician service may be available at the home.
3. Intensive rehabilitation services
   * Daily physical therapy, with access to special equipment which could not be utilized at home, may be available.

290

- Nurses trained in rehabilitation techniques may teach personal care skills
- Aides may assist with daily exercises and keep track of the person's progress.

An eventual benefit for the older person may be more satisfying relationships with family members. Removing the stress and tedium of physical care tasks, placement opens up the possibility for family members to have more substantive conversations with their relative. A daughter previously preoccupied by her mother's care needs may be able to listen to her mother's stories about her past and to her advice about family matters. The leisure and focused attention that was not possible in the pressured home environment may become an asset of their time together in the nursing home. Rather than being oriented to tasks, visits in this context convey the affirmation, "I come because I care about you." By pointing to this advantage when they first propose nursing home placement, families thereby emphasize their intention to extend their care into the new setting.

Under concerted pressure from family members, older people facing placement often try to exact bargains and promises: "If I agree to go, do you promise to take me out if I hate it there?" By making groundless promises in response to pleading, family members put themselves in a deceptive role, later straining their relationship with their relative. A better approach is to support the person's hope that his physical condition will improve and to focus his attention on his rehabilitation efforts, rather than on their plans for the future: "When you're able to transfer in and out of your wheelchair on your own, we'll talk about setting up an independent living situation for you." Even if attainment of a specific rehabilitative goal is improbable, maintaining this kind of hope is a way to ease the adjustment process. Yet it does not imply that family members intend to change their lives to accommodate the existing level of care needs.

Some older people are able to accept placement if family members agree to delay the sale of their home or the breakup of their apartment. The home's continued availability serves as a psychological shield until they establish friendships and adjust to institutional routines. Another benefit of delay is added time to grieve the loss of independence before parting with possessions and memorabilia that have to be packed, distributed, or sold. For families, such delay often means extra yard work, checkup visits to an apartment, and extended home maintenance costs, sacrifices which are often worth their relative's peace of mind. As a symbol of his connection to the outside community, a dwelling and its possessions can make the difference between an older person giving up or staying motivated enough to find a niche in the new environment.

291

Choosing a Nursing Home

As described earlier, if nursing home placement occurs directly from the hospital, it may preclude allowing the family control over the choice of a facility. Another constraining factor is the extent to which private funds are available to pay for the care. Older people and their families often first encounter Medicaid, the major source of public funding for nursing home care, at the point of choosing a facility. Some homes do not admit Medicaid-funded residents, whereas others admit them only after private-pay residents have been accommodated. Since funding is a key determinant in the process of choosing a nursing home, the most commonly asked financial questions are answered here.[1]

1. Why is it often easier to obtain a nursing home bed for someone with private funds than for someone with Medicaid?

The state determines the rate paid by Medicaid to the nursing home. In some states, this amount is substantially less than the charges for private-pay residents. Because of this gap between what Medicaid pays and private rates for care, nursing homes try to maintain a balance of private and public-pay residents. Some nursing homes with Medicaid contracts initially admit only private-pay residents, but allow them to remain with Medicaid funding once their private resources are exhausted. Other facilities may initially admit Medicaid-funded residents, but give preference to private-pay applicants on their waiting lists.

2. What should we do if we only have enough to pay private rates for a limited time?

Selecting a nursing home that participates in the Medicaid program is important if the older person is likely to require Medicaid assistance in the future. Otherwise, transfer to another facility when funds run out can be severely disruptive. Once admitted as a private-pay resident to a Medicaid-licensed facility, the older person cannot be legally transferred to another facility when private funds end.

3. Does a Medicaid beneficiary have to contribute to the cost of care?

The Medicaid beneficiary must pay any income received to the nursing home. The home gives the resident a personal allowance from this amount, with the balance going toward payment of nursing home costs. Medicaid pays the difference between that amount and the rate set by the state.

4. *Does the older person's home have to be sold as soon as he becomes a nursing home resident? Can an apartment be maintained under Medicaid guidelines?*

In some states, the Medicaid program permits a grace period during which a portion of the person's monthly income may be used to maintain a previous dwelling. The grace period's intent is to allow for the possibility of a resident's re-entry into the community, if his physical condition improves or the placement is unsatisfactory. A portion of the person's income may also be reserved for a spouse and dependents living at home. The state financial worker handling the application for assistance should be consulted.

5. *How can financial hardship be prevented for the spouse remaining at home?*

A couple can sometimes split their assets in order for a nursing home resident to become eligible for Medicaid assistance. Since a formal agreement is necessary in some states, the couple should consult a lawyer or the local legal services office.

6. *Are all of the resident's nursing home expenses covered in the Medicaid payment? What is normally included in a home's daily rate and what types of charges are extra?*

The Medicaid payment schedule allows for a daily rate, which generally includes room and board, custodial care, skilled care such as medical consultation and nursing services, and most rehabilitation therapies offered by the nursing home. Dental services, some medications, beautician or barber services, and incidentals, such as facial tissues and hand cream, are usually not covered in the daily rate. Families of both Medicaid and private-pay residents should request a list of items included in the daily rate from the particular nursing home. The contract should also specify conditions for notification of rate changes, refunds, and holding a room in the event of hospitalization.

7. *What is the difference between nonprofit and proprietary homes?*

These terms do not designate type or quality of care, but rather how the home is governed and its earnings distributed. The type of ownership affects who makes major decisions regarding the facility's staff, policies and programs, but not necessarily the standards of care. Nonprofit homes, often sponsored by religious organizations and governed by a board or advisory group, do not pay out profits to the owners or investors. Most homes are proprietary, however, and thus operate as a business providing a profit to the owners. Some nursing homes operate as part of a chain, others are independent.

8. *Can a nursing home refuse to admit anyone?*

Some homes deny admission to certain types of patients because of staffing or facility limitations. Medical or behavioral problems, such as serious drug or alcohol abuse, and wandering or belligerence can prevent admission.

9. *How is an older person's level of care determined, and how does this affect the choice of a nursing home and the fees charged?*

Most states have two licensing levels for nursing home care: intermediate and skilled. A nursing home may be licensed for only the lesser level of care or for both; those licensed for both levels may have a set number of beds available for each level. Medical personnel determine on the basis of the older person's physical and mental status the level of care required. Since private rates can include additional gradations in level of care, family members with private funds should ask homes to explain the methods they use to set fees for private-pay residents.

10. *What is the best way to compare nursing homes in a particular community?*

The county's Area Agency on Aging, senior information and referral hotline, nursing home ombudsman, or the local Medicaid office can be contacted for lists of area nursing homes. Discharge planners in hospitals, social workers in home care agencies, and medical personnel in clinics that serve older people tend to have firsthand knowledge that can save families time. Word of mouth is one of the most common methods families use to gather impressions about specific homes. Other methods are presented in the following discussion.

After financial considerations, the nursing home's location is the most important factor in the selection. More than fancy landscaping or modern rooms, older people facing long-term institutionalization need to be close enough to family members and friends to receive regular visitors. This proximity is even more important when families move their older relative a long distance to a facility in their community. Over time, visitors become the focus of nursing home residents' lives, with the more superficial considerations fading from prominence. For instance, a nursing home that is located between a daughter's home and her place of employment should be chosen over less convenient homes that may be superior in aspects not as crucial to her parent's quality of life. Similarly, whether or not a nursing home is near a bus stop is a key consideration for someone whose spouse no longer drives or whose friends depend on bus transportation.

A fact of life in nursing homes is that residents with regular visitors receive better care than those without. The home's convenience to visitors is vital for reasons beyond a resident's emotional and psychological need for contact. When staff are aware that family members will follow up on a resident's request, they are likely to fulfill it more quickly than in the absence of this expectation. By providing anecdotes about the person's past life and personal habits, family members enhance the staff's understanding of the person in their care and increase their interest in the person's needs. A family's acknowledgment and gratitude toward staff efforts also motivate them to take the time to meet special needs.

When more than one nursing home is convenient to family members' homes, the next most important choice factor is the people in the home who deliver the hands-on care. Nurse's aides spend more time with residents than do other staff, helping with bathing, dressing, grooming and using the toilet. The personal nature of their contact can produce anything from intimate bonds to humiliation, depending upon how they deliver these care tasks. Some of the facilities that look the best channel their funds into expensive mortgages rather than into maintaining a favorable ratio of aides to residents. Overworked aides with too many people to serve cannot take the time to be nurturing or considerate. Contented aides with reasonable workloads will produce a higher quality of life for people in their care. For these reasons, a home with outmoded furnishings and equipment can sometimes be superior to more attractive facilities, if the home's management has set good working conditions for the staff as its priority.

Visiting a nursing home during the evening tends to provide more information about staffing levels than observing the home during official daytime tours. Nursing homes can all seem the same from 7:00 AM to 3:30 PM, before the evening shift comes on duty and the larger daytime staff leaves. During the home's evening visiting hours, family members can time their arrival to observe the way aides serve dinner and how they talk to residents as they escort them back to their rooms. Weekends can also be revealing of staff attitudes and skills, as well as how routines are managed when a predictable scarcity of staff exists. Generally, overworked and burned-out staff talk to each other rather than to the residents they are serving, ignoring residents' needs for verbal contact even when surrounded by these needs at the busy dinner hour. Dedicated, satisfied staff tend to joke with the residents, touch them, and keep a balance between their socializing with each other and paying attention to the people who need their responsiveness.

The availability of rehabilitation therapies and the nature of the facility's equipment to support these services can be as crucial as general staffing levels for people with specific rehabilitation goals. Some homes have extensive physical therapy equipment and can offer state-of-the-art therapy for recovery from strokes, instruction in the use of prosthetic devices, and other services deemed vital by the older person and his family. Asking admissions personnel how often a registered physical therapist services the facility is revealing, because many nursing homes use physical therapy aides to provide the hands-on services. Registered therapists may be available only on a part-time basis for supervision and consultation. This staffing pattern saves money for nursing homes, but detracts from the quality of the rehabilitation program.

The home's attitude toward food can also be an indicator of how residents are viewed. Families may want to inquire about menu variations, residents' access to snacks, coffee, tea, and alcohol for themselves and their guests, whether residents can choose where to sit, and whether they can invite guests to the dining room. Food stored in residents' rooms is an area of contention in most nursing homes. A son may bring in bananas for his mother, assuming they can be kept in a bowl on the table beside her bed until she eats them. Citing a "no food in the room" rule, staff may remove the bananas after he leaves or ask him to stop bringing them. Nursing home residents have so little control over their lives in general, and food in particular, that it can seem unreasonable to deprive them of independent access to snacks in their rooms. The problem is that stored food often leads to insects or to odors when forgotten items rot in night tables and closets. Some homes have refrigerators and storage bins where they will store special treats, allowing residents to ask for small quantities at a time. Families who bring in cooked meals may also be asked to serve the food in an area other than their relative's room.

Whether the outside environment has places to walk, sit and gather, how well-equipped and used the activity rooms appear to be, and whether the home has a social worker to help find solutions to practical and emotional dilemmas are examples of other factors which affect residents' lives. As part of their activity program, most homes offer religious services. A nonsectarian home may provide a chaplain, or bring in clergy from one or more religious groups. For an older person with strong religious or cultural ties, a nursing home with staff and residents from the same denomination or ethnic group can make a difference in the person's level of comfort within the facility.

Some homes have single rooms available on a waiting list basis for private-pay residents, while others only have two- and three-person rooms. When their relative must share a room, family members should inquire about provisions for privacy, such as visiting rooms, screens or curtains. Generally, married couples may share a room, unless their doing so is deemed unadvisable for medical reasons. Homes also vary in establishing areas for smoking and controlled drinking of alcoholic beverages. A factor important to many is whether a home allows residents to bring some of their own furnishings to personalize their living spaces, such as using an antique night table rather than the home's standard bureau or a personal bedspread rather than an institutional one.

Finding a nursing home which does not require the use of in-house physicians and which is convenient for their relative's personal physician is a choice factor rated highly by some families. A family physician's longstanding knowledge of the older person's medical problems and personality style is especially useful during the adjustment period, when so much else is unfamiliar and depersonalizing. Continuity with medication dosage decisions and trust in the doctor's concern and competence can be crucial for someone with complex medical problems. In addition, nursing home residents are more likely to report lapses in the staff's care to nonstaff physicians, perceiving their personal physician as an ally unconnected with the facility. In this regard, outside physicians can serve a valuable advocacy role. The difficulty in retaining a personal physician is that doctors must limit the number of homes in which they follow patients after placement. To make visits cost-effective, they prefer to group patients together in particular homes. In such instances, family members may have to sacrifice their own convenience for the physician's.

The Adjustment Period

After their first few days in a nursing home, older people often engage in desperate bargaining with their families, for example, "If you take me out of here, I promise I won't call you so often" or "Please, just let me have one more chance to try to make it at home." Even those who have entered the home fully agreeing that this is the most practical option may collapse into irrational pleading when faced with the reality of the choice. To be begged for release in this way is extremely painful for families already hurting from the guilt of sacrifices they have chosen not to make, no matter how well-considered these choices have been. As indicated earlier, the best responses are those which focus on physical realities: "Mom, after three or four months, we'll see how much progress you've made with your rehab exercises. In the meantime, we'll hang onto your apartment."

When the hope of leaving is vital to the person, it is better to delay implementing signs of permanence, such as changing the address on magazines, until the person has reached a greater degree of acceptance.

For the first several weeks, families should try to arrange some form of daily contact with the outside world for their relative. Phone calls, notes in the mail, flowers, and visits from friends and neighbors can help out on days when family members cannot visit. Such frequency of contact affirms the continuity of relationships when the person most needs this reassurance. Gradually, contact can be tapered as the person is convinced that she will not be abandoned by family and begins to build ties with people within the facility. The major problem family members face in visiting and with promoting contacts from others is their relative's unhappiness. When most visits and phone contacts consist of listening to complaints and trying to comfort their tearful relative, family members' natural reaction is to avoid contact. Professionals need to remind families that nursing home placement instigates a grieving process which lessens over time and is not indicative of how their relative will react later on.

One of the most difficult adaptations for new residents is the loss of control in their personal hygiene habits. Even in the best nursing homes, residents are unable to control the frequency of their bathing. Assistance with sponge baths is usually available daily, but the relief of getting into a hot tub or shower is regulated by the reality of limited numbers of bathing facilities and staff to assist with this time-consuming task. Most homes assign a weekly bath day to each resident to attempt to manage these limitations in a fair and orderly manner. This scheduling tends to appall lifelong daily bathers when they enter a nursing home. When family members live nearby and can safely transport their relative to their residence, adding an extra bath to the weekly routine is especially helpful during the first weeks as their relative copes with a host of other changes.

Living with at least one roommate is another immediate adaptation. During a hospitalization, most people cope with their roommate's annoying habits by defining them as a temporary inconvenience. For the short-term, intrusions into personal privacy can be endured along with inconsiderateness about noise levels, unduly prolonged bathroom usage, and other irritations. When someone enters a nursing home room, this prospect of relief from a roommate's presence is not available as a coping method. In addition, in the close quarters of most nursing rooms, roommates can intrude on each other in a variety of ways. Whether to leave the window shut or open slightly, when to draw the curtains at dusk, and when the television should be turned off at night are only a few of the many issues requiring that personal preferences be compromised. When a newcomer moves into a nursing home room, she is faced with either asserting her needs into the pre-existing routines or with submitting passively to whatever conditions she encounters. Not surprisingly, complaints about roommates tend to dominate new residents' conversations with their families, provided they can find enough privacy to express dissatisfaction.

Some older people, having coped with roommates in other contexts and learned how to compromise, possess good negotiation skills. In contrast, those who have spent a large part of their lives residing alone or who have lived only with relatives may lack these abilities. Instead of attempting negotiation, they retreat into silent resentment or assail roommates with unreasonable demands. Family members can try to model respectful negotiation by settling the more trivial issues on the older person's behalf. They should be careful, however, not to "gang up" on the roommate in the process or to alienate their relative by offering premature concessions. In instances when conflict between roommates is not resolved after their first few weeks together, family members should request the assistance of the home's social worker or another staff person capable of serving as a mediator.

Sensitivity to the fact that open beds are almost always created by the death of a previous roommate can also help family members interpret a roommate's initial responses to their relative. Typically, only a few days are allowed to elapse between a resident's death and the introduction of someone to fill the opening: "The bed's not even cold yet and they've stuck a new person in with me." Anger toward the person taking a friend's place may be at the root of noncooperation, especially if the roommate was close to the previous occupant. Frustration at yet another uncontrollable change and reluctance to bond again after the loss of a succession of roommates may underlie withdrawn or gruff behavior. Families may want to ask staff about the nature of the roommate's previous relationships and the circumstances ending them, in order to gain insight into the current dynamic.

When negotiation and mediation efforts are unsuccessful, family members count on nursing staff's willingness to arrange a room change. Family members need to remember that until a death occurs somewhere in the facility, moving one person displaces another. Finding someone else who wants to trade rooms is an occurrence over which staff have little control. In addition, if a relative's dissatisfaction with the roommate results from the person's unappealing personality, staff know that they will only make someone else unhappy when they arrange the room change. Since unappealing people cannot be disposed of nor segregated within the facility, staff are constantly faced with the complaints of family members and their relatives who have to cope with selfish or inconsiderate fellow residents. Staff generally manage by placing a resident who does not have the noisy advocacy of family members in these less desirable situations.

One way that homes cope with differing degrees of functional ability among residents is to group people in the various wings or floors according to their level of care. The practical advantage is that the ratio of staff to residents can be adjusted in each area of the home to reflect the severity of needs to be served. The psychological advantage for residents is that the less disabled do not have to be constantly confronted with advanced memory loss, severe effects of strokes, and other conditions that they dread. The painful sequel to this organizational logic, however, is that some residents who start out in a higher-functioning section of the home have to be moved to another area when their health status deteriorates. For instance, the daughter of a woman with Alzheimer's disease may be told that her mother has been wandering into other residents' rooms, picking up their belongings, and asking them repetitive questions. Such behavior necessitates moving her mother to another part of the facility. The daughter may respond angrily to staff, fearing that care in this other section will be of lower quality and that her mother will lose the stimulation from being around higher-functioning people.

Their first glance at the heavy care sections of most nursing homes is a jarring experience for family members. The sight of groups of severely disabled people is in itself upsetting. In addition, human odors are almost always more evident in this part of the nursing home due to the nature of the residents' care needs. Faced with the realities of care management described previously, staff usually do not receive statements such as "You can't put my mother here" with equanimity. A consolation not readily visible to families is that staff in the heavy care areas tend to be the most skilled and experienced in the nursing home. Accordingly, they deliver care to these residents with a high degree of sensitivity and compassion. Another advantage is that families of the residents in such sections, who visit in spite of the difficult sights and smells, tend to be warmly supportive when they encounter each other during visits.

To help their relative cope with the shrinkage of personal space and feelings of intrusion from roommates, families can try to personalize the area around the person's bed as much as possible. The older person's individual identity can be asserted through family photographs posted on a cork board, posters and paintings on the wall or closet door, favorite books and magazines on a night table, and a plant or two that she can nurture. As soon as an older person moves in, decorations and private memorabilia are vital external assurances of who she was prior to entering that room. In the pressure of arrangements and procedures, families tend to put off extensive decoration unless its importance is emphasized by professionals during the first weeks of residence. Prior to admission day, it is advisable for family members to plan with their relative which items will be moved to the nursing home.

The vulnerability of residents' rooms to theft exists in even the best nursing homes. As a result, residents usually exclude from their rooms the objects which hold the most meaning to them. A retired music professor with a precious collection of concert tapes may have to confine her listening to one hour per week when her daughter brings in her tape player and some of her tapes. To protect these items from theft, she limits her access to them and thus the frequency of her enjoyment. Another example is a daughter who is unsure whether to allow her confused mother to wear her wedding ring in the nursing home. Her choice is between risking the theft of this valuable family heirloom and depriving her mother of a link with the past that she can touch and look at each day. This kind of limiting protectiveness is a tragic necessity, given the restricted range of experiences and pleasures accessible to nursing home residents.

Noninstitutionalized individuals are unable to imagine inhabiting a living space which cannot be secured and to which an unknown number of strangers have ready access. This loss of control over their belongings is one of the most frustrating aspects of institutional life to residents and their families. Families can help by their willingness to bring valuable items back and forth for use during their visits. Another option is to obtain a night table with a locked cabinet, if the home permits personal furniture. Even a small locked space serves as a psychological and practical refuge for someone wishing to store private papers and other cabinet-sized items. Older people lacking manual dexterity to handle a lock and key may nevertheless prefer to have precious items locked nearby than at family members' homes. Most nursing homes have safes and deposit boxes for the storage of valuables, but residents still lose contact with items stored in this manner. Providing locks for the doors to resident's rooms is not feasible, since nursing, housekeeping and maintenance staff require ready access to perform their duties.

Loss of discretion over their use of prescribed medications affects many new residents. Those who have gone for years maintaining their own pill boxes and managing incidental omissions and additions to their regimen tend to feel outraged by nurses assuming this function. Pain medications, sleeping pills, and drugs for "nerves" are examples of medications which most people dislike turning over to others' management. Putting on a call light and waiting an uncontrollable number of minutes until someone responds is only the first step in obtaining extra medication during the night. The resident must then wait until the aide finds the nurse in charge of evening medications, and then the nurse must complete the tasks already taking her attention. When appropriate physicians' orders are not listed on the resident's medication sheet, the nurse cannot dispense the requested medication until she contacts the physician by phone. In the meantime, someone accustomed to reaching into a night table and taking an extra pill to relieve pain must lie there unable to control her suffering.

This loss of control over medications can be just as infuriating for families, especially when they were previously able to dispense relief at will. A common scene at the nursing stations of most homes is an angry and upset family member attempting to hasten the dispensing of medications needed by their relative. Staff coping with multiple demands on their time may respond to such anger defensively: "Look, I've got thirty other people besides your mother to worry about." Family members are often overwhelmed to the point of tears by the helplessness entailed in asking staff busy with other priorities to attend to a beloved person's needs. They are humiliated by having to plead with or cajole staff to get them to meet a relative's request, a necessity which also drives home the fact that their relative's care is no longer in their hands. To a large extent, the family's losses mirror those of their relative as they confront the same institutional inflexibilities.

Care over the Long Run

The first several weeks and sometimes months of placement are filled with coping efforts. Loss of control over personal hygiene, privacy, possessions, and medications are only a few of the changes to which residents must adapt. Eating mass-produced foods at set times, having a loudspeaker intrude on naps, television viewing and conversations, and accepting help from people of different ethnic groups also challenge their capacity to adjust. During the initial period, family members are usually caught up in helping with these adjustments. As a result, they find they have plenty to talk about with their relative and ample tasks to fill their time. Simply bearing their relative's unhappiness and waiting for it to subside can sap even the most energetic family member's coping capacity.

The long run, or the months and years following the adjustment period, presents a different set of challenges for residents and their families. In some ways, the long run may be more emotionally trying for both. The older person gradually abandons the hope of leaving the facility, and family members confront the very changes in their relative which accompany the acceptance of nursing home life as a permanent reality. Defining exactly what it means to extend their care into this institutional setting is the next question for families. Their answer may shift as personal circumstances and the effects of time change the terms of the question.

Facing a surplus of tedious hours, day after day, and repeated defeats of their will, nursing home residents gradually shut down their sensory and emotional receptors. They begin to experience the boredom and the intrusions less acutely by blunting their sensitivity. Family members, who arrive for an hour's visit once or twice a week, want their relative to rise out of this protective numbness in response to their presence. They especially want their relative to show some signs of gladness upon their appearance in the doorway of the room. Instead, they may be hurt when their relative immediately makes a set of requests without offering a greeting or acknowledging that the family member is not a staff person. From the resident's standpoint, leaving her receptors in their customary unfeeling status may be easier than to become stimulated for an hour, only to feel a sense of absence more deeply for having taken in the pleasure of the visit. Nursing home residents often comment "I want them to visit, but I feel more lonely after they leave."

Unlike meals, which can be counted on as a source of gratification three times a day, family visits occur in unpredictable and sometimes unreliable patterns. Family members are often stunned the first time a relative asks to be taken to the dining area a half hour in advance of serving time, despite their having just arrived for a visit or their willingness to stay until mealtime: "Why do you want to go down there when all you'll do is sit there?" This seemingly disrespectful and uncaring preference hurts family members who have made the effort to visit, often after deferring other plans or conquering their feelings of revulsion about even entering the nursing home. Without firsthand experience with institutional life, most people cannot conceive of how routine events, such as meals, become anchors for getting through the day. The habit of gathering near the dining area to wait for the meal gradually becomes part of the event itself. Asking their relative, "Mom, can't you just get to lunch a little late today?" generally evokes distress. In some instances, an older person may vehemently resist this disruption in her anchoring routine.

As they focus on what oppresses them in the new environment, nursing home residents often stop seeing beyond themselves. They may lose interest in others' lives to the point that they change the topic back to themselves when family members try to tell stories about their own situations. One strategy is for families to take relatives home with them for an overnight or all-day visit once or twice a month. Time away from the institutional milieu jolts people back into awareness of the outside world. It helps them renew their acquaintance with the stresses confronted by their families. For instance, as a mother sits at the kitchen table and hears her daughter tend to a series of phone calls, she gains an immediate view of life circumstances that are unrelated to her needs as a nursing home resident. This view may renew her interest in her daughter's life.

As their relative's complaints about being in the nursing home begin to subside, these signs of lessened responsiveness and inability to disengage from routines generally increase. The price of adaptation tends to be some degree of personality change. Giving in to the way of life in a nursing home protects residents from misery, primarily because they shed personal characteristics that do not fit into the environment. Those who hang on tenaciously to their individuality have to continue to experience pain each time staff assail their distinctive needs as troublesome and inconvenient: "Mrs. Jones, you know you're not the only person here. We've got a lot to do." It is no accident that those who retain a spark in their eyes, compared to the dullness in other residents' eyes, tend to be the "difficult" ones according to the standards of busy staff members. The same vitality that enables a resident to force an institution to bend to her demands also empowers her to seize onto remaining sources of meaning, where others see only a wasteland.

An illustration of this dynamic is a ninety-eight-year-old woman with urinary incontinence who refuses to allow aides to change her in the afternoon unless they come prior to her two o'clock departure for the coffee hour. Although coffee is not served in the lounge until 2:30, the woman finds that it takes her nearly half an hour to propel her wheelchair the full distance. A disruption of this time sequence evokes her fury, to the point that the aides are careful to arrive prior to two o'clock. Although the staff perceive her two o'clock deadline as an annoying and unreasonable imposition, she clings to this capacity to transport herself as an essential component of her dignity. Capitulating to their convenience would make her a "good" resident, but would eventually rob her of her aliveness.

Despite many of these painful changes, family members can employ a number of comforting practices. To compensate for the blandness of institutional food, they can establish a weekly routine of bringing in a home-cooked meal. By providing their relative with the opportunity to choose the contents of this one weekly meal, family members restore a partial sense of control. Bringing in food is also a powerful way for family members to satisfy their need to nurture their relative, especially when they watch her enjoy surprise treats. Nursing home residents, confined to eating what is placed before them, often become envious of the family's ability to go to a grocery store at will and select any item off the shelf. Taking a nursing home resident to a restaurant, even to a drive-in where she need not leave the car, supplies a chance to make choices and to consume foods normally not served in nursing homes.

Another helpful practice is for family members to visit once a week on a particular day rather than intermittently or unpredictably. This routine allows their relative to anticipate that day: "Tomorrow is Saturday, the day my daughter comes." Such regularity gives the person a reason to keep track of the days as well as a feeling of security once the schedule is established. Choosing a day that is most convenient for them, family members should avoid restricting themselves to a set time in order to retain maximum flexibility for other plans. The less intrusive the visit feels to them, the more receptive they will feel toward their relative's needs. The understanding can be that unless family members phone to cancel, they will appear sometime on that day, eliminating the need to call in advance.

Week after week, it can be difficult to make conversation with a relative who has little to say due to the uneventful nature of her life. Reporting on their personal news and asking for ideas on specific problems they are facing is one way family members can stimulate conversation and give the older person a sense of participation in their lives. Generally, older people benefit from being included in difficult family decisions rather than being artificially shielded from life outside the nursing home. Even if unable to attend, many older people enjoy planning future family events, such as a wedding or trip. The family can include them in parts of the event by sending postcards, taking pictures, or bringing some of the decorations and food to the nursing home.

Forming rituals for visits is also helpful, such as drinking a glass of wine together after reading a few pages of poetry or jointly working on an oral history. Rituals provide a structure for visits which is especially useful when families have little to say or need a sequence of things to do during each visit. Assisting with letter-writing, listening to a favorite radio show, going for a walk outside, and looking through mail order catalogs for gifts are other ways to make visits more satisfying. Another is to read magazine articles aloud and share reactions to the issues presented, thereby spurring their relative's interest in current political and social events. The naturalness of young children can also serve to fill awkward silences during visits. When they are permitted in the facility, pets can be especially evocative of memories and the urge to nurture.

In an effort to counter the self-centeredness inherent in institutional living, family members may find it helpful to encourage activities that involve their relative's reaching out to others. A wheelchair-bound resident may be able to read to a visually impaired roommate or assist another with writing letters or recording audiotapes. A long-time community activist may find her niche in the facility's resident council or in assisting with the newsletter. Family members can join with their relative in visiting other residents, planning special holiday activities, leading sing-alongs, stuffing envelopes for the home's fund-raising effort, or making handicrafts for the home's bazaar. Transporting a resident to vote, to a former club, or to church tends to be well worth the family's effort in terms of maintaining the person's sense of connection to the community.

Over time, family members may learn to be more comfortable with quiet activities or silences during visits. Simply being present and gently touching their relative can convey their caring. Washing her hair, massaging her back or hands with lotion, or manicuring her nails can be a powerful means of communication. Families who are pained by the changes in their relatives may avoid physical contact, without realizing how important touch can be.

People who work in nursing homes for several years witness the phenomenon of adaptation over and over again. The new resident enters, complains vociferously for weeks or months, and gradually incorporates aspects of the institution into herself. As they watch their relative change, family members experience sorrow, but also relief from the lessening of complaints and depictions of unhappiness. It takes time to learn not to be hurt by a relative's nonresponsiveness and to accept the loss of personality traits discarded for the sake of adaptation. A year after admission, families often marvel at the pain of the first months contrasted with the adjustment of later months.

Note

1. Adapted from Marty Richards, Nancy Hooyman, Mary Hansen, Wendy Brandts, Kathy Smith-DiJulio, and Lynn Dahm, *Nursing Home Placement: A Guidebook for Families* (Seattle: University of Washington Press, 1984).

Suggested Resources

American Health Care Association, 1200 15th Street N.W., Washington, DC 20005, 202-833-2050.
> Provides publications on nursing homes.

BURGER, SARAH GREENE, and MARTHA D'ERASMO. *Living in a Nursing Home: A Complete Guide for Residents, Their Families and Friends* (New York: Ballantine Books, 1976).
> Descriptive, helpful hints.

Collation. National Citizens' Coalition for Nursing Home Reform, 1309 L Street N.W., Washington, DC 20036, 202-393-7979.
> A journal for advocates working on nursing home issues. Includes legislative updates, organizational strategies, and litigation experiences. National Citizens' Coalition for Nursing Home Reform is a coalition of groups and individuals committed to improving the quality of life and care for nursing home residents.

HORN, LINDA, and ELMA GRIESEL. *Nursing Homes: A Citizen's Action Guide* (Boston, Mass.: Beacon Press, 1977).

An advocacy guide on how to organize, plan, and achieve nursing home reform.

RICHARDS, MARTY, MARY HANSEN, LYNN DAHM, and MICHAEL BEERS. *Understanding Families: A Guidebook for Trainers of Nursing Home Staff,* (Seattle: University of Washington Press, 1984).
Oriented to training nursing home staff to interact more effectively with family members.

RICHARDS, MARTY, NANCY HOOYMAN, MARY HANSEN, WENDY BRANDTS, KATHY SMITH-DiJULIO, and LYNN DAHM. *Nursing Home Placement: A Guidebook for Families* (Seattle: University of Washington Press, 1984).
Discusses choosing a nursing home, the transition to nursing home life, and ways for families to work effectively with nursing home staff.

VLADECK, BRUCE, *Unloving Care. The Nursing Home Tragedy* (New York: Basic Books, 1980).
Historical analysis of nursing homes, development of Medicare and Medicaid, and reasons for many of the problems faced by homes.

Conclusion

Throughout this book, the questions commonly raised by families and professionals have been addressed, without minimizing the complexity and diversity of the lives of older people and their families. Although easy answers to caregiving dilemmas do not exist, concise replies to frequently voiced concerns are suggested here along with references to the substantive discussions in the book. Both professionals and families can use these questions and responses as a format for family meetings and individual discussions. The process of working through these questions is often more important than the course of action chosen, since fully satisfying solutions are rare. The appropriateness of any solutions will depend upon the family's size and history, socioeconomic status and ethnicity, and geographic location. The larger community context, particularly the nature of support services and housing options, also determines the choices available to families.

Frequently Asked Questions

1. How can a family member bring up these difficult topics?
2. How can it be determined whether someone can safely live alone?
3. How can a family member explain to her relative that she has given all she is able to give?
4. How can a family member get his siblings more involved in the care of their parents?
5. How can families get professionals involved?

6. How can families deal with their relatives' irrationality about money?
7. What if the older person rejects help provided or arranged by family members?
8. What if a family member just does not want to provide care?

1. Bringing Up the Difficult Topics

Long in advance of the actual need, families tend to worry about what will happen when a spouse or parent requires care. A statement such as, "Mom, there's some planning that we can do now that will give us more choices later" is a nonthreatening way to remind someone of future concerns. A prime opportunity for this kind of discussion is when a change of residence is being considered, as often occurs upon retirement. The family can suggest that the later life residence be wheelchair accessible, near public transportation, and close to shopping areas and medical services. Another opportunity is when a relative talks about a friend's sudden illness. During such conversations, natural transitions to the relative's circumstances can be made: "Dad, you're probably wondering what you would do if that happened to you." Other constructive ways to stimulate discussion about the future are through reviews of financial management options (Chapter 8), the checklists for home safety adaptations (Chapter 9), and alternative living arrangements (Chapter 11). These can be read in the older person's presence, with family members reacting to the ideas presented in the text. The objective at this stage should be the airing of issues rather than making promises about the family's future contributions.

When such difficult topics are broached, older persons often change the subject or respond with painful silence. Families need to move slowly in such instances, gently raising appropriate topics and recognizing that their relative has probably heard what they said, even when not responding. Families at a geographic distance generally find writing about such issues easier than trying to discuss them on the phone. The advantage of letters are that they give the older person time to think about the issues raised, without feeling pressured to respond immediately. Family members are more likely to get a response to their concerns if they directly state "It is very important to me that I hear from you about this."

2. Determining the Safety of Living Alone

The question of safety depends more on the family and older person's willingness to tolerate danger than on objective aspects of the person's circumstances. For the special needs of people with memory problems, a professional assessment may be helpful as an adjunct to the family's evaluation (Chapter 7). In other instances, the question of safety has to be negotiated between the older person's desire to remain in a long-term home and the ability of relatives and friends to support that desire. A preliminary step toward answering this question is to investigate community resources that can supplement their supportive efforts (Chapter 9). Another helpful approach is to identify the natural helpers performing voluntary services for the older person. Natural helpers' perceptions of the older person's safety and their willingness to continue to provide support should be assessed (Chapter 4).

In the end, the older person may prefer to accept the risk of accidents and the problems resulting from insufficient help rather than enter a more protected setting. Family members' expression of care may mean holding back from taking actions for their older relative, thereby acknowledging the older person's right to make decisions about her own life, despite their disagreement (Chapter 7).

3. Reaching the Limits of Giving

When a relative phones too often to gain relief from loneliness or to seek reassurance, family members often feel a knot in their stomachs, even within the most loving and respectful relationships. The older person's voice may evoke the family's worry about incomplete care tasks and generalized guilt about "not doing enough." Taking care of themselves as caregivers often means that family members must assert their right not to be called during certain time periods, such as during dinner or right before bed. By recognizing that they cannot take away their relative's loneliness, family members can begin to find a realistic level of contact with the person (Chapter 5).

Participating in a family support group may provide families with the advice of others who have also felt overextended by caregiving demands. Family members may find it helpful to hear others weigh the emotional costs and rewards of providing care before they attempt to explain their weariness to their relative. When the older person's demands seem unreasonable, caregivers may need to protect themselves with limit-setting techniques (Chapter 7) or to consider the possibility of nursing home placement (Chapter 13). Discussing nursing home placement as an alternative early in the decision-making process allows the older person to become accustomed to the idea. Decisions of this magnitude should not involve only one party's preferences, but rather be the culmination of a joint decision-making process in which needs are voiced as openly as possible.

4. Getting Siblings More Involved in the Care

Sending a copy of this book or one of the suggested readings may stimulate siblings' motivation to become involved. Understanding the reasons behind a sibling's resistance to being part of the direct care effort usually helps in devising alternative forms of contribution, such as paying for hired services or handling phone calls to agencies (Chapter 3). Siblings peripheral to the family may not have known how to be involved and may benefit from concrete suggestions. Similarly, long distance relatives may not have considered the variety of ways they can contribute in spite of geographic limitations (Chapter 1). Family meetings sometimes motivate previously uninvolved relatives to offer their support (Chapter 3). The potential to heal differences through giving care to parents may induce embittered siblings to try to come together for the care effort. In some instances, it may be preferable for a family member to rely primarily on natural helpers and community services rather than be repeatedly disappointed by an uncooperative sibling.

5. Getting a Professional Involved

Families are often at a loss about how to obtain appropriate professional assistance. Such services tend to be most available to families whose relatives have been hospitalized or under a doctor's frequent care. When an older person is hospitalized, family members can ask to meet with the staff arranging their relative's discharge. Hospital discharge planners have a wide knowledge of community resources, alternative housing arrangments, and nursing home placement procedures. Home care professionals can be utilized when a relative qualifies for the Medicare-covered services of a physical therapist or nurse, or when private funds are available to pay for these services. At this point, the additional service of a visiting social worker can be requested. Family physicians can not only refer families to home health care services, but also to other community contacts. Some physicians employ social workers as consultants to work with families on care management problems.

When an older relative is not ill, obtaining appropriate services can be more difficult. The best starting point is the community's senior information and referral hotline, the area agency on aging, or department of social and health services. A growing number of organizations are sponsoring educational programs about aging and support groups for family members. These are mechanisms for families to contact professionals in the sponsoring agencies (Chapter 5). Increasingly, social workers in private practice are specializing in working with families caring for older relatives. These private practitioners are available on a fee-for-service basis to do home assessments and to make referrals to community resources. Some universities have gerontology centers, which provide information about community demonstration projects as well as relevant continuing education workshops for families and their older relatives. Unfortunately, many of these services are limited in rural areas.

6. Dealing with an Older Person's Irrationality About Money

Attitudes toward money are rarely rational. Styles of spending and saving learned in childhood are often maintained throughout a person's lifetime. Attempts to change such deeply embedded styles tend to meet with determined resistance. Addressing specific worries about health care costs can help relieve a person feeling threatened by them. Similarly, establishing a medical bill accounting system establishes a degree of order in the array of paperwork. Feelings evoked by the need to apply for medical assistance from the state may require family members' concerted reassurances (Chapter 8). When siblings disagree about how to spend money for care needs, it is helpful to initiate open discussions of inheritance concerns and ways to achieve fairness for those contributing the most time and labor (Chapter 3). Family members can suggest steps to ensure their access to financial documents in the event of incapacitating illness (Chapter 8). When the older person remains adamant about maintaining control over her money, family members must generally respect their relative's right to preserve boundaries around this part of her life.

7. When the Older Person Rejects Help

Understanding the reasons why help is rejected is the first step in deciding how to respond. Some older parents, unable to grant their adult children equal status as adults, avoid relying on them until they have no other choice (Chapter 1). Others reject services out of fear that family contact will diminish, or due to inexperience with hired people working for them in their home (Chapter 9). Worried about imposing on adult children or becoming burdensome, many older people prefer to exhaust other sources of support before accepting relatives' help. When first discharged from the hospital, older people usually need time to discover their limits before becoming receptive to additional help in the home. Tenaciously clinging to independence, some conceal their care needs from family out of worry that nursing home placement might be discussed. Refusals of assistance also arise from the desire to have something to do and contribute, a form of resistance which older people are not always able to articulate directly.

Family caregivers who demonstrate their own willingness to accept help may prod their older relative to try out in-home help. In some instances, when family members let go of responsibilities, it creates a void which the older person realizes must be filled by others' assistance. When relatives ignore their families' suggestions, or sabotage helping systems they have arranged, families often have to respect this expression of independence and withdraw outside help.

8. Ambivalence Toward Caregiving

Adult children frequently question the nature of their caregiving obligations. They may harbor anger toward parents for poor relationships during childhood or for current value differences and personality clashes. Caring for a parent may interfere with the adult child's priorities, such as accepting a job transfer or vacationing with his children. Another source of resistance for both adult children and spouses is the fear of being stuck with caregiving responsibilities for years. Assisting a relative for a month or two may seem manageable compared to sacrificing for an unknown number of years. On one level, family members may dread a relative's death, but on another look forward to it as a release from responsibilities.

Family members struggling with their ambivalence may find it helpful to imagine themselves in the future, looking back on what they did to assist their relative and whether they felt they acted decently. Another helpful guideline is to consider their own children's reaction to the degree of respect they accord older relatives. How family members resolve these dilemmas changes with their shifting life circumstances as well as with their older relative's needs. What is crucial is for family members to clarify their own priorities and then, within those parameters, to do as much as they can.

Index